T0345185

SCHOOL REFORM IN AN ERA OF STANDARDIZATION

School Reform in an Era of Standardization explores how teachers and school-based administrators navigate the processes of accountability and standardization in schooling systems and settings. It provides clear insights into how the work and learning of teachers and students in schools have been dramatically reconstituted by increased pressures of external, political scrutiny and accountability. The book reveals in detail the nature and effects of standardization processes upon schools and schooling systems. Specifically, it shows how curriculum development, teaching and assessment practices have all been recalibrated under conditions of increased external scrutiny of teacher and student work and learning, and how such processes are manifest in curriculum dominated by attention to literacy and numeracy, more 'scripted' pedagogies and standardized testing.

However, the research not only elaborates the detrimental effects of such processes, but also how those responsible for educating in schools – teachers, heads of curriculum, deputy-principals and principals – have responded proactively by interpreting, interrogating and challenging these conditions. In this way, it provides resources for hope – evidence of what are described as more 'authentic accountabilities' – and at the same time it provides a clear portrait of the difficulty of fostering substantive curriculum, teaching and assessment reform during an era of increasingly reductive accountability processes. It will be an invaluable resource for understanding and enhancing practices in schools and school systems in the decades to come, and for giving hope to educators in the ongoing work of rebuilding trust in public education.

Ian Hardy (PhD) is Associate Professor of Education at the School of Education, The University of Queensland, Australia. Dr Hardy researches the relationship between education and society, particularly the broader socio-political contexts that influence educators' work and learning, and educators' responses to the policy and political settings in which their work is undertaken.

SCHOOL REFORM IN AN ERA OF STANDARDIZATION

Authentic Accountabilities

Ian Hardy

Routledge
Taylor & Francis Group

LONDON AND NEW YORK

First published 2021
by Routledge
2 Park Square, Milton Park, Abingdon, Oxon OX14 4RN

and by Routledge
52 Vanderbilt Avenue, New York, NY 10017

Routledge is an imprint of the Taylor & Francis Group, an informa business

© 2021 Ian Hardy

British Library Cataloguing in Publication Data
A catalogue record for this book is available from the British Library

Library of Congress Cataloging-in-Publication Data
A catalog record has been requested for this book

ISBN: 978-0-367-89324-8 (hbk)
ISBN: 978-0-367-89327-9 (pbk)
ISBN: 978-1-003-01858-2 (ebk)

Typeset in Bembo
by Taylor & Francis Books

To Allan Luke, Bob Lingard, Stephen Kemmis and Wilfred Carr, for pointing the way ...

CONTENTS

ACKNOWLEDGEMENTS

Many scholars, colleagues, family and friends have influenced the ideas presented in this volume, more than I can hope to adequately acknowledge here. However, I will flag several groups without whom this work would not have been possible.

First, I would like to extend my sincere thanks to the many teachers, principals, deputy-principals, heads of curriculum, various teaching 'coaches', teacher aides and support personnel in schools throughout Queensland who gave generously of their time and insights into the nature of their work over the past decade. I also thank personnel within Education Queensland who assisted the progress of this research, including flagging schools where interesting work was being undertaken throughout the state.

Secondly, I would like to thank my many local, national and international academic colleagues and interlocutors whose generosity of spirit has helped foment many of the ideas presented here. I would particularly like to thank colleagues from my former workplace at the Faculty of Education, Charles Sturt University (particularly in Wagga Wagga), and current colleagues and students at the School of Education, The University of Queensland. I also acknowledge the continued associations and friendship of members of the Pedagogy, Education and Praxis (PEP) international network.

Thirdly, this work would not have been possible without the significant financial support provided through the Australian Research Council. The data from more than 400 interviews informing this work were collected as part of two substantial grants: Discovery Early Career Researcher Award (DECRA: DE120100086, *Teachers' learning in complex times: Theorising teacher professional development practices under globalised policy conditions*; 2012–2014), and Future Fellowship (FT140100018, *How do teachers learn to enact the Australian Curriculum? A question of policy in practice*; 2015–2018).

Finally, I acknowledge the unwavering support of my family and friends whose continued encouragement have enabled the production of this volume. Thank you.

1

INTRODUCTION

The rise of accountability and audit in schools

Introduction

This book explores how the increased focus on more standardized approaches to educational accountability has influenced key aspects of schooling policy and practice. This includes particular attention to the organization of curriculum, teaching and, perhaps most obviously, assessment.

In the overview of their account of education, Robertson and Dale (2015) argue for an understanding of educational practices that brings into conversation processes of political economy with various forms of cultural analyses. Such an account seeks to understand education as not simply a provider of educational qualifications, but as 'a complex and variegated agency of social reproduction, broadly conceived' (p. 150). While the nature and extent to which educational practices are reproductive is contested, there is clear evidence that educational practices are deeply reflective of broader social processes in which they are embedded, and of which they are simultaneously constitutive. Robertson and Dale (2015) argue that practices and processes that constitute an educational ensemble are not always readily apparent, even as they have very real effects:

> Given its stratified ontology, not all of what goes on in any education ensemble is visible. As a result, our explanations of education ensembles need to take into account those mechanisms and processes that are not observable but which have real effects.
>
> *(p. 150)*

In this volume, I argue that key components of such ensembles in recent times are the accountability practices and processes that seek to manage and monitor schooling. Such practices and processes are manifest in a variety of ways. This includes, drawing upon what Bernstein (1971) described almost five decades ago, as the three 'message systems' of schooling: curriculum, teaching and assessment. These message systems are the conduits through which that which is valued is communicated in schooling. These message systems flag which knowledge is most powerful, and how such knowledge is organized, conveyed and evaluated. They also reveal the inherently political nature of curriculum, teaching and testing practices.

This book seeks to explore the nature of these power relations, and particularly how those influenced by broader accountability processes in relation to curriculum development, teaching and assessment practices have responded. The research endeavours to reveal the nature of educators' responses to accountability practices in and across these domains, and the extent to which they exert agency under such circumstances. At the same time, these ensembles are characterized by broader, global processes of governance that are increasingly complex and that exert influence in multiple and varied ways.

Accountability and audit technologies

An important part of the managerial and bureaucratic apparatus that seeks to exert control over the work and learning of educators is the ability to 'account' for the practices of those engaged in schooling settings. Under conditions in which social practice has become increasingly influenced by economic prerogatives, there has also been an emphasis on economic productivity over other forms of being, elevating modes of financial rationality. This, in turn, has led to the rearticulation of practice, characterized by a need to 'keep track' of the success or otherwise of this approach, necessitating forms of counting and 'accounting'. Importantly, this has led to a substantive change in practice and conformity to a financial logic, regardless of the parameters of the actual practice in which such logics have come to exert influence:

> This overlaying of financial rationality did not leave the organizations as they found them. Organizations had to be rendered accountable, and the terms of that accountability were not professional but those of accounting. They were reorganized, transformed into aggregations of accountable spaces, reshaped into cost-centres and the like, rendered calculable in financial terms.
>
> *(Rose, 1999, p. 152)*

These processes of accountability are greatly enhanced by various forms of 'audit' technologies that seek to render knowable forms of knowledge and practice that may appear complex or problematically irregular from the outside. Processes of audit dramatically change that to which they are directed:

> Rendering something auditable shapes the process that is to be audited: setting objectives, proliferating standardized forms, generating new systems of

record-keeping and accounting, governing paper trails. The logics and technical requirements of audit displace the internal logics of expertise.

(Rose, 1999, p. 154)

Power (1997) refers to an 'audit explosion' to try to capture the dramatic increase in focus on such prerogatives, and how they alter more established relations. While auditing has traditionally been considered 'distinctly unglamorous' (Power, 1997, p. xi), the dramatic increase in processes of auditing and applications well beyond the financial practices and processes to which they were originally directed reflects how audit technologies have taken on a life of their own, influencing all aspects of social life, including education. Rose (1999) argues that through processes of new public management, new forms of governing of practice have come into being. New processes of 'costing' and accounting mean that processes of professional autonomy no longer hold sway. The consequence is that new forms of commensurability become possible. Each decision is made 'knowable', often through the use of numbers. Such numbers enable processes of comparison, and 'can be transported to centres of calculation, aggregated, related, plotted over time, presented in league tables, judged against national averages, and utilized for future decisions' (Rose, 1999, p. 153). Through such practices, an air of objectivity can be conveyed that fosters a sense in which an elevated air of neutrality can always be maintained, and that such neutrality is a mark of the success of processes of audit and accountability. On such renderings, professional judgement and autonomy become much less consequential, and may be construed as inherently limited and limiting.

Accountability and audit in school education

In recent decades, since such processes have become increasingly apparent, a variety of technologies have arisen that serve as various sorts of 'infrastructures' that contribute towards the management and modulation of accountability and audit processes, and these are clearly evident in schooling practices today. In their account of the uses of data and their effects on schooling practices in the United States, Anagnostopoulos, Rutledge and Jacobsen (2013) refer to an 'infrastructure of accountability' to try to capture the nature of various forms of surveillance and control mechanisms in contemporary schooling practice. As with so many recent accounts of schooling, with their focus on pedagogies of standardized testing (Kempf, 2016), and various forms of 'globalized educational accountabilities' (Lingard, Martino, Rezai-Rashti and Sellar, 2016), Anagnostopoulos et al. (2013) emphasize the effects of testing practices. They focus particular attention on the 'information infrastructure' associated with testing – the many systems designed to develop, produce, monitor and manage the multitude of data produced through various forms of school, district, state, national and international testing systems. These data have been used for a variety of purposes, including as a vehicle for public accountability, via the mass media:

> Test-based accountability has spurred states to create large-scale information systems that gather, process, and disseminate information on the characteristics and performance of schools, teachers, and students. Data from these systems are made available to ever-widening audiences and used to inform decisions across and beyond the educational system.
>
> *(Anagnostopoulos et al., 2013, p. 1)*

However, and even as testing is central to contemporary accountability regimes, closer inspection of current policy, curricula and approaches to teaching also reveal evidence of standardization of not just testing, but also how knowledge is presented in and to schools and schooling systems, and the nature of the teaching that is particularly valued and valuable under these circumstances. In this sense, arguably, infrastructures of accountability are also readily apparent across the three message systems of schooling.

It is the displacement of forms of accountability and audit expertise which has had such an influence on these three message systems. Meyer, Tröhler, Labaree and Hutt (2014) argue that accountability is becoming a 'normal', accepted part of educational practice, focused on economic growth and development, rather than democratic participation; accountability is 'a pervasive normalizing discourse, legitimizing historical shifts in educational policy from a social and cultural project of facilitating democratic citizenship to an economic project of engendering usable skills and "competences"' (p. 1). There is also a sense in which the current trends in accountability involve processes of redirecting influence for education from the local level of practitioners to a national and global cadre of policy actors operating from more economic and statistical backgrounds. Rather than focusing on a local 'practical' – practice-based – conception of education, this broader political and professional assemblage of policy protagonists focus attention on local practices insofar as they are responsive and reflective of broader, national and international markers of attainment and achievement. Such a focus has the effect of eliding contextual difference and contingency, and cultivating a homogenous conception of education that is far removed from the complexity of actual educational practice. At the same time, this process has involved a 'tightening into' these national and international markers of attainment – a shift from 'softer' forms of governance to 'harder' more specific and measurable modes of achievement, as expressed through these more centralized indicators.

Policy processes: Policy development and enactment

So how have such accountability practices and processes been able to exert such influence? A key reason for the effects of accountability and audit technologies is the way in which they have proved so attractive at the level of national and sub-national policy-making. This has been enabled through processes of policy-borrowing at a global level.

Global education policy-borrowing as a vehicle for audit and accountability

Even as much of the literature, data and analysis presented in this book are focused on schooling practices of policy-making, curriculum, teaching and assessment as locally situated (i.e., in specific sub-national systems and school sites), these practices are simultaneously understood as exhibiting characteristics of both national and more global practices and processes. This is evident through the way in which particular foci and practices are reflected in multiple educational settings in different parts of the world, albeit always mediated by the particular histories and spatialities that characterize each unique site (Rizvi & Lingard, 2010). Such knowledges often constitute forms of 'knowing capitalism' (Thrift, 2005) in which government and non-government organizations are engaged in processes of constantly monitoring practices and collecting information about practices to inform their work, for broader economic prerogatives.

Curriculum, teaching and assessment practices do not simply exist in isolation. Rather they are both product and productive of broader processes of audit and accountability that have come to characterize schooling. While a considerable focus of attention in this book is how these processes of accountability are enacted in schools in specific national and sub-national contexts – and particularly empirical research from one sub-national government school system (Queensland, Australia) to illustrate these processes – these empirical insights are provided as instances of broader processes of the standardization of public schooling practices in different countries and educational systems throughout the world. The tensions referred to in the Queensland context are reflective of broader pressures and processes operating globally that seek to exert influence on more 'local' practices. These effects are particularly felt in Anglo settings, but increasingly in European contexts, as well as operating (albeit differently) in other national and cultural settings.[1] The seemingly ubiquitous focus on processes of audit and accountability across national contexts is supported at a global level by policy processes of global policy-borrowing on the part of governments (Phillips & Ochs, 2003). These processes of 'borrowing' policy entail that some form of learning has occurred in the first instance; indeed, this capacity to learn from other cultures and contexts is a fundamental premise on which research into comparative education might best be understood (Phillips, 2000). However, the extent to which this is actually the case is very much an empirical issue, and open to question.

The challenges associated with notions of 'borrowing' begin with the very nature of the term itself, and the impermanence of whatever it is to be 'borrowed' that is implied by the term: '[the term borrowing] clearly implies temporariness, and temporary solutions to educational problems are more often than not unsatisfactory' (Phillips, 2000, p. 299). Drawing on the work of Steiner-Khamsi (2004), Lingard (2010) also refers to processes of policy-borrowing to capture the way in which educational reforms at the national (and sub-national) levels have been taken up in the context of broader, global, pressures for increased economic performance.

Such processes involve taking up particular initiatives from specific contexts, but without necessarily 'learning' from the experiences of the application of these ideas. In the push to ensure responsiveness to what are construed as 'successful' practices, or practices arising in response to particular jurisdictions' struggles to reform education, this disjuncture between policy-borrowing and actually learning from the experience of the adoption of particular policy prerogatives in different contexts seems to be elided.

In large measure, this process of global policy-borrowing is a result of the increased influence of the Organisation for Economic Co-operation and Development (OECD), and in schooling settings, particularly the impact of the OECD's Program for International Student Assessment (PISA). Given the OECD is an intergovernmental body that exerts influence on member countries, but without the capacity to directly set policy, this focus on PISA as a vehicle for reform represents a form of 'soft power' (Nye Jr, 2004) that can be deployed to achieve desired ends; in the case of the OECD, these ends entail increasing influence on national policy prerogatives, ultimately oriented to improved economic performance, as a marker of its own esteem amongst member states.

A key part of this process is the ability to foster understanding in relation to efforts to compare educational practices and outcomes across national contexts. Nóvoa and Yariv-Mashal (2003) refer to the increased interest and focus on comparative education, and how this increased attention may be undertaken for multiple, and contradictory, purposes. On the one hand, such practices may help inform individual jurisdictions' understandings of their own educational practices, and may serve as a stimulus to learn from the experiences of others, with a view to developing their own, indigenous responses to the needs of their particular communities. On the other hand, such foci may be a product of the desire of national and state governments and associated entities to govern the educational practices that transpire in jurisdictions that are increasingly constituted in relation to broader supra-national and 'global' relations of attainment and capacity. Again, the OECD PISA initiative as well as the International Association for the Evaluation of Educational Achievement's (IEA) Trends in Mathematics and Science Study (TIMSS), and other earlier initiatives such as those supported by the European Quality of School Education initiatives, all have the potential to have more or less beneficial or deleterious effects.

Under such circumstances, Nóvoa and Yariv-Mashal (2003) refer to the way in which education is understood and analysed through both a 'global eye' and a 'national eye', particularly given the way in which national governments are construed as continuing to exert influence in this domain, even as broader global processes are clearly (and, depending on the jurisdiction, increasingly) at play. In their rendering of the effects of the increased focus on comparative education, Nóvoa and Yariv-Mashal (2003) argue there is increased attention to what they describe as the 'society of the international spectacle', and the 'politics of mutual accountability' (p. 427). The notion of the international spectacle transforms historical resonances and practices into a token or symbol, and this symbol acts and is presented as if it were a centralized point of control. Importantly, this process of the spectacle is simultaneously one of surveillance, in which the surveillance occurs at an international level. These processes of surveillance entail practices of audit, to monitor performance. At the same time, a politics of mutual accountability is also prominent, characterized by a process of developing multiple methodologies to compare schools and schooling systems. This leads to a constant process of measuring and monitoring performance in relation to other schools and systems – a 'perpetual comparison to the other' (Nóvoa and Yariv-Mashal, 2003, p. 427) – resulting in a hierarchical relationality between systems and sites. These processes of comparison become sufficient grounds for the involvement of bodies devoted to this international comparative work, and foster a sense in which the status of each participant is made possible, indeed essential, through such work.

These processes of international spectacle and mutual accountability are enabled through processes of comparison, which serve as vehicles for governing practices that come to dominate in schooling settings. The development of such technologies as PISA have instantiated a new form of educational accountability not just at a global level – cultivating a global policy field characterized by constant comparison, and making possible the involvement of other policy actors, including private firms seeking to exert influence at an international level (Lingard, Martino, Rezai-Rashti & Sellar, 2016) – but have also reconstituted how education is enacted in schooling settings. Even as they may not be recognized as such by teachers and other personnel working in schools, local, school-based practices are reconstituted in ways that ensure constant processes of comparison between school sites, and intervention where such comparisons are found wanting.

Policy-in-practice: The politics of policy enactment processes

In seeking to understand how more accountability logics have come to exert influence locally, it is crucial to better understand how such broader policy processes are enacted in practice. A brief history of processes of policy implementation, or what Ball, Maguire and Braun (2012) more accurately refer to as 'enactment' in education settings, enables such understandings.

In relation to policy processes more broadly, Rein's (1983) earlier work provides some very useful insights into the dilemma of what he refers to as policy implementation. His focus on implementation emerged at a specific period when policy analysis in the US had shifted from how policies developed to how policies influenced practice – from 'inputs' to 'outputs'. However, what is most significant, argued Rein, is the relationship between the two: 'But between the inputs and the outputs there lies a terrain that is still fairly unexplored: the question of how policies change as they are translated from administrative guidelines into practice' (p. 113). Rein described this process as 'what I call "the politics of implementation"' (p. 113). Also, importantly, Rein was modest in his analysis of this work: 'I do not intend to propose a theory, but to develop a perspective' (p. 113). Furthermore, '[a]ttending to the implementation process makes it possible to consider the point at which intent gets translated into action and where and why slippage and reformulation occur' (p. 114). Rather than focusing on the roles of leaders, interest/pressure groups or the general public in influencing policy implementation, Rein focused on the relationship between the policy process and its outcomes/outputs/products.

This approach emphasizes implementation as the result of considerations of feasibility in settings where 'there is little practical experience and little cognitive understanding about how best to achieve the goals of legislation' (p. 115). This is a contested process involving legislators, administrators and various groups influenced by outcomes. This process is messy, but also involves learning about how decisions influence various aspects of programs and initiatives as they unfold. New problems arise as part of this unfolding, and this is particularly the case as practitioners seek to resolve various inconsistencies and ambiguities that characterize the original policy-making process: 'One of the consequences of passing ambiguous and inconsistent legislation is that the arena of decision making shifts to a lower level. The everyday practitioners become the ones who resolve the lack of consensus through their concrete actions' (p. 117). This means that ultimately, 'implementation becomes the strategic stage for the resolution of problems' (p. 116).

In educational settings, Odden's (1991) work also provided evidence of the conflicted understanding of policy implementation/enactment processes in his analysis of what he identified as three stages of education policy implementation in the United States context. The first stage related to programs instigated in the late 1960s and 1970s, and referred to how conflict over implementation of federal and state policy initiatives at the local level stymied policy intentions. Local governments were described as lacking the desire and capacity to ensure fidelity of policy implementation: 'The expectations and hopes of state and federal program designers were dashed on the shoals of local resistance and ineptness' (p. 5). For Odden (1991), the second stage of education policy implementation involved more longitudinal studies to ascertain how policy implementation processes changed over time. Odden (1991) described varying implementation outcomes for redistributive versus developmental programs, with the former proving more contentious and contested in their enactment. However, over time, higher-level programs and policies were implemented at the local level, with bargaining processes leading to outcomes acceptable for both local and higher-level governments. Importantly, policies do have impact, even if in unpredicted and unpredictable ways. Finally, Odden (1991) identified a third stage of policy implementation as characterized by not only how to get programs and policies implemented, but how to ensure they had the desired effects, as originally intended – 'how to make them "work"' (Odden, 1991, p. 8).

More recently, in their focus on how schools 'do policy', rather than focusing on 'how to make [policies] work', Ball, Maguire and Braun (2012) take a more critical approach to policy implementation as 'enactment' to try to capture the multiplicity and hybridity that characterizes actual engagement with policy. Rather than focusing on 'implementation' with its connotations of linear adoption of policies developed elsewhere, and implemented in schools, Ball et al. (2012) evince 'a dynamic and non-linear aspect of the whole complex that makes up the policy process' (p. 6). Enactment processes are complicated by the plethora of policies that exist in school sites; Ball et al. (2012) identified 170 policies across the four school sites that comprised their research. Many of these policies pertained to a range of issues, such as behaviour and uniform, not immediately associated with the core practices of teaching and learning. Under such circumstances, those in schools also adopt various roles. These roles include interpreters of policies to be emphasized, translators who seek to achieve particular actions and outcomes, critics, and policy entrepreneurs who develop or support particular policies and foci.

However, how various policies play out in relation to more accountability logics is an always open question, and subject to the particular circumstances and conditions that characterize any given instance of educational practice. It might be anticipated that, as with conceptions of policy more broadly, the way in which education policy enactment is understood in relation to more accountability logics may also be contested.

Accountability logics in practice in schooling settings

In relation to schooling, analyses of accountability practices have indeed revealed considerable uncertainty and variability in outcomes. Accountability logics have tended not to have the effects intended. In relation to student learning, this has included focusing disproportionate attention on student performance at the lower levels of attainment. Perhaps this is because of a penchant to diagnose failure, and perhaps because there is less attention to the needs of poorer performing students more broadly:

> the benefits of K–12 accountability seem to be concentrated among the most disadvantaged students in the lowest-performing schools, both perhaps because failure is easier to diagnose than success and because lower-performing schools face less scrutiny from stakeholders in the absence of government monitoring.
> *(Deming & Figlio, 2016, pp. 34–35)*

These processes of accountability have very real effects on schools, administrators, teachers and students to whom they are directed. In his critique of the increased privatization of public education, David Hursh (2016) points out how standardized testing is central to making the case for a crisis in education, and for the subsequent importation of various private enterprise approaches to govern 'public' education. The result is a democratic deficit in which the extent to which public schools are genuinely reflective of the school communities, districts/boards, students, teachers and parents in specific locales is increasingly open to question. In recent history, legislation such as *No Child Left Behind* (NCLB) in the United States has been associated with significant sanctions, including the removal of school administrators and school closure. Such policies constitute forms of 'consequential accountability', involving various forms of rewards or sanctions based on student performance (Hanushek & Raymond, 2005). Such sanctions can encourage problematic behaviours as those in schools seek to avoid their negative effects, or seek to minimize the circumstances in which sanctions could be employed. This has problematic effects on the broader aims of education that might not be so readily quantified, measured or 'ac/counted' for:

> Schools are trying to accomplish many objectives – higher student achievement on certain tests, but also achievement in those areas that may not be well-captured by performance on standardized tests, performance in other academic areas that do not appear on the accountability test, and more abstract goals such as critical thinking, open-mindedness, maturity, and citizenship. When faced with strong incentives to concentrate on some metrics but not on others, schools might be expected to focus on short-run gains in what is being measured – sometimes obtained through strategic behavior such as 'teaching to the test' – at the expense of long-run skill acquisition.
>
> *(Deming & Figlio, 2016, p. 38)*

Deming and Figlio (2016) draw on Neal's (2013) criticism of using one assessment system to pursue two objectives; Neal (2013) argues standardized testing systems used to measure individual student achievement are not designed to provide accurate information about the performance of teachers and principals. The latter encourages manipulation of the evaluation processes for students to ensure a more beneficial outcome in relation to the evaluation of educators, which ultimately diminishes the learning experiences for which such measures are supposed to serve as accurate proxies.

In their summary of the effects of accountability in schooling settings, Deming and Figlio (2016) isolate four lessons: 1) organizations tend to respond to pressure for short-term improvements in specific measures, rather than seeking to attain long-term outcomes, particularly when public reporting or various forms of rewards or sanctions are imposed; 2) the particular locus of attention of the accountability system has effects on the behaviours of personnel in schools and schooling systems; 3) the volume of high-stakes accountability targets influences the scope for strategic responses to accountability pressures; and 4) accountability systems tend to influence the outcomes for lower-performing students rather than other students. There is also a sense in which 'external accountability works best when institutions would not otherwise face strong internal or community pressures to improve' (Deming & Figlio, 2016, p. 43). This also suggests broader public accountability logics are less influential in relation to more affluent communities, in which internal monitoring pressures are at play, compared with less affluent areas in which such pressures may not be exercised so readily.

In the context of the push for more accountability, recent school reforms in school organization, curriculum, teaching and testing have been substantive.

Testing processes have been particularly significant. Indeed, the very purposes of schooling have been transformed under increasingly test-centric conditions:

> We need to understand that the education reforms are not a minor change in how schools are administered, or how tests and curriculum are created, or how teachers are evaluated. Instead, the current reforms have transformed the purpose of schooling, teaching, and learning. The curriculum is being reduced to what will be tested, teaching reduced to implementing lessons designed to resemble the test questions and often scripted by someone else, and learning reduced to test-taking strategies and memorizing for the test.
>
> *(Hursh, 2016, p. 2)*

Under such circumstances, an earlier, broader social democratic social imaginary, oriented towards students as citizens, seems to have been superseded by a more corporate managerial approach that focuses on competition, individual choice and free markets. Education is construed as essential for continued economic growth, and schools and schooling as fundamental for the development of skills to foster necessary economic development. Under conditions of increasing accountability – indeed, 'globalizing educational accountabilities' (Lingard, Martino, Rezai-Rashti & Sellar, 2016) – schools are seen as falling behind in the competitive race that schooling has become. In the context of continuous calls for improvement as part of the international spectacle of comparing and contrasting not simply different national performances, but also state/provincial performances, right down to school-level performances (witness the rise of PISA-for-Schools in recent years), the focus on developing mechanisms to audit and track outcomes, and to 'contain' potentially problematic practices (such as through the promotion of various kinds of teaching templates e.g. 'explicit teaching', 'direct instruction'), has become much more overt.

Governing policy and practice through audit and accountability

However, how are processes of governing through accountability actually expressed under current policy conditions, and how might they be expressed in practice in schools? What is the nature of the contestation that characterizes policy and practice/policy enactment at present? How is such contestation manifest in different school settings influenced by ostensibly similar policies?

Empirical realities

To help answer such questions, this book draws on recent research into the nature of schooling policy and practice in the state of Queensland, Australia. It does so not to present an authoritative account of schooling policy and practices in that state, but to shed light on the nature of accountability logics more broadly. That is, the book draws on examples presented from the Queensland case to stimulate reflection, and shed further light, on the nature and effects of dominant conceptions of audit and accountability in different national and sub-national contexts, more broadly. The Queensland data involved in-depth interviews with more than 405 teachers and school-based administrators in 14 schools located in geographic/administrative regions spread throughout the state. This included schools serving remote, predominantly Indigenous communities, other rural schools scattered throughout the state, suburban schools in northern, central and southern regions of the state, and schools serving affluent middle- to upper-class communities in inner city locations. These interviews were collected between 2012 and 2017 – a period of significant reform, and some turmoil in relation to education provision in Queensland.

The interviews were typically 30 minutes to 1 hour, undertaken by the author and complemented by the collection of relevant systemic and school policies, reports and documentation at this time. They were also complemented by attendance at a series of ongoing professional development meetings involving teachers from one school in the northern regions of the state, in particular, where staff were seeking to enhance the quality of educational provision at this time. While all participants and schools are anonymized throughout, pseudonyms for school names have been chosen to provide insights into the geographic distribution and demographic character of schools across the state (but still at a sufficient level of generality to preserve anonymity). Collectively, these data reflect important insights in the schooling practices occurring in Queensland at this time as a case study of educational reform more broadly. The data reveal how educators interpreted these practices, and particularly in relation to the nature of schooling provision that governed the enactment of curriculum reform, teaching approaches and testing practices of these teachers.

Importantly, and reflecting the contestation that attends policy enactment more broadly, and in relation to accountability processes in schooling settings more specifically, the book also seeks to highlight points of hope, possibility and resistance in relation to more performative accountability logics. To this end, the book seeks to make the case, via empirical evidence, and associated theorizing and literature, for what are described as more 'authentic accountabilities' that can and should attend discourses of accountability in schools and schooling settings more broadly. These more authentic accountabilities are found to be hard-won, and characterize processes of not only interpretation and analysis on the part of educators in schools, but deep interrogation of their circumstances. The multifaceted nature of these empirical insights also require an array of pertinent conceptual resources to more effectively make sense of these empirical realities.

Conceptual resources

To help understand current school policies and their enactment in practice, the book draws on a variety of conceptual resources that explicitly address issues of governance in the context of increased accountabilities, including how governance processes are understood – interpreted – by those to whom they are directed, and how they are contested. This includes earlier Foucauldian-inspired work about governing and technologies of government by Rose (1999), and later work by Rhodes (2012) about network governance, meta-governance and particularly interpretive governance. In building towards a case for more authentic account-abilities, Rhodes' notion of 'interpretive governance' (Rhodes, 2012) was particu-larly helpful for understanding the expression of accountability logics under current policy conditions, and alternatives to more performative approaches and foci. Bourdieu's (1990) notion of the logics of practice as contested was also critical to help understand the contestation that attended these governance processes.

From the outset, it is important to note that processes of governing continue to be influenced by the state, even as they exist in more hybridized forms, with greater influence from the private sector. In his efforts to better understand the political power that characterizes the state, Rose (1999) foregrounded various instruments or 'technologies of government' that seek to influence the conduct of populations. This includes what he described as 'human technologies' to fore-ground how it is 'human capacities' that are both the object of understanding, and on which various 'technologies' might seek to exert influence:

> Technologies of government are those technologies imbued with aspirations for the shaping of conduct in the hope of producing certain desired effects and averting certain undesired events. I term these 'human technologies' in that, within these assemblages, it is human capacities that are to be understood and acted upon by technical means.
>
> *(Rose, 1999, p. 52)*

Under such circumstances, governing processes entail engagement with various 'technologies' of government, which exist in a plurality of forms. This includes as:

> an assemblage of forms of practical knowledge, with modes of perception, practices of calculation, vocabularies, types of authority, forms of judgement, architectural forms, human capacities, non-human objects and devices, inscription techniques and so forth, traversed and transacted by aspirations to achieve certain outcomes in terms of the conduct of the governed (which also requires certain forms of conduct on the part of those who would govern).
>
> *(Rose, 1999, p. 52)*

Such an approach seems to foreground such technologies as broadly encompassing of the conditions in which policy actors find themselves, and who appear as 'hemmed in' by the possibilities and preclusions of such technologies. The 'con-duct' of those involved appears as open to influence by broader processes beyond the control of those to whom they are directed. And such 'encompassing' con-ceptions of practice seem to postulate that the practices of those to whom they are directed are indeed subject to intervention – indeed perceived as requiring intervention in some way: 'If the conduct of individuals or collectivities appeared to require conducting, this was because something in it appeared problematic to someone. Thus, it makes sense to start by asking how this rendering of things problematic occurred' (Miller & Rose, 2008, p. 14).

Through such processes, audit and accountability represent new modes of governing that influence individual and group action. However, such processes also involve new players, beyond government, and entail significant meaning-making and interpretation on the part of those governed.

More recently, Rhodes' (2012) multi-pronged conception of governance has proved useful for understanding the analytical potential of governance studies, even as his work has not been deployed in depth to help make sense of more recent processes of standardization in schooling settings. Rhodes (2012) refers to processes of governance as a shift in relations between governments, the private sector and various voluntary organizations. He also flags how 'the informal authority of networks supplements and supplants the formal authority of government' thereby exposing the limits of the state (p. 33). This work also involves exploring what Rhodes (2012) describes as 'the paradox of strong states confounded by implementation gaps and unintended consequences' (p. 33). In this volume, I argue some of these unintended consequences include the rise of individuals and companies seeking to influence schooling practices through the provision of specific approaches and programs (see the emphasis on various 'explicit teaching' programs in Chapter 5 for a particularly cogent example).

The involvement of new actors has entailed a shift from bureaucratic or hierarchical relations to more networked modes of operation. The resulting 'network governance' is the first of what Rhodes (2012) refers to as three modes of governance in the broader literature on governance processes to try to capture the nature of relations between forces that seek to exert influence on situated practices, and those materially affected by such forces. Processes of network governance are associated with the incursion of increasingly neoliberal practices into the public sector, most obviously since the 1980s. Various forms of markets and quasi-markets have subsequently come into being to deliver aspects of public service that had traditionally been undertaken by the state. In education, Hursh (2016) refers somewhat dramatically to 'the end of public schools' to portray how standardized and high-stakes testing processes supported by private sector provision in particular serve as key technologies of audit and accountability for governing schooling practices.

Such an approach complements those analyses of institutional processes that see public enterprises and entities as governed through an increasing mix of state, market and civil processes. In this sense, processes of governance entail significant and important inter-relations between these entities, and considerable interplay on the part of policy actors occupying dominant positions in each sphere. On such a rendering, as Kooiman (2003) puts it, governance is:

> an instrument for conceptualising issues on the boundary between the social and the political, or in current terminology, between state, market and civil

society. Many governing challenges cannot be handled by each of these societal realms or institutions in isolation. The character and nature of these challenges – either problems or opportunities, is such that they 'trespass' traditional
boundaries between them. Thinking about modern governance in a systematic
manner, requires a set of concepts that show each of them to be parts of such
governing, forming a coherent framework that enables a picture of governance
as a societal quality to emerge.

(Kooiman, 2003, p. 8)

In this earlier rendering of governance processes, Kooiman (2003) sought to
convey what he described as 'a "rich" picture of the totality of such governing
without losing sight of the parts and aspects it consists on' (Kooiman, 2003, p. 8).
This book shares Kooiman's (2003) enthusiasm for such richness of the various
organizations and entities that seek to govern educators' work, but also argues that
in the effort to try to foreground these associations, the voice of those involved has
become somewhat subdued.

In contrast with more network governance approaches, more meta-governance
approaches explicate the development of increasingly and varied relationships and
interactions between various actors and agencies as indicative of more complex forms
of governance, and of evidence of hyper-governing of practices. Essentially, on such
a view, 'the state governs the organizations that govern society' (Rhodes, 2012,
p. 37). The state has various means of exerting influence, including via establishing
the 'rules of the game', such as facilitating the development of quasi-markets for
provision of services. It can also engage in various practices of 'storytelling', whereby
it can foster and sanction various forms of narratives about the nature of the work of
the organization. The state also steers practices via its capacity to distribute resources – most obviously money and various forms of authority (Rhodes, 2012). In many
ways, those affected by these new forms of governing and those engaged in 'steering
from a distance' (Kickert, 1995) are part of this work.

Significantly, however, Rhodes (2012) argues that such broader network and
metagovernance approaches are insufficient for making sense of current processes of
governance and governing. There is a need to 'put the people back into governance' (Rhodes, 2012, p. 33), to reflect the need to acknowledge how both
understandings of practices of governance are heavily influenced by those engaged
in such processes, and to better acknowledge those to whom such processes are
directed. In a more 'interpretive' account of governance, beliefs and practices are
made sense of in light of actors' own interpretations and understandings. Within
this approach, various 'dilemmas' cause pause for thought and consideration, and
recognizing 'contingencies' and critiques of various narratives are important
(Rhodes, 2012). Such an account also seeks to make sense of the perspectives of
those seeking to rule, the rationalities involved in such work, and processes of
resistance.

In keeping with Rhodes' (2012) argument that an interpretive approach ascribes
necessary attention to those engaged in and influenced by processes of governance,

this book seeks to take up Rhodes' challenge by drawing explicitly on the insights of educators in schooling settings, and how they make sense of the broader policy, curriculum, teaching and testing practices that have come to characterize their practice. However, it does so in ways that seek to acknowledge the always necessarily precarious conditions of possibility in which individual and collective educational actors seek to exercise agency, and understanding. It does not simply deny the broader practices and processes of audit and accountability that have sought to govern educators' work in schooling settings, but instead seeks to portray how such processes are always and everywhere 'in the making' through educators' practices, even as they are simultaneously contested by educators' work and learnings.

A toolbox approach

The research presented here is heavily informed by broader practices and processes of governance and techniques for government by those engaged in such practices. These processes of governing are exercised through various forms of audit and accountability. Such accountability is enabled through the technical expertise and infrastructures that make it possible to collect, store and draw on various forms of data as 'evidence' of the need for further policy reform.

At the same time, the research does not seek to simply reinforce the nature of such governing processes of accountability, and the more economistic and managerial logics that attend the advocacy and collection of data for this purpose. Instead, it also asks whether and how those being governed also seek to simultaneously influence the conditions in which they work. The book endeavours to shed light on the various forms of accountability that have come to characterize schooling practices in recent times – in policy, curriculum, teaching and assessment/evaluation.

To this end, broader understandings of governance under current policy conditions, including Rhodes' (2012) notion of interpretive governance are deployed, and are particularly generative for thinking anew the inter-relations between processes of governance through various audit, accountability and standardization practices, and how these processes might be understood and engaged by those to whom they are directed. Such an approach also seeks to focus attention on the more localized practices of educators as they work and learn in educational contexts increasingly governed by broader accountability logics, particularly through the development and application of various forms of data at school sites. On this rendering, such an approach is akin to research that also seeks to foreground more 'micro-processes' (Little, 2012) associated with teachers' use and engagement with data.

Given the contestation that attends accountability processes, after Bourdieu (1990), the research also seeks to delineate the nature of the dominant logics that have come to characterize practices in each of the domains of policy, curriculum, teaching and assessment/evaluation. It seeks to reveal the competing and contested logics that attend these processes, and why and how particular logics come to dominate. Such contestation is an intrinsic part of not only the policy development processes but also policy enactment, and seeking to provide insights into the nature of the contested logics that characterize the governance of schooling practices is crucial to gaining fuller insights into the plurality of practices that attend the enactment of educational policy in relation to the three message systems of schooling of curriculum, teaching and assessment (Bernstein, 1971).

Consequently, the book adopts a broadly political theory approach which draws on literature on processes of government, governance, and policy and practice, from political and social theory, and education, to help make sense of how processes of audit and accountability have become so dominant in current schooling practices. It also provides resources for hope by drawing on notions of interpretive governance that reveal possibilities beyond those accountability logics that seem to restrain more educative practices and insights. Through development of more 'educative' conceptions of what are described as 'interrogative governance' on the part of educators, the book seeks to provide insights into more 'authentic accountabilities' that should and could characterize schooling settings. Such an approach combines a social–political theoretical analysis of practices with a philo-sophical normative articulation of what schooling and professional learning might look like from the 'real-world' understanding and perspective of educators working and learning in schools under current policy conditions.

The purpose of this book

This book seeks to explore how teachers and school-based administrators in schools navigate the vicissitudes of increased processes of accountability in increasingly neo-liberal and managerial conditions in schooling settings, and in ways that provide evidence of more hopeful approaches to accountability, even as this is challenging work. The book draws on data into schooling practices in the state of Queensland, Australia, to exemplify how educators make sense of their work under strong pressure for increased accountability, auditability and enumeration of education. As out-lined earlier, such an approach is not simply reflective of the particular conditions that have characterized schooling in Queensland in the 2010s, but serves as a vehicle to help scholars and educators understand schooling practices more fully in their own circumstances. This includes to help substantiate evidence of the broader practices of curriculum development, teaching and assessment referred to here, as well as to potentially challenge established understandings and claims about dominant practices in other settings. On this last point, the book is not simply a descriptive account of existing practices, but an analysis of existing practices that resonates in large measure with the wider literature, while at the same time revealing these practices as perhaps more nuanced, complex and contradictory than existing accounts of how policy, curriculum, teaching and testing are construed under current conditions of increased accountability and standardization of practice. This analysis is provided not simply to critique existing accounts for the sake of critique, but to better understand the spe-cific practices to which they refer, how particular practices come to exert significant influence under current policy conditions, as well as how those constituted through these practices make sense of – interpret and interrogate – the particular conditions in which they find themselves. Such an approach serves as a necessary foil that can be deployed by others to help make sense of associated practices in other cultural contexts, and to see how schooling practices might be analysed anew, and practised differently, and become more oriented towards what are described as more 'authentic accountabilities'.

The book also takes seriously Ball et al.'s (2012) call to move beyond more traditional conceptions of policy 'implementation' as some sort of simplistic, one-way 'unfolding' of centralized policy prerogatives that are somehow 'put into practice' in schooling sites. Given policy is not simply a text or set of texts to be faithfully and unproblematically developed by educational authorities and bureaucrats, and automatically and uncritically adhered to by educational administrators, principals, teachers and other system- or school-based personnel (Taylor, Rizvi, Lingard & Henry, 1997), the way in which policies play out is multifaceted, complex, unanticipated and unpredictable.

In the current context of increasing emphasis on 'what works' (Slavin, 2008), the book seeks to challenge decontextualized approaches that fail to take into account the contingencies that characterize policy enactment. Honig (2009) argues her reviews of decades of implementation research indicate that:

> whether or not a policy works is not an inherent property of the program or intervention itself. Rather, its outcomes depend on interactions between that policy, people who matter to its implementation and conditions in the places in which people operate.
>
> *(p. 333)*

With this in mind, Honig (2009) argues 'educational researchers should reframe their "what works" debates to ask: what works for whom, where, when and why?' (p. 333). Such an approach is 'far more nuanced than many present debates about what works suggest and calls researchers' attention to the importance of uncovering various implementation contingencies' (pp. 333–334). It is with these interests and foci in mind that the research that informs this book is presented.

Overview: Philosophy, policy, politics, curriculum, teaching and testing

In the first part of the book, following this introductory chapter, and to better 'set the scene', Chapter 2 provides an overview of a brief history of political theory to help situate how practices and processes of governing for and through accountability have become so prominent. This includes an account of earlier theorizing in relation to the establishment of the state, and its evolution, to theorizing in relation to accountability as a form of governance.

This is followed, in Chapter 3, by an account of the broader policy conditions that have contributed to the rise of more accountability-oriented logics and foci.

This includes an overview of how more neoliberal and managerial approaches and foci have become so prominent, including in the Queensland context. The latter contextual material in this chapter also helps situate the subsequent accounts of policy enactment in the Queensland case.

The second part of the book, focusing on policy-in-practice, commences with an overview (Chapter 4) of how more accountability logics have influenced curriculum development practices. This includes an analysis of the Queensland iteration of the Australian Curriculum, known as 'Curriculum into the Classroom', or C2C, and how this sought to govern teaching practices throughout the state.

Chapter 5 provides an account of how more accountability logics have influenced teachers' teaching practices. Again, as well as drawing on the broader cognate literature in relation to the standardization of teaching more broadly, specific examples from the Queensland context are used to inform broader discussions about the nature and contestation surrounding more standardized approaches to teaching that have arisen in response to more accountability logics.

Chapter 6 focuses necessary attention on assessment practices in schooling contexts, revealing how accountability practices have become heavily instantiated with standardized testing practices, and how the latter have sought to reorient schooling, more broadly, and teaching and learning in particular. Again, data from Queensland are provided to exemplify the broader processes evident in the literature, as well as to reveal the need for further scrutiny and critique of this literature.

The concluding chapter provides an overview of dominant logics of practice under current policy conditions of increased accountability for educational practices and outcomes, and how such conditions have substantively altered schooling practices in sometimes problematic ways. However, the chapter also seeks to serve as a stimulus for the cultivation of alternative practices – more 'authentic accountabilities' – beyond more reductive accounts of standardization in schooling. The chapter provides 'resources for hope' in the way it reveals how such accountabilities were evident through the active interrogation of teachers and school-based administrators in their work, even as this was challenging work for those involved.

Conclusion: Resources for hope

At the same time that this volume reveals the challenges that attend increased pressures and demands towards accountability, it also seeks to reveal instances and opportunities for resistance to more totalizing, standardized practices and processes. In educational settings, perhaps Rizvi & Lingard (2010) summarize such hopefulness best when they argue that while processes of neoliberal governance have had substantive effects in educational settings, such processes are not uniform in their influence, but are instead always subject to negotiation and change, at local sites:

> Ideologies now play a greater role, for example in relation to the ideas of individual choice and markets. In this way, the processes of the allocation of

values and the structure of state authority are transformed. However, this shift to governance is not uniform around the world but is negotiated locally, as these processes are mediated by local histories, cultures and politics.

(p. 117)

This book seeks to indicate where these points for intervention, and hope, lie, even as it reveals how the conditions in which teachers' work and learning transpire are heavily influenced by logics of accountability associated with more neoliberal and managerial influences. It is important not to simply concede the seemingly totalizing influence of such practices of 'control' but instead to observe and articulate where and how processes of resistance and meaning-making are exercised that give credence to more agentic and optimistic ways of engaging with the world. Rhodes' (2012) notion of interpretive governance is revealed as a useful starting point for identifying such interrogative possibilities, and how they might give rise to more authentic accountabilities.

Note

1 I acknowledge from the outset that the data presented in the book is situated within a very specific national and sub-national context at a particular point in time. However, by situating this data in relation to international literature about the nature of public schooling provision more broadly, the volume seeks to serve as a stimulus for readers to consider the nature, extent and effects of various accountability processes within the particular education systems with which they are most familiar.

References

Anagnostopoulos, D., Rutledge, S., & Jacobsen, R. (2013). Introduction: Mapping the information infrastructure of accountability. In D. Anagnostopoulos, S. Rutledge & R. Jacobsen (Eds), *The infrastructure of accountability: Data use and the transformation of American education*. Cambridge, MA: Harvard Education Press.

Ball, S., Maguire, M., & Braun, A. (2012). *How schools do policy: Policy enactments in secondary schools*. London: Routledge.

Bernstein, B. (1971). On the classification and framing of educational knowledge. In M.F.D. Young (Ed.), *Knowledge and control: New directions for the sociology of education* (pp. 47–69). London: Collier-Macmillan.

Bourdieu, P. (1990). *The logics of practice*. Stanford, CA: Stanford University Press.

Deming, D., & Figlio, D. (2016). Accountability in US education: Applying lessons from K-12 experience to higher education. *The Journal of Economic Perspectives*, 30(3), 33–55.

Hanushek, E., & Raymond, M. (2005). Does school accountability lead to improved student performance? *Journal of Policy Analysis and Management*, 24(2), 297–293.

Honig, M. (2009). What works in defining 'what works' in educational improvement: Lessons from education policy implementation research, directions for future research. In G. Sykes, B. Schneider & D. Plank (Eds), *Handbook of education policy research* (pp. 333–347). New York: Routledge.

Hursh, D. (2016). *The end of public schools: The corporate reform agenda to privatize education*. New York: Routledge.

Kempf, A. (2016). *The pedagogy of standardized testing: The radical impacts of educational standardization in the US and Canada.* Basingstoke: Palgrave Macmillan.

Kickert, W. (1995). Steering at a distance: A new paradigm of public governance in Dutch higher education. *Governance: An International Journal of Policy and Administration,* 8(1), 135–157.

Kooiman, J. (2003). *Governing as governance.* London: Sage.

Lingard, B. (2010). Policy borrowing, policy learning: Testing times in Australian schooling. *Critical Studies in Education,* 51(2), 129–147.

Lingard, B., Martino, W., Rezai-Rashti, G., & Sellar, S. (2016). *Globalizing educational accountabilities.* New York: Routledge.

Little, J.W. (2012). Understanding data use practice among teachers: The contribution of micro-process studies. *American Journal of Education,* 118, 143–166.

Meyer, H-D., Tröhler, D., Labaree, D., & Hutt, E. (2014). Accountability: Antecedents, power and processes. *Teachers College Record,* 116, 1–12.

Miller, P., & Rose, N. (2008). *Governing the present.* Cambridge: Polity Press.

Neal, D. (2013). The consequences of using one assessment system to pursue two objectives. Working Paper 19214. National Bureau of Economic Research. Downloaded 18 January 2018 from: http://www.nber.org/papers/w19214.pdf

Nóvoa, A., & Yariv-Mashal, T. (2003). Comparative research in education: A mode of governance or a historical journey? *Comparative Education,* 39(4), 423–438.

NyeJr, J. (2004). *Soft power: The means to success in world politics.* New York, NY: Public Affairs.

Odden, A. (1991). The evolution of education policy implementation. In A. Odden (Ed.), *Education policy implementation.* Albany, NY: State University of New York Press.

Phillips, D. (2000). Learning from elsewhere in education: Some perennial problems revisited with reference to British interest in Germany. *Comparative Education,* 36(3), 297–307.

Phillips, D., & Ochs, K. (2003). Processes of policy borrowing in education: Some explanatory and analytical devices. *Comparative Education,* 39(4), 451–461.

Power, M. (1997). *The audit society: Rituals of verification.* Oxford: Oxford University Press.

Rein, M. (1983). *From policy to practice.* London: Macmillan.

Rhodes, R. (2012). Waves of governance. In D. Levi-Faur (Ed.), *The Oxford handbook of governance* (pp. 33–44). Oxford: Oxford University Press.

Rizvi, F., & Lingard, B. (2010). *Globalizing education policy.* London: Routledge.

Robertson, S., & Dale, R. (2015). Towards a 'critical cultural political economy' account of the globalising of education. *Globalisation, Societies and Education,* 13(1), 149–170.

Rose, N. (1999). *Powers of freedom: Reframing political thought.* Cambridge: Cambridge University Press.

Slavin, R. E. (2008). Perspectives on evidence-based research in education: What works? Issues in synthesizing educational program evaluations. *Educational Researcher,* 37(1), 5–14.

Steiner-Khamsi, G. (Ed.) (2004). *The global politics of educational borrowing and lending.* New York: Teachers College Press.

Taylor, S., Rizvi, F., Lingard, B., & Henry, M. (1997). *Educational policy and the politics of change.* London: Routledge.

Thrift, N. (2005). *Knowing capitalism.* London: Sage.

PART I
Philosophy, policy and politics

2

GOVERNING FOR AND THROUGH ACCOUNTABILITY

A brief history

Introduction

The state has always sought to exert influence, to govern, even as this has been resisted. In relation to schooling, this is most evident in efforts to control educational practices via particular policy settings. Such policies seek to prescribe the nature of the curriculum, teaching and assessment which characterize schooling. While the specificities of how policy is deployed, and how it influences practice, are the subjects of the following chapter and subsequent chapters, this chapter helps to situate the circumstances that enable educational policy to exert influence in the first place. The chapter argues that it is within the realm of ideas – of what Taylor (2004) describes as a social imaginary – that particular modalities of understanding come to exert influence, and that eventually find their way into policy. This chapter seeks to give expression to some of the key ideas informing trends in educational policy practices as social practices, and particularly how broader tendencies to control and govern have been manifest at different periods in time, but always expressed variously, depending on the particular circumstances and social conditions that dominate. This lineage of ideas helps to usefully inform current educational debates by situating such insights in broader historical debates about the best ways to ensure productive social, political and economic organization.

This chapter provides an overview of earlier and later political theorizing to help situate current emphases on accountability as a dominant logic. It summarizes an array of political theories, from ancient societies to the Enlightenment, through to the current moment, to account for the variability with which social processes, including education, have been governed. Given the vast array of debates over social practices, and how these can be understood, the chapter does not and cannot provide a definitive account of such practices, but seeks to highlight key conceptual resources during different periods of time to indicate how more accountability logics can be understood to have exerted influence, and how current manifestations have exerted influence differently from previous expressions.

A brief history of political theory: From ancient times to the present

The ancients: Governing the 'good society'

Since ancient times, governing the population has been construed as entailing placing limits on individual and collective practices. While the ancients were animated by thinking about and articulating the notion of the 'good society', they also conceived of a notion of society which was inherently limiting for most of their populations. Plato's (1987) notion of the good society espoused in *The Republic* was a justification for a form of government which reified conceptions of some sort of 'natural' division between humans based on innate natural ability and aptitude. It is this 'naturalness' of the capacity of particular individuals and groups which predisposes them to particular roles in society, and which, in turn, determines the nature of the education most applicable to their needs. For Plato, the good society is founded on three essential needs: economic needs, for the material well-being and prosperity of its members; the need for protection through an able and reliable military; and administrative needs to ensure the populace is effectively and appropriately governed. Those who were inclined towards satisfying immediate pleasures were best suited to become labourers and business people, in order to foster economic growth and development. Those with a disposition to bravery were most suited to become soldiers to protect the city-state, alongside an executive for this purpose ('Auxiliaries'). And those driven by the search for meaning and knowledge, and with the virtues of wisdom and understanding, had the intellectual capacity to be philosophers, and were most suited to ruling over others ('Guardians'). In this way, workers/those engaged in commerce, soldiers and ruler/philosophers were seen as having natural proclivities which would be revealed by an educational system designed to these multiple ends.

The type of education which would enable such a society to come into being was one which provided various gradations of educational experience, accessible to each according to his [sic] abilities and capacity to engage. A basic education entailed the development of fundamental reading and writing skills, physical education and a later period of secondary or 'literary' education. This latter phase served as a vehicle for the inculcation of moral and theological training. This was followed by a period of military training. However, to become a ruler – a 'philosopher ruler' – further education in five mathematical disciplines (arithmetic, plane and solid geometry, astronomy and harmonics) was required. This phase was followed by training in pure philosophy ('Dialetic'). For the working classes, their education ceased after the first phase of acquisition of basic reading and writing skills; for soldiers, subsequent literary education and military training were undertaken. Only those deemed to possess the requisite understandings and proclivities, and displaying the necessary intellectual capacity, could enter the latter stages to become political leaders. In this way, the education system was deeply implicated in the construction of a particular kind of society, and was instrumental in maintaining the conditions for its perpetuation.

For Plato, governing society entailed application of notions of justice (his ostensive focus in *The Republic*) through enactment of the virtues of wisdom, courage, discipline and temperance. This final ascription of justice was exercised through each person fulfilling the role assigned to him [sic], and to which he [sic] was 'naturally' predisposed. This was expressed in terms of 'minding one's own business':

> So perhaps justice is, in a certain sense, just this minding one's own business … I think that the quality left over, now that we have discussed discipline, courage and wisdom, must be what makes it possible for them to come into being in our state and preserves them by its continued presence when they have done so.
>
> *(Plato, 1987, p. 145)*

Plato goes on to reinforce the point about the need for each group to sustain its role as part of a functioning society:

> Interference by the three classes with each other's jobs, and interchange of jobs between them, therefore, does the greatest harm to our state, and we are entirely justified in calling it the worst of evils … So that is what injustice is, and conversely, when each of our three classes (businessmen, Auxiliaries, and Guardians) does its own job and minds its own business, that, by contrast, is justice and makes our state just.
>
> *(pp. 146–147)*

In this way, an ordered political system was enforced which enabled little digression. The Platonic position ensured the continuation of a highly regulated, classed and gendered society in which some were preordained to govern others. Variations of this approach were sustained throughout the Middle Ages, manifest through a stable feudal order which sought to cement established regimes, and resiled against practices and processes which challenged its maintenance.

The Enlightenment: Reconstituting governance

While the push towards control and increased influence over the governance of practice has a long history, reconsideration of processes of governing and governance were perhaps most evident during the Enlightenment. Understanding the nature of social control, and relations of control, proved fertile ground for political philosophers and social theorists, with manifestations of such influences expressed differently in different periods, and providing insights into the nature of dominant practices at any given moment.

In 1651, Thomas Hobbes of Malmesbury published his celebrated work *Leviathan or The Matter, Forme and Power of a Common Wealth Ecclesiasticall and Civil,* more commonly referred to as *Leviathan.* A biblical sea monster, Leviathan was an object of fear and foreboding in the Christian Old Testament and the Tanakh – the canon of the Hebrew bible. In *Leviathan,* Hobbes makes the argument for strong central government as a means of overcoming the 'state of nature' of humanity which tended towards anarchy as a result of disagreements about what constituted the greatest good for its members. Influenced by the English Civil War, for Hobbes, the penultimate state of confusion is characterized by a state of conflict and perpetual torment between all as each pursues his [sic] own ends. This is because rather than focusing on and assuming evidence for some form of 'the common good' (*summum bonum*) as had been (assumed) the case in earlier times, Hobbes argued that there was a need to redress the *summum malum,* or 'greatest evil'. This greatest evil constituted fear of a violent death, and was the product of a perpetual condition of anarchy.

The only way to redress these concerns was to establish a political community, the purpose of which was to mitigate against a state of perpetual violence and anarchy. This is the source of the oft-quoted reference attributed to Hobbes of *bellum omnium contra omnes* [1] 'the war of all against all'. A state of perpetual conflict was not sustainable, and detrimental to all forms of productive human endeavour:

> In such condition there is no place for Industry; because the fruit thereof is uncertain: and consequently no Culture of the Earth; no Navigation, nor use of the commodities that may be imported by Sea; no commodious Building; no Instruments of moving, and removing such things as require much force; no Knowledge of the face of the Earth; no account of Time; no Arts; no Letters; no Society; and which is worst of all, continuall feare, and danger of violent death; and the life of man, solitary, poor, nasty, brutish and short.
>
> *(Leviathan, Ch. XIII; Hobbes, 1996/1651, p. 70).*

However, more enlightened perspectives sought to challenge rigid, established hierarchies and forms of governance that sought to 'rule over' people. Rousseau's *The Social Contract* perhaps best characterizes this challenge to the established order, arguing for a form of governance in which those governing agree to submit to the 'general will' of the people. This general will is characterized by a sense of singular unity over the nature of what is deemed important. The general will is expressed as a consensus position about the requirements for the general well-being and preservation of any given group of people. This will is of value in that it is the product of robust engagement about the nature of what the group values:

> So long as several men [sic] assembled together consider themselves a single body, they have only one will, which is directed towards their common preservation and general well-being … A state thus governed needs very few

laws, and whenever there is a need to promulgate new ones, that need is universally seen.

(Rousseau, 2004, p. 122)

Even under those circumstances in which states become corrupted, this capacity for productive will-formation remains intact, awaiting the opportunity for renewal:

> In the end, when the state, on the brink of ruin, can maintain itself only in an empty and illusory form, when the social bond is broken in every heart, when the meanest interest impudently flaunts the sacred name of the public good, then the general will is silenced … Does it follow from this that the general will is annihilated or corrupted? No, that is always unchanging, incorruptible and pure, but it is subordinated to other wills which prevail over it … Even in selling his vote for money, he does not extinguish the general will in himself; he evades it. The fault he commits is to change the form of the question, and to answer something different from what is asked him; so that instead of saying, with his vote, 'It is advantageous to the state', he says, 'It is advantageous to this man or to that party that such or such a proposal should be adopted'. For this reason, the sensible rule for regulating public assemblies is one intended not so much to uphold the general will there as to ensure that it is always questioned and always responds.
>
> *(Rousseau, 2004, p. 124)*

Unlike Hobbes' conception of a 'natural' human state as depraved and requiring close government, Rousseau's conception of the social contract was one premised on a positive articulation of human nature which could only be realized by shaking off the constraints of formality which hemmed it in.

Educationally, this much more equitable arrangement was reflected in the need to develop the capacity for participation in the process of the 'general will' formation. Such capacity could help to counter the 'negative freedom' associated with the individual proclivity to satisfy one's own interests; the 'positive freedom' involved seeking a mode of living with others which would enable them to live productively, collectively. Rousseau's account of the education of the hypothetical child, *Émile,* provides insights into his philosophy of education. For Rousseau (3011/1762), the form of education most appropriate for the child was one which enabled him [sic] to exercise control over his self, and to do so in a virtuous way regardless of the corrupting influences which exist in society at large. The development of the natural proclivities of the child were seen as most likely to be able to be developed in a context away from these corrupting influences – typically associated with urban areas. The more natural environment, remote from large urban areas, was seen as providing the necessary conditions to cultivate a 'natural' education – one associated with first-hand experiences in the world around him. As Carr and Harnett (1996) argue, 'only by first capturing his "natural innocence" will Émile learn to accept the General Will and seek the common good' (p. 35).

As with Plato, Rousseau's student moves through various phases. The education of the child moves from first-hand experiences of the environment around him up to age 12, followed by a period of engagement in practical knowledge development by engaging with specific problems relevant to his environment. This is followed by a final stage of engagement in historical analyses of alternative societies and subsequently political philosophy as a vehicle to understand the issues and problems of politics, government and public morality to which the general will-formation is oriented. To this end, notions of education were central to realizing more egalitarian position-taking.

In keeping with more utilitarian approaches (most notably associated with Jeremy Bentham), later notable philosophers also advocated the role of education as a vehicle for the cultivation of the greatest good for the greatest number. However, the approach supported was one which foregrounded the significance of the individual in society, rather than any given collective. This more liberal approach to social organization was one in which the liberal individual was accorded primacy over notions of 'society'. By virtue of this support for the individual, the social was construed as a collective of individuals whose needs could only be satisfied by social organizations which enabled individual profit and agency, at the expense of the development of more collective concerns. Under these circumstances, only those who have been predisposed, through their social circumstances, to engage in this competitive process, were able to profit from it. The rewards of this competition were therefore disproportionately allocated to a minority of the population at the expense of the majority. This minority was able to establish the parameters in which social practices, including education, were exercised, and to participate in those fractions of the educational enterprise which accorded them greatest effect, exerting influence over the majority through their decisions and decision-making.

The sense of freedom attached to liberal thinking was associated with the restriction of forms of imposition and control over individuals' actions and liberties. This 'negative' definition implied a sense of freedom achievable through the removal of any form of restriction on individual actions. This contrasted with more collective forms of self-actualization associated with classical notions of freedom as occurring through participation in the public sphere, in making decisions about what was construed as logical and relevant through deliberation and dialogue. From a more utilitarian Benthamite perspective, the aim was to ensure that individuals could pursue, without limits, their own happiness, and that the 'good society' was one characterized by the greatest happiness for the greatest number.

However, orchestrating such a process was fraught with difficulties, as it was clear that establishing a functioning government would necessitate a mechanism to ensure that those governing did not simply satisfy their own interests, as a utilitarian approach assumed they would, but that the interests and happiness of those governed could be advanced. James Mill's *Essay on Government* (2015/1828) made the case for a representative democratic approach which he argued could better secure such an ideal. Annual parliaments, secret ballots and universal voting would enable the people to ensure that their individual wants and desires were protected.

However, and subsequently, J.S. Mill's elaboration of these utilitarian practices and principles took a different approach to determining the nature of human happiness, arguing that happiness was a product of the capacity of individuals to comprehend their own circumstances, rather than a more basic desire to address baser conceptions of pleasure and pain, associated with Jeremy Bentham's original utilitarian approach: 'Nature has placed mankind under the governance of two sovereign masters, *pain* and *pleasure*. It is for them alone to point out what we ought to do, as well as to determine what we shall do' (Bentham, 1879, Ch. 2, p. 1). While committed to the principle of people developing their moral and intellectual capacities through engaging in the democratic process, J.S. Mill's philosophy also harboured concerns about the extent to which the general population was indeed capable of making the best possible decisions. This was evident, for example, in his arguments that the most educated should have the capacity to cast several votes, by virtue of their dominant intellect.

This concern about governing through liberal ideals, and the contrast with actual governing practices in the name of liberalism, led to a revision of such ideals during the 19th century. T.H. Green's development of liberal theory recognized rights and freedoms – 'positive freedom' – as always existing in some conception of shared social life, and that this common life necessarily influenced how such freedoms and rights can be understood. Freedom entailed engaging in actions and activities with others, and in ways which maximize the opportunity for all 'to make the best of themselves' (Green, 1906, p. 372). In this way, liberalism came to be defined in terms of what it enabled, rather than what it prevented or abhorred. In the English setting, Green drew on the implementation of the Education Act of 1870 as a primary example of government action which greatly influenced human action, but which simultaneously promulgated human freedoms by enabling access to a variety of modes of living and being, including in relation to careers, and without which these same individuals would have been greatly limited in their freedoms.

Such a stance was in direct contrast with elitist conceptions of governance processes through participatory democracy advocated in the mid-20th century, which were influenced by a notion of democracy involving an ill-informed and disinterested populace deciding who should rule for them. In this vein, Schumpeter (1947/1942) advocated a notion of participation which accounted for perceptions of apathy and limited understanding about the political process amongst the general population. Under these circumstances, the best that could be hoped for was a conception of democracy which provided the opportunity for a limited few to exercise control over the majority, and with as minimal input and deliberation by the latter over the decisions of the former. In this way, a conception of political engagement was advocated which had little to do with the cultivation of the population for active involvement in the decision-making which would influence their lives and work.

Governing to and through neoliberalism: The dominance of economism

More recently, and in spite of the Keynesian post-war settlement that advocated much more social-democratic reforms in education and society more broadly, educational governance has been further influenced by liberal governance traditions, albeit differently. This has been expressed in the form of a much more interventionist economic rationality. A heavily contested concept (Dunn, 2017; Venugopal, 2015), such an economic rationality is commonly described as 'neoliberalism'. Stuart Hall (2011) argues the term is deeply problematic, and necessarily provisional in nature, yet useful as a means of identifying a particular set of characteristics. For Connell, Fawcett and Meagher (2009) these characteristics are founded on an economic logic associated with the free market:

> 'Neoliberalism' broadly means the project of economic and social transformation under the sign of the free market. It also means the institutional arrangements to implement this project that has been installed, step by step, in every society under neoliberal control.
>
> *(p. 331)*

For Connell et al. (2009), the free market is the central motif of neoliberalism, and markets are always seeking to expand into new arena. As a result, and through a process of commodification, products and services become available which were not previously considered possible. Public services and institutions have been increasingly privatized as a means of ensuring increased efficiency and effectiveness.

Importantly, neoliberalism is not simply an economic rationality, but also 'an agenda of cultural change and institutional change, extending – at least in potential – through every arena of social life' (p. 333). By supporting increased choice, entrepreneurial approaches, individualism and competitive mechanisms for effecting change and improvement, a more neoliberal rather than collective ethos becomes apparent. Through a process of 'fractal organizational logics' (p. 333), in which 'each part of an organization is a microcosm of the larger unit in which it is embedded' (p. 333), Connell et al. (2009) argue that processes of competition and entrepreneurialism pervade all facets of an organization, which can be divided into units that mirror the same competitive principles and practices which characterize the whole.

To a certain extent, Connell et al.'s (2009) assessment of neoliberalism conflates an economistic ethos with more managerial technologies – technologies which, in many ways, are the antithesis of the free enterprise approach supposedly associated with neoliberalism. In truth, the neoliberal project contains in it significant dissonances and contradictions which challenge its integrity. Nevertheless, these contradictions are not sufficient to derail the neoliberal telos. Indeed, neoliberalism has been construed as a form of governance in which governing processes require technical solutions rather than political or ideological consideration (Rose & Miller, 1992).

Larner (2000) interprets neoliberalism as a policy agenda, as an ideology and as a form of governmentality. When understood as a policy agenda, Larner (2000) drawing on Belsey (1996) refers to the shift in policy emphasis as a product of a particular set of ideas – an ideology – which is underpinned by a specific set of five values: 'the individual; freedom of choice; market security; laissez faire, and minimal government' (Larner, 2000, p. 7 after Belsey, 1996). Significantly, 'while neoliberalism may mean less government, it does not follow that there is less governance' (Larner, 2000, p. 12). From a governance perspective, neoliberal strategies 'encourage people to see themselves as individualized and active subjects responsible for enhancing their own well-being' (p. 13). Such an approach foregrounds a society in which all are actively working on themselves and processes of audit and accountability are central to such work; indeed, '[w]elfare agencies [indeed all agencies] are now to be governed, not directly from above, but through technologies such as budget disciplines, accountancy and audit' (p. 13). Under such conditions, '"degovernmentalization" of the welfare state, competition and consumer demand have supplanted the norms of "public service"' (p. 13).

For Ong (2006), neoliberalism is a mode of governing designed to streamline government – a form of government which seems the antithesis of state power, but which is actually an 'exception' to such oppositions to state power:

> Indeed, neoliberalism considered as a technology of government is a profoundly active way of rationalizing governing and self-governing in order to 'optimize'. The spread of neoliberal calculation as a governing technology is thus a historical process that unevenly articulates situated political constellations.
>
> *(p. 3)*

It is this 'interventionist aspect of neoliberalism' which Ong (2006) describes as 'neoliberalism as exception', and which influences practices of citizenship in settings, such as in emerging countries, which are not typically governed through such practices. However, this linking of neoliberalism and exception also makes it possible to realize how processes of neoliberalism exert influence in multiple ways, and are also resisted because of the particular conditions and circumstances in context.

Such a position resonates with Peck's (2010) account of 'neoliberal reason' as a constructed entity. Drawing on Friedman (1951), Peck argues neoliberalism had many iterations in the various locations and times in which it developed. However, what is distinctive about neoliberalism is the way in which it corrals the state to its aims. Peck draws incisively on Friedman's (1951) argument that a 'new liberalism' needed to be radically different from earlier forms of 19th century liberalism based on laissez-faire principles that shunned the state. Instead, the state needed to 'lead the way' in fostering competition as the undergirding principle of neoliberalism:

> [The] fundamental error in the foundations of 19th Century liberalism [was that it] gave the state hardly any other task other than to maintain peace, and

to foresee that contracts were kept. It was a naïve ideology. It held that the state could only do harm [and that] laissez-faire must be the rule ... A new ideology must ... give high priority to limiting the state's ability to intervene in the activities of the individual. At the same time, it is absolutely clear that there are truly positive functions allotted the state. The doctrine that, on and off, has been called neoliberalism and that has developed, more or less simultaneously, in many parts of the world ... is precisely such a doctrine ... [I]n place of the nineteenth century understanding that laissez-faire is the means to achieve [the goal of individual freedom], neoliberalism proposes that it is *competition* that will lead the way ... The state will police the system, it will establish the conditions favourable to competition and prevent monopoly, it will provide a stable monetary framework, and relieve poverty and distress. Citizens will be protected against the state, since there exists free private markets, and the competition will protect them from one another.

(Friedman, 1951, pp. 91–93)

Importantly, the perspective put forward by the neoliberals of the mid-20th century – Friedman, Hayek, Mises, Buchanan, amongst others – differed significantly from the tenets of Adam Smith himself, whose work is so often invoked in the name of 'freedom' of the market, but whose moral sensibilities also challenged the adoption of market principles in some sort of 'pure' state. As Stedman-Jones (2012) argues, '[i]t was a virulent faith in the individual and his economic behaviour under market conditions rather than any conception of cultivated behaviour, manners, or Smithian moral sympathy that was important to neoliberal thinkers' (p. 115). Smith (1979/1776) argued that government should take responsibility for education and infrastructure rather than it being left to the market, for example, through vouchers.[2] Furthermore, historically, neoliberalism was far from a 'done deal'. As Peck (2010) argues, 'the neoliberal ascendency was never a sure thing' (p. 4). Rather, 'capturing and transforming the state was always a fundamental neoliberal objective' (Peck, 2010, p. 4):

Only at its wildest, anarcho-capitalist fringe did the neoliberal project venture to imagine life without the state. Notwithstanding its trademark antistatist rhetoric, neoliberalism was always concerned – at its philosophical, political, and practical core – with the challenge of first seizing and then retasking the state.

(Peck, 2010, p. 4)

Indeed, Peck (2010) also notes, in his account of the challenges of establishing neoliberal policies and principles in various 'frontier' communities – Chile in the 1970s, Iraq after the US-coalition intervention in the early 2000s – that establishing such goals requires active intervention and is far from a 'sure thing'. Such 'frontiers' 'may … be zones *both* of audacious experimentation and catastrophic failure', but also always advancing forward (p. 6):

> There are unique and contextually specific features of every such experiment, each of which reshapes the contradictory 'whole' of actually existing neoliberalism. Certainly, there is no neoliberal replicating machine. Rather, each experiment should be seen as a form of reconstruction, representing a conjunctural episode or moment in the contradictory *evolution* of neoliberal practice. The analytical – not to say political – challenge is to figure out how these have chained together over time, how they have become interwoven, how the project has achieved a form of evolutionary consolidation. It is both an indictment of neoliberalism and testament to its dogged dynamism, of course, that the laboratory experiments do not 'work'. They have nevertheless tended to 'fail forward', in that their manifest inadequacies have – so far anyway – repeatedly animated further rounds of neoliberal invention. Devolved governance, public-private partnership, management by audit, neopaternalism … all can be seen as examples of institutional reinvention spawned as much by the limits of earlier forms of neoliberalization as by some advancing 'logic'.
>
> *(Peck, 2010, p. 6)*

Consequently, neoliberalism has to be an active project if it is to exert influence, and must alter and adapt to do so. It cannot simply be taken for granted, and does not exert influence unchallenged. This process of active construction is taken as a summary lesson for how to foster alternative accountabilities from those dominated by a more neoliberal logic. In the case of education, and, more specifically, schooling, such work must be similarly ongoing and active, and oriented towards achieving an end-point of more robust professional judgement.

Managerialism and neoliberalism

As mentioned briefly above, alongside these neoliberal influences, there has been a concomitant process of importing various management practices, often associated with the corporate world, to govern educational, including schooling, practices. This 'New Public Management' (NPM), as it is often described, entails a process by which 'schemes of organization and control are imported from business to public institutions' (Connell, 2010, p. 25). This entails increased emphasis on neoliberalism occurring alongside concomitant, and contradictory, practices of 'managing' behaviours. As Hall (2011) explains (in the context of the rise of New Labour in Great Britain), this entails all manner of mechanisms to regulate, monitor and surveil actors via various targets:

> New Labour thus embraced 'managerial marketisation'. The economy was actively 'liberalised' (with disastrous consequence for the coming crisis), while society was boxed in by legislation, regulation, monitoring, surveillance and the ambiguous 'target' and 'control' cultures.
>
> *(p. 19)*

Competition, and increased management, went hand-in-hand, even as these management practices were sometimes found wanting, and, in the context of economic regulation, did not necessarily actually regulate the sector in ways intended. However, this did not stop the rise of various forms of regulation in government more broadly, in all aspects of public provision, including education. A key element of these increased managerial influences was the focus on accountability.

The 'new' governance: Governing through accountability

In the introductory chapter of *The Oxford Handbook of Public Accountability*, Bovens, Schillemans & Goodin (2014) lead with the sentence: '[a]ccountability is the buzzword of modern governance' (p. 1). While research into accountability studies is very diverse, and the field lacks a more cumulative approach to understanding the concept, subject as it is to a proliferation of perspectives, and disparate understandings regarding its nature and circumstances, research reveals how accountability is heavily associated with practices of book-keeping – of both keeping a count of/counting particular phenomena deemed important, as well as providing a description/'accounts' of how phenomena have been 'counted' (Bovens et al., 2014). This implies the composition of various forms of 'storytelling in a context of social (power) relations in which enforcement of standards and the fulfilment of obligations is a reasonable expectation' (Bovens et al., 2014, p. 3). This notion of accountability implies having to give 'account' for one's actions. It implies a sense of 'answerability' – of having to be able to justify particular practices, how they were undertaken, and to what ends: '"Accountability" refers to being answerable to somebody else, to be obligated to explain and justify action and inaction – how mandates, authority, and resources have been applied, with what results, and whether outcomes meet relevant standards and principles' (Olsen, 2014, p. 107).

Etymologically, the concept of accountability has a long lineage, ascribed by Dubnick (2007) to the translation of the French term *comptes a rendre* in the Domesday books of William I in 1085. The connotation of accountability associated with this volume is significant, given its ostensive capacity to 'account' for all the king's goods i.e., the sum total of all goods in the kingdom at that time. The result is a conception of accountability that implies ascription to particular norms, and under some sense of compulsion. In these medieval times, accountability:

> refers to the counting of possessions and classifying information on the basis of implicit or explicit norms and conventions ... [A]gents were *obliged* to provide answers to the questions posed to them by the accountants on behalf of their master ... Accountability thus has a relational core to it; it refers to the obligation to provide an account *to*, usually, a superior or at least someone with a legitimate stake.
>
> *(Bovens et al., 2014, p. 3)*

Numbers have always been central to this capacity to give an account, and these numbers have been construed as important vehicles for ascribing value to activity.

In similar vein, Poovey (1998) demonstrates how double-entry bookkeeping was construed as evidence of mercantile virtue amongst merchants in the late 15th century. Virtue and the capacity to give account through graphicacy were significant bedfellows. Such accounts served as a mode of government to which merchants sought to conform:

> Proclaiming mercantile virtue was necessary in 1494, both because in the late fifteenth century merchants were generally held in low esteem and because status mattered as much as wealth, if not more, and salvation ultimately mattered more than worldly goods. The system of double-entry books displayed virtue graphically, by the balances prominently featured at the end of each set of facing ledger pages and by the order evident in the books as a system. Thus the entries in the double-entry system seemed simply to refer to the particulars of a merchant's trade, while the system as a whole, which subordinated those particulars to the all-important balance, produced meanings that exceeded even the veracity of the individual entries. Most immediately, the balances produced by this system of writing proclaimed the creditworthiness of the individual merchant; more generally, the system's formal coherence displayed the credibility of merchants as a group. In this embryonic variant of the modern fact, then, we see particulars harnessed to a general claim, whose acceptance required believing that the precision of the formal system signalled virtue itself.
>
> Implicitly, at least, double-entry bookkeeping was both a system of writing and a mode of government, for if merchants were to benefit from the aura of credibility cast by the rectitude of the formal system, they had to obey the system's rules.
>
> (pp. xvi–xvii)

However, the practices used to keep account can also have specific and sometimes problematic effects. Scott (1998) refers to the rendering of forests as primarily sources of revenue for the early modern European state, and how this came to influence the actual forests themselves. While the logic of accounting for what constituted the forest was not particularly distinctive, Scott argues that: 'What is distinctive about this logic, however, is the narrowness of its field of vision, the degree of elaboration to which it can be subjected, and above all ... the degree to which it allowed the state to impose that logic on the very reality that was observed' (p. 13). This 'narrowness of the field of vision' enabled forest workers to be employed, using grids developed about the layout of the forest, to actually reconstitute the nature of the forests themselves. An early attempt to standardize the measurement of sustainable forestry yields involved estimating the revenue provided by forests on the basis of sample plots in which commercial-grade timbers were identified. This estimation process, initially involving forestry workers allocating colour-coded nails to the sample plot, was one thing. However, it was the next step which was truly significant in terms of how accountability processes came to reconstitute that for which they sought to account:

> That step was to attempt to create, through careful seeding, planting, and cutting, a forest that was easier for state foresters to count, manipulate, measure, and assess. The fact is that forest science and geometry, backed by state power, had the capacity to transform the real, diverse, and chaotic old-growth forest into a new, more uniform forest that closely resembled the administrative grid of its techniques. To this end, the underbrush was cleared, the number of species was reduced (often to monoculture), and plantings were done simultaneously and in straight rows on large tracts. These management practices, as Henry Lowood observes, 'produced the monocultural, even-age forests that eventually transformed the Normalbaum from abstraction to reality. The German forest became the archetype for imposing on disorderly nature the neatly arranged constructs of science. Practical goals had encouraged mathematical utilitarianism, which seemed, in turn, to promote geometric perfection as the outward sign of the well-managed forest; in turn the rationally ordered arrangements of trees offered new possibilities for controlling nature'. ... At the limit, the forest itself would not even have to be seen; it could be 'read' accurately from the tables and maps in the forester's office.
>
> *(Scott, 1998, p. 15)*

Importantly, and at the same time, even as these more accountability practices had the effect of standardizing a particular phenomenon – in this case, natural forests – alternative practices and processes continued to operate, reflective of the particular environment in which these change processes were undertaken, and the influence of those whose work was reconstituted through these processes:

> This utopian dream of scientific forestry was, of course, only the *immanent* logic of its techniques. It was not and could not ever be realized in practice. Both nature and the human factor intervened. The existing topography of the landscape and the vagaries of fire, storms, blights, climatic changes, insect populations, and disease conspired to thwart foresters and to shape the actual forest. Also, given the insurmountable difficulties of policing large forest, people living nearby typically continued to graze animals, poach firewood and kindling, make charcoal, and use the forest in other ways that prevented the foresters' management plan from being fully realized.
>
> *(Scott, 1998, p. 19)*

In this way, at the same time as more dominant accountability practices exert influence, such practices are also subject to critique and interrogation, and the specificity of practices *in situ*. My argument in this book is that such specific practices 'on the ground' may give rise to more productive, substantive and 'authentic' responses on the part of those involved. This has implications for the nature and particularly the effects of educational policy, as outlined in the second half of this volume.

Accountability: Understanding the concept, in context

In spite of little consensus about what constitutes 'accountability' in the cognate literature (including in fields as diverse as social psychology and accounting), there is still a broad conception of accountability as entailing having to provide an account of practices and/or perspectives, typically to some individual or entity occupying a position of relative authority (Bovens et al., 2014). This is reflected in what Jann and Lægreid (2015) refer to as the 'well-known definition' (p. 941) of the concept outlined in earlier work by Bovens (2007); on such a rendering, accountability entails:

> A relationship between an actor and forum, in which the actor has an obliga-
> tion to explain and justify his or her conduct, the forum can pose questions
> and pass judgment, and the actor may face consequences
>
> *(Bovens, 2007, p. 452)*

Reflecting the importance of context, Jann and Lægreid (2015) refer to this push for accountability as a reflection of disillusionment with the 'inefficienc[ies]' of the welfare state. This focus on accountability is reflected in: multiple forums, including political, administrative, legal, professional and social; multiple focus areas, including legal, procedural, financial and performance; and multiple forms, including 'vertically' (hierarchical accountability), 'horizontally' (e.g. social and professional accountability) and 'diagonally' (involving giving accounts to various forms of audit offices, administrative and regulatory bodies) (Bovens, 2007). While there may be no direct lines of accountability or sanction, such as in relation to more vertical accountability, the effects of more diagonal relations can still be significant.

There is also a sense in which the complexity surrounding accountability practices and processes is ever increasing, with new forms of accountability not simply replacing older forms, but being added to the mix of more traditional approaches and foci:

> In many cases, the new reforms build on old reforms, leading to even more
> complex and mixed relations between public-sector organizations on the one
> hand and the government and parliament on the other. Traditional forms of
> hierarchical (vertical) accountability are combined with new forms of hor-
> izontal or diagonal accountability – for example, to regulatory bodies, audit
> offices as well as to stakeholders and the public in general, for example,
> through the media.
>
> *(Jann & Lægreid, 2015, p. 943)*

However, there are also concerns about whether there is 'too little' (Mulgan, 2014) or 'too much' (Halachmi, 2014) accountability. Perhaps more cogently, Olsen (2014) refers to what he describes as 'the politics of accountability' to help make sense of the ambiguity that attends accountability. Olsen (2014) makes the point that the traditional compliance-control approach to understanding accountability (including measuring the extent to which actors deviate or do not 'comply' with particular expectations/demands) does not give adequate attention to the politics that surround accountability processes. While organizations are construed as 'tools of rationality, effectiveness, and efficiency characterized by clear and consistent goals' (Olsen, 2014, pp. 107–108), actual practices do not conform to these more rationalized approaches and foci. Rather, ambiguity is an inherent part of all social practices, and cannot be somehow excised.

Such politics are evident in different traditions that inform studies of accountability. From a moral philosophy standpoint, for example, Butler (2005) equates moral philosophy as conduct, with the everyday of 'doing'; she seeks to explore 'how it might be possible to pose the question of moral philosophy, a question that has to do with conduct and hence, with doing, within a contemporary social frame' (p. 3). For Butler (2005), such questions are a product of social relations, and reflect the very conditions in which they are framed, and frame them, accordingly, to reflect these conditions. Interestingly, Butler (2005) also makes the point that the problem lies not so much with conceptions of universality in relation to what constitutes an appropriate way to live, but rather with the extent to which such universality is cognisant of the specificity of the context to which it relates:

> [T]he problem is not with universality as such but with an operation of universality that fails to be responsive to cultural particularity and fails to undergo a reformulation of itself in response to the social and cultural conditions it includes within its scope of applicability.
>
> *(p. 6)*

Furthermore, given the significance of the social context in which practices unfold, any effort to account for one's practice as an individual will also necessarily reflect the particular social conditions in which such an account is rendered:

> When the 'I' seeks to give an account of itself, it can start with itself, but it will find that this self is already implicated in a social temporality that exceeds its own capacities for narration; indeed, when the 'I' seeks to give an account of itself, an account that must include the conditions of its own emergence, it must, as a matter of necessity, become a social theorist.
>
> *(p. 8)*

Often, this social context involves comparison. In comparative educational sociology, notions of accountability are evident in the way in which individuals and groups are called on to constantly compare themselves in an effort to constantly improve performance. Nóvoa and Yariv-Mashal (2003) refer to a 'politics of mutual accountability', and how comparative research acts as a mode of governance for how practices of accountability are expressed. They argue a 'politics of mutual accountability' is evident in the way in which processes of continual comparison are encouraged in educational settings. Such a politics:

> brings a sense of sharing and participation, inviting each country (and each citizen) to a perpetual comparison to the other. In fact, much more than a horizontality of exchanges, this process brings a kind of verticality, that is a system of classification of schools according to standards that are accepted without critical discussion.
>
> *(p. 427)*

These comparative logics play out in substantive ways, perhaps most overtly through the use of OECD PISA results which are employed as part of the 'global education race' (Sellar, Thompson & Rutkowski, 2017) and that have so much influence over how national governments 'give account' of educational provision.

Public accountability

These various forms of accountability are typically expressed as needing to be made public. In the schooling sphere, the mediatization of national PISA results, and attention to PISA more broadly, is a particularly apposite example of this 'public-ness'. The emphasis on public accountability reflects the increasing complexity of government, and associated governance processes (Bovens et al., 2014). The variety of groups and individuals involved contributes to this complexity, and associated challenges of determining to whom, and how, accountability should be rendered. A large part of these governance processes is focused on the provision of services by independent and quasi-independent organizations and entities operating in similarly quasi-marketized environments. Various forms of networks involving private and public actors contribute towards this complexity.

In what Bovens et al. (2014) describe as the 'minimal conceptual consensus' about what constitutes understanding of accountability, accountability is fundamentally a relational concept involving providing answers to those deemed in a position to demand them; accountability is 'about answerability towards others with a legitimate claim to demand an account' (p. 6). Accountability implies the enactment of some form of activity, and has consequences (Bovens et al., 2014). The 'public-ness' of these activities is significant. In relation to 'public accountability', this entails some form of openness to scrutiny on the part of the 'general public':

> That is to say the account is not rendered discreetly, behind closed doors. Rather, it is in principle open to the general public. The information provided

about the actor's conduct is generally accessible, hearings and debates are open to the public, and the forum promulgates its judgement to the public at large.

(Bovens et al., 2014, p. 7)

First, the person giving the account needs to detail his/her actions and practices, their outcomes and, if necessary, to justify these outcomes (particularly if deemed problematic). Secondly, the option of being able to interrogate this account, and the extent to which it is deemed adequate, needs to exist. And finally, there is a sense in which some form of judgement has occurred, and/or particular sanctions or rewards put in place as a result of the account. This conception of 'public' also implies a focus on concerns deemed to be of a 'public' nature – of consequence to a broader citizenry. It also pertains to various accounting standards, and entails the actual process of giving an account 'for matters of public interest' (Bovens et al., 2014, p. 7).

The nature of the audience to whom the account is directed is also important. This includes political accountability, in which accounts are given to various branches of governmental apparatus (members of parliament, constituents/voters, political parties); managerial/hierarchical accountability in which accounts have to be given to more senior managers/personnel; administrative accountability in which accounts have to be given to various administrative and regulatory entities; legal accountability involving accounts to courts, judges, magistrates, juries; professional accountability to professional peers/entities; and social accountability in which accounts have to be rendered to a variety of stakeholders in social arrangements, including clients, various third parties and interest groups (Bovens et al., 2014). In schooling settings, 'rich accountabilities' require such accounts be given and received by all involved in schooling practices, including parents, school administrators and students – and members of the broader community (Lingard, Sellar & Lewis, 2017). Such accounts need to reflect how teachers are accountable to broader schooling systems, just as these systems are simultaneously accountable to teachers.

The content of accountability processes is significant. This includes accountability related to financial probity, procedural processes/appropriate conduct, the development of particular products and outputs/outcomes. This content is also associated with the particular standards by which individuals and groups are held to account. Such standards reflect particular forums/audiences (bureaucratic; legal; professional; political) to which an account must be rendered. Various outcomes-focused standards may also be applied, such as in relation to efficient governance, effective practice and professional conduct (Bovens et al., 2014). Similarly, the content and standards are also associated with the extent to which actors are required to give account of their perspectives and practices. Bovens et al. (2014) contrast mandatory accountability, involving actors compelled to give account of their practices as a result of formal, typically hierarchical arrangements (a form of 'vertical mandatory accountability'), with more voluntary forms of accountability associated with forms of social accountability, and not involving any form of compulsion to do so. Various forms of 'quasi-voluntary forms of accountability' also exist between these mandatory and voluntary spectra, and may be character- ized by agents putting in place accountability regimes in response to the likelihood of increased scrutiny or as more 'light-touch' approaches encouraged by govern- ments or associated authorities (Bovens et al., 2014).

The limits and limitations of accountability: Perverse accountabilities

Importantly, accountability can also be problematic in nature, and demands close scrutiny of actual practices. In an analysis of political voting in Argentina, for example, Stokes (2005) refers to how party-political activists engaged in forms of 'perverse accountability' when they threatened voters with punishment if they suspected them of failing to vote for their parties after they had provided them with benefits, and for which they had earlier expressed their allegiance and support. Forms of accountability might be considered 'perverse' in other ways, particularly for how they encourage outcomes in the form of penalties that do not rightly take into account the particular conditions and circumstances at play in all manner of circumstances. The way in which 'adequate yearly progress' (AYP) is used as a mechanism for questionable high-stakes decision-making in schooling settings, including in relation to teacher pay, and retention and termination of staff, is a good example of such perverse forms of accountability (Amrein-Beardsley, 2014).

Perhaps rather than fostering 'perverse accountabilities', educational policies and practices currently lack a sense of the limitations of accountability, or what Messner (2009) refers to, in the context of financial accounting, as the 'limits of accountability'. These limits pertain to the relatively restricted way in which accountability processes are exercised, and the formulaic ways in which they encourage accounts of practice to be proffered. Given these restrictive practices, Messner (2009) raises an ethical argument about whether 'more of the same' forms of accountability are morally conscionable. Drawing on and elaborating work by Judith Butler, Messner (2009) argues that the accountable self is 'an opaque, exposed, and mediated self that is inherently limited in its ability to give an account of itself' (p. 918). These limits are palpable, and occur in perhaps unforeseen ways as people seek to give an account of their practices. Excessive demands for ever increasing accountability practices foster what Butler (2005) refers to as 'ethical violence', encouraging the production of an account about particular aspects of practice for which it is very difficult, perhaps impossible, to develop, because of the complexity of actual practice. More context-responsive approaches are advocated, that encourage 'situation-specific sensitivity for the "particular other" whose interests and values cannot be appropriately accounted for by a system of general rules and principles' (Messner, 2009, p. 919). As the remainder of this volume indicates, the work of educators and educational prac- tice fits well in the remit of such 'particular others'.

Importantly, accountability processes themselves are not simply denied. Instead, what is advocated is a form of accountability that accounts adequately for the complexity of practice, and does so in ways cognizant of this specificity of actual practice:

> This paper does not deny that, in many situations, it is reasonable to demand more accountability. It does, however, remind us that accountability itself may become a problematic practice, if it does not acknowledge its own inherent limits as an ethical practice. These limits are constituted by the burden that accountability may place on the accountable self who is expected to provide a convincing account even in situations where this is extremely difficult or even impossible.
>
> *(Messner, 2009, p. 919)*

Furthermore, those circumstances where there are constant pressures to account for one's practice can lead to the infiltration of a logic of accountability that is overly burdensome. Demands to somehow account for what constitutes more tacit forms of knowledge and understanding that are not readily recognized as contributing to and constitutive of practice are also problematic. Messner (2009) also raises the issue of conflicting pressures, and how the demands of multiple/varying bodies/entities can lead to a conflictual understanding of practice, and constitute an ethical dilemma in itself. The accountable self can be 'opaque' in that it is: not able to provide an adequate account of the complexity of lived experience; 'exposed' to demands for accountability that impacts on its particular practices; and 'mediated' by these demands for particular kinds of accounts of practice that are not grounded in its own experiences of practice (Messner, 2009). Any form of understanding is always necessarily inhibited by the limitations of the individual in understanding just why particular actions have been undertaken in particular circumstances; that is, understandings of both the capacity to effect change, and the nature of the social circumstances in which that change transpires, are always necessarily limited. Consequently, there is a sense in which the nature and extent of accountability can be deeply problematic.

In the field of politics, Flinders (2011) argues accountability in the form of an increasingly 'monitory' democracy – one characterized by the proliferation and increased influence of various authorities, agencies and other bodies to monitor the progress and actions of various groups and individuals – has had deleterious effects on democratic practice. At the same time as accountability practices in relation to politicians, politics and the bureaucratic apparatus have increased, trust in various institutions and processes have declined. At the same time as there has been increased scrutiny and accountability, there has been a concomitant decline in confidence in the value and validity of politics and the political process. These circumstances have arisen as a result of: the increasing politicization of accountability to serve narrow political and/or economic interests; individualized accountability processes that have lessened understanding of the nature of collective democratic engagement; and inadequate involvement on the part of scholars to educate the broader public about the political process, and challenging unsubstantiated critique of politicians and associated bureaucrats (Flinders, 2011).

Significantly, even as it is described as '*the* uber-concept of the late 20th and early 21st centuries' (p. 597), the consensus in relation to accountability is that the shift from processes of government to governance has resulted in less trust in the broader political process, and the need for ever more accountability, and that such accountability is implicitly a good thing:

the transition from *government* to *governance* has undermined traditional mechanisms of democratic accountability;
↓
as a result, politicians have become more untrustworthy and bureaucracies less responsive;
↓
new modes and mechanisms of accountability therefore need to be implemented; and
↓
any individual or organization that argues against greater accountability must have something to hide.

(Flinders, 2011, p. 599)

Flinders (2011) highlights the importance of what Anechiarico and Jacobs (1996) refer to as the integrity/efficiency trade-off, and how the emphasis on accountability can deleteriously affect actual service provision. While individuals and groups emphasize how to present themselves for purposes of audit or internal scrutiny, they run the risk of placing much greater emphasis on the representation of their work, rather than the substance of their work *per se*.

Such responses are encouraged by attention to accountability as often associated with a form of 'attack politics', involving 'an aggressive focus on failure over success, the exploitation of perceived personal or organizational vulnerabilities' (Flinders, 2011, p. 602); under such circumstances 'any willingness to listen or compromise is interpreted as a sign of weakness' (Flinders, 2011, p. 602). Such an attack politics places an emphasis on having to justify practices and outcomes, rather than seeking ways of addressing or overcoming shortcomings. The emphasis is on retribution, rather than redemption. On the one hand, when all is going well, concerns about accountability are diminished; when this is not the case, this more retributive logic comes into play: 'Those whom we want to hold accountable have a clear understanding of what accountability means: accountability means punishment' (Behn, 2001, p. 3). In this way, 'The promise to hold someone or something "to account" is therefore symbolically interpreted as a threat; as a promise to make someone pay for an error, omission, or mistake' (Flinders, 2011, p. 602).

The audit culture

As mentioned earlier, an important part of the accountability agenda is the pressure to quantify. Shore and Wright (2015) argue that the use of various forms of rankings, measurements and 'indicators' have become dominant modes of both representing the capacities and performance of organizations to external stakeholders, as well as mechanisms to measure and manage the activities of those in organizations. The way in which these technologies have proliferated, and how they have affected those to whom they are directed, has led to what professor of accountancy Michael Power (1994) and anthropologist Marilyn Strathern (2000a; 2000b) have described as the 'audit culture'. It is not only the use of various enumerative indicators and modes of ranking that have become significant modes of governance in contemporary organizations. Rather, there is also evidence of how broader processes of modern accountancy and finance have been taken up in settings very different from those in which they originated. Such processes effectively reframe the work of those to whom they are directed as beyond contestation – as subject to expert, technical intervention; as a result, they diminish the much more complex political and professional judgements that are actually undertaken as part of many domains (Shore & Wright, 2015). Such professional judgement is particularly crucial in the complex, uncertain and multifarious contexts of schools and schooling systems.

Alternative accountabilities

In this context of contestation over accountability, Shore and Wright (2015) ask whether and how more dominant processes of audit can be challenged:

> Just as Weber (2002/1904) wrote about the iron cage of bureaucracy and its inevitable onslaught as both a cause and effect of rationalization and modernity, is audit an unstoppable 'glass cage' of coercive transparency? How can we reclaim the professional autonomy and trust that audit practices appear to strip out of the workplace? Is it possible to sustain critical practice when what counts in modern rankings no longer reflects the central role and purpose of a professional and public institution?
>
> *(p. 422)*

Such an approach resonates with efforts to develop various 'alternative' forms of accountabilities. In educational settings, O'Neill (2013) refers to 'intelligent accountability', while Roberts (2009), drawing on O'Neill's (earlier) work, refers to 'an ethic of intelligent accountability'. These more intelligent conceptions of accountability do not entail some sort of 'fully transparent' understanding of one's practice, but instead are a recognition and understanding of the fallacy of such an approach, and a necessarily much more humble and conscientious understanding of the limits and possibilities of any call for increased accountability and transparency more broadly. A relentless focus on accountability as open to ever increasing processes of transparency is a form of self-consciousness and self-absorption that focuses attention on attaining an impossible ideal of transparency with consequently deleterious outcomes for all involved; Strathern (2000b) rightly refers to the 'tyranny of transparency'.

Roberts (2003) argues more 'hierarchical' modes of accountability exist when 'individuals take it for granted that their value and worth depends on their position in the organizational hierarchy and on the fulfillment of imposed targets' (p. 922). The constant processes of comparison have a distancing effect on the worth of the individual in relation to their work, as this work is tied increasingly tightly into more instrumental arrangements. These more individualizing forms of accountability contrast with more 'socializing' forms of accountability that promote open engagement and dialogue rather than instrumental action (Roberts, 2001). Through processes of developing mutual understanding about particular activities and actions, participants are able to develop better informed and more substantive accounts of practices. The necessarily collective work of educating in schooling settings suggests that more 'socializing' forms of accountability hold promise for enhanced learning than more 'hierarchical' approaches, even as schools and schooling systems are heavily influenced by such hierarchies.

These efforts at developing understanding in conjunction with others entail various forms of interpretation. Under such circumstances, Rhodes' (2012) notion of 'interpretive governance' provides the possibility for rethinking notions of accountability as currently constituted. Unlike a network approach to governance (where power and authority for delivery is understood as distributed amongst different forms of private, public and voluntary organizations), and a 'metagovernance' approach (where such networks are construed as evidence of the reassertion of governing capacity of governments through their ability to indirectly 'steer' various public instrumentalities), an interpretive approach shifts the focus from various forms of institutional structures and processes, even as these are recognized as important, to those to whom such structures and processes are directed. More interpretive approaches give greater attention to the beliefs and practices of those engaged in particular activities, and the 'narratives that relate actions to beliefs and desires that produce them' (p. 40). The emphasis is on how those influenced by various reforms seek to make sense of these reforms, and the specific and contingent influences that affect them. Such an approach foregrounds the actions of those involved, and more 'bottom-up' approaches in the context of 'particular traditions and in response to specific dilemmas' (p. 40); as Rhodes (2012) describes it: 'we have to adopt an actor-centred or bottom-up approach to explaining any pattern of rule' (p. 40). Various forms of 'dilemmas' serve as a stimulus for this meaning-making, which is conditional on the particular experiences and broader traditions that characterize a given society. Such an approach provides resources for hope by eliciting the perspectives of those to whom accountability logics are directed. To this end, Rhodes' (2012) notion of interpretive governance seems particularly generative for thinking anew the inter-relations between broader processes of control through various audit, accountability and standardization practices in schooling settings, and how these processes might be understood and contested by those to whom they are directed.

Conclusion: Towards more 'meaningful' accountabilities

In the broader literature on accountability, particularly public accountability, there is considerable critique of more functionalist understandings. Olsen (2014) argues for a conception of accountability that extends 'beyond compliance and control', and instead adopts a more overtly political approach to making sense of accountability in practice. He argues for a much more nuanced conception of accountability that takes into account the real-politic of actual instances of accountability in action, particularly during periods of significant change:

> The compliance-control perspective is too static, treating too many aspects of accountability as exogenous to politics and accountability processes. For example, principal-agent approaches usually assume pre-determined principals and agents. Authority and success criteria are embedded in normative theories and formal-legal institutions prescribing chains of delegation/authorization and representation/accountability. *A priori* assumptions are made about information asymmetry and conflict and the mechanism through which accountability works. These assumptions about political institutions and agency are likely to apply to some political orders, settings, and situations, and not to others. They are in particular unlikely to capture accountability in polities in transformation.
>
> *(p. 106)*

Such an approach foregrounds ambiguity, and accountability as consistent with efforts to clarify purposes and goals. Actual practice is characterized by a plurality of stimuli and outcomes, and not always or readily associated with particular approaches or foci. Indeed, accountability in western democracies is difficult to gauge because of the pluralism that characterizes such democracies. Consequently, again, more interpretive approaches to governance practices seem fruitful for cultivating alternative understandings of practice. At the same time as there is a shift in attention from more deficit to overload studies of accountability (Bovens et al., 2014), there is also recognition of a more pressing need to explore questions of what Bovens and Schillemans (2014, p. 17) refer to as 'meaningful accountability'. Such accountabilities are premised on practices of meaning-making *in situ*, and aim to reveal the circumstances in which processes of accountability are actually effective, rather than focusing on notions of deficit.

This requires deep empirical inquiry in a specific field – in this case, schooling – to shed light upon how those influenced by accountability governance processes make sense of, or 'interpret', such processes. To this end, the next chapter outlines the nature of schooling policies that constitute key conditions within which these governance processes transpire, and that are key influences upon educators' practices. This is followed in subsequent chapters with analyses of curriculum, teaching and assessment practices in this educational policy context, and how educators interpret such practices in the context of an increased culture of accountability in schooling settings more broadly.

Notes

1 A phrase originally used by Hobbes in the preface of *De Cive* ('On the Citizen').
2 See Smith (1979/1776) *Book 5*, Ch. 1, Articles 1 and 2.

References

Amrein-Beardsley, A. (2014). *Rethinking value-added models in education: Critical perspectives on tests and assessment-based accountability*. New York: Routledge.

Anechiarico, F., & Jacobs J. (1996). *The pursuit of absolute integrity: How corruption control makes government ineffective*. Chicago: University of Chicago Press.

Behn, R. (2001). *Rethinking democratic accountability*. Washington, DC: Brookings Institution.

Belsey, A. (1996). The New Right, social order and civil liberties. In R. Levitas (Ed.), *The ideology of the New Right*. Cambridge: Polity Press.

Bentham, J. (1879). *Introduction to the principles of morals and legislation*. London: Oxford University Press Warehouse.

Bovens, M. (2007). Analyzing and assessing accountability: A conceptual framework. *European Law Journal*, 13, 447–468.

Bovens, M., Goodin, R., & Schillemans, T. (2014). *The Oxford handbook of public accountability*. Oxford: Oxford University Press.

Bovens, M., & Schillemans, T. (2014) Meaningful accountability. In M. Bovens, R. Goodin & T. Schillemans, *The Oxford handbook of public accountability* (pp. 673–682). Oxford: Oxford University Press.

Butler, J. (2005). *Giving an account of oneself*. New York: Fordham University Press.

Carr, W., & Harnett, A. (1996). *Education and the struggle for democracy: The politics of educational ideas*. Buckingham: Open University Press.

Connell, R. (2010). Understanding neoliberalism. In S. Braedley & M. Luxton (Eds), *Neoliberalism and everyday life*. Montreal & Kingston: McGill-Queen's University Press.

Connell, R., Fawcett, B., & Meagher, G. (2009) Neoliberalism, New Public Management and the human service professions: Introduction to the special issue. *Journal of Sociology*, 45(4), 331–338.

Dubnick, M. (2007). Situating accountability: Seeking salvation for the core concept of modern governance. Unpublished paper. Downloaded 8 October 2018 from: mjdubnick. dubnick.net/papersrw/1007/situacct.pdf

Dunn, B. (2017). Against neoliberalism as a concept. *Capital and Class*, 41(3), 435–454.

Flinders, M. (2011). Daring to be Daniel: The pathology of politicized accountability in a monitory democracy. *Administration and Society*, 43, 595–619.

Friedman, M. (1951). Neoliberalism and its prospects. *Farmand*, 17 February, 89–93.

Green, T.H. (1906). *Works of Thomas Hill Green: Volume III*. London: Longmans, Green & Co.

Halachmi, A. (2014). *Accountability overload*. In M. Bovens, R. Goodin & T. Schillemans, *The Oxford handbook of public accountability* (pp. 560–573). Oxford: Oxford University Press-Oxford: Oxford University Press.

Hall, S. (2011). The neoliberal revolution. *Soundings: A Journal of Politics and Culture*, 48, 9–27.

Hobbes, T. (1996/1651). *Leviathan, or the matter, forme, and power of a common-wealth ecclesiasticall and civil*. New York: W. W. Norton & Co.

Jann, W., & Lægreid, P. (2015). Reforming the welfare state: Accountability, management, and performance. *International Journal of Public Administration*, 38(13–14):941–946.

Larner, W. (2000). Neo-liberalism: Policy, ideology, governmentality. *Studies in Political Economy*, 63(Autumn), 5–25.

Lingard, B., Sellar, S., & Lewis, S. (2017). Accountabilities in schools and school systems. In G. Noblit (Ed.), *Oxford research encyclopedia of education*. doi:10.1093/acrefore/9780190264093.013.74

Messner, M. (2009). The limits of accountability. *Accounting, Organizations and Society*, 34, 918–938.

Mill, J. (2015/1828). *An essay on government*. Cambridge: University of Cambridge Press.

Mulgan, R. (2014). Accountability deficit. In M. Bovens, R. Goodin & T. Schillemans, *The Oxford handbook of public accountability* (pp. 545–559). Oxford: Oxford University Press.

Nóvoa, A., & Yariv-Mashal, T. (2003). Comparative research in education: A mode of governance or a historical journey? *Comparative Education*, 39(4), 423–438.

O'Neill, O. (2013). Intelligent accountability in education. *Oxford Review of Education*, 39, 4–16.

Olsen, J. (2014). Accountability and ambiguity. In M. Bovens, R. Goodin & T. Schillemans, *The Oxford handbook of public accountability* (pp. 106–123). Oxford: Oxford University Press.

Ong, A. (2006). *Neoliberalism as exception: Mutations in citizenship and sovereignty*. Durham, NC: Duke University Press.

Peck, J. (2010). *Constructions of neoliberal reason*. Oxford: Oxford University Press.

Plato (1987). *The Republic*. London: Penguin.

Poovey, M. (1998). *A history of the modern fact: Problems of knowledge in the sciences of wealth and society*. Chicago: The University of Chicago Press.

Power, M. (1994). *The audit explosion*. London: Demos.

Rhodes, R. (2012). Waves of governance. In D. Levi-Faur (Ed.), *The Oxford handbook of governance* (pp. 33–44). Oxford: Oxford University Press.

Roberts, J. (2001). Trust and control in Anglo-American systems of corporate governance: The individualizing and socializing effects of processes of accountability. *Human Relations*, 54(12), 1547–1572.

Roberts, J. (2003). The manufacture of corporate social responsibility: Constructing corporate sensibility. *Organization*, 10(2), 249–265.

Roberts, J. (2009). No one is perfect: The limits of transparency and an ethic of intelligent accountability. *Accounting, Organizations and Society*, 34, 957–970.

Rose, N., & Miller, P. (1992). Political power beyond the state: Problematics of government. *British Journal of Sociology*, 43(2), 1–19.

Rousseau, J-J. (2004). *The social contract*. London: Penguin Books.

Rousseau, J-J. (2011/1762). *Emile, or on education* (trans. Barbara Foxley). London: Dent.

Schumpeter, J. (1947/1942). *Capitalism, socialism and democracy*. London: Allen & Unwin.

Scott, J.C. (1998). *Seeing like a state: How certain schemes to improve the human condition have failed*. New Haven: Yale University Press.

Sellar, S., Thompson, G., & Rutkowski, D. (2017). *The global education race: Taking the measure of PISA and international testing*. Edmonton: Brush Education Inc.

Shore, C., & Wright, S. (2015). Audit culture revisited. *Current Anthropology*, 56(3), 421–444.

Smith, A. (1979/1776). *The wealth of nations*. London: Penguin.

Stedman-Jones, D. (2012). *Masters of the universe: Hayek, Friedman, and the birth of neoliberal politics*. Princeton, NJ: Princeton University Press.

Stokes, S. (2005). Perverse accountability: A formal model of machine politics with evidence from Argentina. *American Political Science Review*, 99, 315–325.

Strathern, M. (2000a). Introduction. In M. Strathern (Ed.) *Audit cultures. Anthropological studies in accountability, ethics and the academy* (pp. 1–18). London: Routledge.

Strathern, M. (2000b). The tyranny of transparency. *British Educational Research Journal*, 26(3), 309–321.

Taylor, C. (2004). *Modern social imaginaries*. Durham: Duke University Press.

Venugopal, R. (2015). Neoliberalism as concept. *Economy and Society*, 44(2), 165–187.

Weber, M. (2002/1904). *The protestant ethic and the spirit of capitalism, and other writings*. Harmondsworth: Penguin.

3

EDUCATIONAL POLICY AND POLITICS IN AN ERA OF STANDARDIZED ACCOUNTABILITY

Introduction

This book seeks to make sense of how educators in schools have responded to policy and political pressure for increased accountability, and the more standardized educational practices that have subsequently ensued. These include in relation to curriculum, teaching and testing. However, to make sense of such practices, it is firstly necessary to understand the nature of the particular policy and political conditions within which such practices have unfolded. This chapter seeks to provide such necessary contextual framing, beginning with an overview of the nature of educational policy at present. The chapter provides a brief overview of the various ways in which policy has been theorized more briefly, including under more neoliberal and managerial conditions, and how this is manifest in relation to increased accountabilities. It concludes with an account of the political and policy context in the state of Queensland, Australia, as an example of the effects of these more managerial, neoliberal accountability logics, and how these conditions set up the circumstances for potentially more homogenized educational practices, which are elaborated in subsequent chapters.

Theorising policy: Establishing the policy 'problem'

The conception of policy presented here is one that claims that policy is actively constituted, and the product of particular decisions at specific moments in time. Furthermore, as Schön (1979) argued earlier, and Bacchi (2009) has argued more recently, social policy is less a matter of problem solving than one of problem setting. Similarly, Beilharz (1987) argues 'Problems are not *given*, but *constructed*, agendas are not self-evident but are *produced* as though they were; policymaking is an instrumental exercise which necessarily fails to see itself as such' (p. 389; emphasis original). He goes on to point out that these problems are constituted as if they were self-evident, and that they have somehow 'set themselves', rather than recognizing the much more technocratic practices that have often been involved in their establishment:

> [T]he problem-solving *mentalité* is itself technocratic – those who know, the specialists, identify the *real* social problems, subject them to research, offer appropriate advice on intervention, prognosis to accompany diagnosis. The logic involved, again, is instrumental: it views problems as obvious and argues only over the appropriate response ... we set the agenda, behaving as though it has *set itself*.
>
> *(Beilharz, 1987, p. 389)*

This process of problem construction is therefore a reflection of the concerns, perspectives, stance – the values – that inform policy-makers' work. In one of the earlier and most significant articulations of policy and political systems, Easton (1981/1953) emphasized the place of values. Easton (1981/1953) argued politics entailed 'a web of decisions and actions that allocates values' (pp. 129–130). Building on this conception, Prunty (1985) argued policy as 'the authoritative allocation of values' (p. 136). In this way, policy becomes a vehicle for the inscription of selective ways of being, and reflects the particular normative assumptions and standpoints from which it was developed.

Recently, this problem setting has come to be associated with concerns about ensuring increased accountability amongst those engaged in educational provision. The 'problem' that is construed as needing to be addressed (cf. Bacchi, 2009) is that there is not enough oversight and accountability of and amongst educators.

The 'solution' to this problem is the establishment of much more overt mechanisms to ensure compliance amongst educators in relation to what are deemed acceptable educational practices and outcomes. In this context, the rhetoric of accountability comes to take on a life of its own, such that any mechanism to ensure increased accountability is deemed beneficial. Drawing on a Foucauldian-inspired governmentality analysis of educational policy in the US, Suspitsyna (2010) reveals how the forms of rhetoric evident in US federal Department of Education speeches construe accountability as a form of what Degeling (1996) described as 'sacred language'. Such language involves identifying gaps between the ideal or theory, and actual practice. It entails specifying criteria for effective practice and how current practice falls short of attaining such criteria (Tenbensel, 2002). However, even as such language may be construed as 'sacred', the way in which those to whom this language is directed respond is far from given, and always open to debate and contestation. Indeed, this contestation reflects a challenge to the way in which policy is traditionally understood.

Theorizing policy as contested under global neoliberal and managerial conditions

Such stances of policy as always in flux, characterized by contestation, and reflecting particular value positions, are in contrast with more traditional definitions of policy, which emphasize a more functionalist interpretation of policy, policy production and enactment. Harman (1984) exemplifies such traditional approaches, arguing policy is:

> The implicit or explicit specification of courses of purposive action being followed or to be followed in dealing with a recognised problem or matter of concern, and directed towards the accomplishment of some intended or desired set of goals. Policy also can be thought of as a position or stance developed in response to a problem or issue of conflict, and directed towards a particular objective.
>
> *(p. 13)*

However, the view of policy drawn on in this book is more critical in orientation, akin to that proffered by Taylor, Rizvi, Lingard and Henry (1997):

> In contrast [to functionalist accounts], our view of society draws on a conflict approach which sees society as consisting of competing groups having different values and access to power. Thus, in relation to power, we need a definition which reflects the political nature of policy as a compromise which is struggled over at all stages by competing interests.
>
> *(p. 24)*

Taylor et al. (1997) go on to criticize more functionalist accounts such as Harman's (1984) for their positivist overtones, and assumptions that applications of scientific method will lead to ready 'solutions' to policy problems. They emphasize that any form of policy analysis needs to take into account the broader circumstances and background which influence policy development processes, as well as key texts which comprise any given policy, and the outcomes and effects of these policies. That is, a more encompassing account of policy can be achieved by accounting for and explicitly identifying the 'contexts, texts and consequences of policy' (p. 44).

Context is construed as the broader circumstances and conditions which contribute towards the identification of some sort of policy 'problem' requiring a 'solution'. Such contextual circumstances pertain to a variety of social, political and economic influences. Importantly, it is crucial to consider both the historical circumstances and conditions which contributed towards the current policy moment, as well as the contemporary factors and influences which have foregrounded current policy foci (Taylor et al., 1997). These contextual factors also relate to the actual text production process, and the steps involved in the establishment of the particular texts which eventuate.

Texts refer to the actual policy texts which come to be associated with a particular policy. The nature of policy texts make it possible to identify whether the policy in question is substantive or merely symbolic – funded to ensure outcomes, however difficult to predict or define, or simply construed as rhetorically important, but lacking any mechanism to have effect. Texts may contain substantive background information to contribute productively to implementation, or they may lack such material. Final production of the texts themselves – use of colour, font size, layout – all influence engagement with the policy and its effects. The nature of the discourses evident in the policy are also identifiable through more detailed analyses of the language employed in the policy. Silences – absences in the text – are also vitally important, and provide insights into whether and how policies may be taken up.

The consequences of policy contexts and texts represent a third significant analytical dimension (Taylor et al., 1997). Policy consequences refers to the effects of policies, revealing the multitude of ways in which policies may be enacted. Policies are complex in their gestation, textual representation, and effects: 'predicting the effects of policy is never easy' (Taylor et al., 1997, p. 50). It is the interplay between contexts, policy texts and effects in relation to schooling practices, particularly those associated with increased pressures of accountability and standardization in relation to curriculum, teaching and testing, which are the focus of attention of this book.

The influence of managerial, bureaucratic and new public management conditions

A key part of the context of influence associated with more accountability logics is more managerial influences that seek to control educational practices. As outlined in the previous chapter, these foci are key components of the broader social imaginary in which educational policy-making and enactment are currently undertaken. There is considerable evidence of increasing control and regulation of schooling practices. The management of schooling practices which such control processes encourage is manifest across school sites and systems, impacting upon whether and how those at local sites can influence schooling and systemic processes and practices.

Such control and regulation is perhaps most evident in relation to testing practices. Drawing upon Stobart (2008), and writing from an Australian perspective, Lingard and Sellar (2013) argue that national and international testing regimes form part of a globalized educational policy discourse and such tests complement one another, with each reinforcing the other:

> The development of NAPLAN[1] in Australia is also part of a globalized education policy discourse that argues that standards can only be driven up by such testing (Stobart 2008). Furthermore, the development of national high stakes testing around the globe is driven by and complements international testing programs and comparisons.
>
> *(p. 4)*

While national tests indicate improvement or decline at a national level, international measures are construed as necessary to ensure comparison between nations so as to ascertain national positioning on a broader global basis; a comparative logic drives the governance of schooling in this way (Nóvoa & Yariv-Mashal, 2003).

The development of various comparators of performance, both nationally and internationally, also foster competitive processes *within* institutions, which further encourage the establishment of various measures and markers of achievement to ensure competitiveness *beyond* individual institutions, and in relation to the broader market of which they have come to be a part. To this end, the setting of various performance measures has become a ubiquitous governing practice in public sector reform:

> The emphasis on outcomes and performance in the new public management has seen the proliferation of performance indicators and various league tables of performance measures across the last two decades or so in all public–sector departments.
>
> *(Rizvi & Lingard, 2010, p. 122)*

In relation to schooling, these new public management approaches are also characterized by a lack of trust in the teaching profession and the continual surveillance of student (and teacher) performance through testing; such response are a clear manifestation of more neoliberal and managerial practices (Ball, 2017). More managerial foci also emphasize cost control, and a focus on transparency of costs, and economic efficiency.

However, while new state structures might be considered 'post-bureaucratic', actual practices reflect an amalgam of more bureaucratic, and managerial, and new public management approaches. As Rizvi and Lingard (2010) argue, post-bureaucratic does not entail a phase after a more bureaucratic period, but instead a reflection of how more managerial and new public management models have built on, and added to, more bureaucratic ways of organizing social services – in this case, education, and particularly schooling. The state continues to reflect many bureaucratic features and functionalities, alongside newer, more management- and neoliberal-oriented approaches and foci.

Consequently, educational institutions are a hybrid mix of more overtly market-oriented, managerial and bureaucratic influences, all coalescing in a complex amalgam of sometimes contradictory processes. Even as the mechanisms by which the work and learning of teachers and students in schools are understood is subject to contestation, such learning is clearly constructed within administrable domains, subject to intervention by the state, which is itself influenced by and reflective of broader, more economistic national and global influences – particularly calls for increased productivity, and greater control over how to measure and monitor such productivity.[2]

The commodification and privatization of education

At the same time, alongside more managerial influences, schooling practices have been heavily influenced by more overt instances of marketization through increased commodification and privatization of education. Connell (2010) argues the commodification of education reflects broader processes of neoliberalism, which are most evident through the privatization of services and entities traditionally understood as part of the public realm, including airlines, telecommunications systems and banks. This process of privatization is understood to have occurred in surreptitious ways, including in education:

> Privatization of public institutions is only the beginning. Neoliberals have been quite inventive in finding ways to commodify services. Under neoliberal regimes, more and more spheres of social life are colonized by the market. Education, for instance, is commodified by subsidizing private schools to compete with public schools, forcing all schools to compete with each other for students and funds, forcing public universities to charge their students fees, and then forcing the fees up.
>
> *(pp. 23–24)*

In her description of how public health service provision has become increasingly privatized, Connell (2010) makes the point that the result is a situation in which 'private care becomes normative, and public health care becomes the residual system, the second-best choice for those who can't afford the real thing' (p. 24).

Similarly, for education, the private option is becoming increasingly normative, and public education a residual system for those unable to conform to the 'norm'. In this sense, it is important to recognize how neoliberalism '"does us" – speaks and acts through our language, purposes, decisions and social relations' (Ball, 2012, p. 29). Ball (2012) argues it is useful to consider how we are changed by neoliberalism, and how internal changes in the public sector enable neoliberal ideals to become established in slow and insidious ways: 'Neoliberal technologies work on us to produce "docile and productive" teacher and student bodies, and responsible and enterprising teacher and student selves' (Ball, 2012, p. 29). After Jessop (2002), and similarly reflective of Rhodes' (2012) conception of governance, Ball (2012) talks about metagovernance, and how neoliberal technologies serve as 'aspects of metagovernance, forms and means of governing by organising the conditions for governing – metaorganisation, metaexchange and metaheterarchy' (p. 30). As well as providing useful insights into how ideas, ideoscapes (after Appadurai, 2006), help constitute a neoliberal imaginary, Ball (2012) also flags how the neoliberal imaginary is expressed as 'a set of specific, located and embodied practices, both as policy and as business and philanthropy, rather than as an abstract juggernaut of ideas' (pp. 66–67). However, as has been argued in earlier chapters, and as will be pointed out again in subsequent chapters about educational policy-in-practice, it is the way in which such ideas are materialized via specific and embodied practices in situ that also give hope for how alternative practices and approaches can gain traction.

In the field of education, this more neoliberal imaginary is evident through the development of various markets for specific educational goods – e.g. professional development programs, software packages for various organizational and budgetary purposes, consultancy 'expertise' to address areas designated as requiring reform – as well as through the way in which the educational landscape has itself become expressed as a broader 'market'. The former is evident in the prevalence of various programs and packages sold to schools, and how such packages encourage teachers to become what Luke (2004) describes as 'commodity fetishists', as they 'adopt' and 'adapt' various pre-packaged, 'commodified' learning materials and resources. Such an approach entails seeking to minimize risks, and employing business practices to do so – construing education as something of a 'risky business' (Hardy, 2013). This includes in relation to various forms of curriculum, provision of resources to assist with remedial instruction of students, teacher professional development, storage of data, and a plethora of tests and testing related resources (including for marking and the distribution of results) (Burch, 2009; Verger, Fontdevila and Zancajo, 2016; Lingard, Sellar, Hogan and Thompson, 2017; Rizvi, 2016). At the same time, this commodification of education is also evident through the way in which individual educational institutions and systems have also sought to promote themselves as superior to others in the 'market'. At the more macro level, this commodification is most evident in various forms of league tables, and ways of measuring and monitoring institutional and systemic outcomes.

Part of this process has also entailed the increased privatization of education. Again, this is evident in both the provision of schooling, and the practices that occur within schools. Regarding schooling provision, the increased influence of charter schools in the United States, academies in England, and the proliferation and increased share of private schools in Australia reflect the increased privatization of education. In the United States, there has been significant investment in charter schools, with approximately 7000 such schools serving 3 million students (Gleason, 2017); this is the case even as the results have been very mixed, often negative for particular populations (Clark, Gleeson, Clark Tuttle & Silverberg, 2015), and unrelentingly competitive for all involved (Stahl, 2018). Through various forms of 'edvertising', involving branding and advertising, expansive marketing campaigns enable corporations to gain a foothold in public schools; such approaches involve promoting various 'choice' policies which in turn enable these organizations to provide products to promote schools, and sell their wares for profit (DiMartino & Jessen, 2018). The effects of privatization processes have also been increasingly heavily critiqued, including how corporations seek to reframe schooling for profit-taking, including through use of tax-payer financed vouchers to support private schools (Molnar, 1996; Verger et al., 2016). Nevertheless, privatized models of school provision have become widespread, with various models evident to different degrees in many countries around the world, including in countries where such practices might not be expected to be so prevalent, such as in Scandinavia and Canada (Verger et al., 2016).

In relation to the practices that occur in schools, the increased trend towards private-public partnerships has also seen the outsourcing of various aspects of school practices to private companies. This includes the building, cleaning, and maintenance of the physical plant necessary for schooling; these contracts associated with the design, build, finance and maintenance of infrastructure have proved challenging in different contexts (e.g. as evident in van Gestel, Willems, Verhoest, Voets and van Garsse's (2014) account of public-private partnerships in Flemish schools).

The increased privatization of schooling has also been expressed through continual audit of schools through standardized testing, which is often constructed as the best way to address the outcomes of students, and particularly poorly performing students. And such tests, through their use in the marketing of schools, feed directly into more marketized conceptions of schooling in which the privatization of public education plays a major role, and are seen as addressing and redressing existing educational and broader social problems. Consequently, as Hursh (2016) puts it, 'because standardized testing and school privatization will, goes the argument, result in improved schools for all, testing and privatization are part of the new civil rights movement' (p. 27). Through such processes of infiltration, it is possible to see how more neoliberal principles have come to dominate the current educational imaginary, and the challenges of 'thinking differently' about how educational provision might be enacted, including for more equitable outcomes.

The policy and politics of educational accountability

In relation to education policy, processes of accountability are a key mechanism by which more neoliberal and managerial practices can be instantiated, with consequential effects at the level of practice. Accountability as pertaining to a sense of 'answerability' is also associated with processes of having to answer in multiple directions. From the standpoint of educators, such answerability pertains to having to give account of practices at various scales of the educational apparatus – including at local (school; principal), regional (local educational authority; school board; region), state/provincial and national levels. Such answerability also pertains to giving accounts of practices to members of the community in which schools are physically located.

The notion of educational accountability has a long history. In the United States context, for example, Mehta (2013) refers to how educational accountability is not a recent phenomenon but can instead be seen at very different periods during the past 150 years. He describes such processes as evident during the Progressive Era of the late 19th and early 20th century, when concerns were expressed about the quality of education provision – typically by business and professional figures beyond the field. The concomitant push for increased efficiency through Taylorist approaches encouraged the measurement of educational outcomes in ways homologous to current foci on the use of standardized testing, and scripted teaching practices. More tightly constrained practices were construed as necessary to inject sufficient discipline into the teaching corp. A focus on both the costs of schooling, and its outcomes, spawned a push for increased accountability of such practices.

Reflecting the inherently socially constituted nature of schooling, this focus on accountability shifted to more state-based foci during the 1960s and 1970s, and reflected concerns about the effectiveness of more progressive educational approaches, a need to re-focus on basics in education; this was reinforced by perceptions of US students falling behind in maths and science (as evident in the successful Sputnik launch in 1958) (Mehta, 2013). Arguably, these reforms did not have the effects of earlier and later reforms because of the greater influence of countervailing forces, such as strong national debates and contestation about desegregation and more local community control of education.

However, the more recent set of reforms, described as occurring from the 1980s to the present, have exerted considerably more influence. Again, from a United States perspective, the publication of *A Nation at Risk* in 1983 (The National Commission on Excellence in Education, 1983) reflected a plethora of concerns about American students' capacities which were sheeted home to concerns about their schooling; the nation's economic pre-eminence was at threat because of high rates of illiteracy, falling SAT scores and poor outcomes on international tests in comparison with students from other countries. The way in which the report connected education and economic productivity ensured much greater scrutiny on the part of state and national legislators and industry and business groups.

More recently, calls for enhanced accountability have also garnered support across the more traditional political divide in the United States, with supporters from both Democratic and Republican parties. However, it has nevertheless created tensions between supporters of accountability mechanisms who favour more centralized approaches to reform (such as state standards), and those who claim reform of schools needs to be generated from within schooling settings themselves. Mehta (2013) also argues that schooling is dominated by a technocratic rationality that dominates such practices, and through such a rationality, more performative accountability logics have gained the ascendency. These logics, in turn, operate in conflict with teachers themselves:

> The penchant for rationalizing schools is better understood as a process by which a technocratic logic comes to penetrate the educational sphere … we see a recurring pattern: schools are declared to be in crisis by an authoritative source; a high status epistemic community offers a solution premised on what it claims are scientifically validated premises of management practice; a wide variety of actors external to the schools supports such a logic as a way to control schools and create greater standardization from the outside; objections from teachers, who resent accountability and see aspects of their professional autonomy being compromised, do not prevail because of the low status and weak institutionalization of a feminized profession … [T]hese patterns remain remarkably consistent across periods.
>
> *(pp. 27–28)*

However, while it is possible to generalize about the nature of educational policies and the politics of accountability from what has occurred in settings such as the United States – which together with England, has acted as an influential comparator in other countries, such as Australia – it is only through the specific expression of such policies and politics that it becomes possible to better understand why and how particular logics of accountability are evident as they are in schooling settings. To this end, the next section focuses on the case of the Queensland, Australia, as an example of how accountability logics may be expressed at the level of the state/sub-state,[3] and as a precursor to analysis of accountability logics in practice, described further in relation to curriculum, teaching and testing practices in the remaining chapters of the book.

Policy and politics in context: The case of schooling in Queensland

From the outset, it is important to note that schooling is the constitutional responsibility of the individual 'states' in Australia, rather than the federal government. In the Australian context, the term 'state' typically refers to the six individual political regions that, together with two territories, comprise Australia as a federated nation. As it pertains to analyses of educational practices in Queensland, where education is the constitutional responsibility of the individual states, rather than the nation, the term 'state' typically refers to the state of Queensland, rather than a broader, post-Westphalian conception of state as synonymous with the nation-state.

With more than 5 million people, Queensland is the third most populous state in Australia (total population in excess of 25 million people). Located in the northeast quadrant of the country, the state covers a vast area – almost 2 million square kilometres – making it the sixth largest sub-national entity in the world. The majority of the state's population (3.6 million people) reside in the south-east corner (covering just over 22,000 square kilometres). Consequently, the provision of services, including schooling, is a large-scale enterprise, but also one requiring careful consideration of the geographic and demographic diversity that characterizes the state.

A national approach to schooling provision: Testing, teaching and curriculum

Under the Australian constitution, education is the responsibility of the individual states and territories. However, because of a significant vertical fiscal imbalance, arising from the federal government's superior capacity to raise taxation revenue vis-à-vis the states, the federal government has typically been able to exert considerable influence on state provision of services, including education. Since 2008, this influence has become increasingly 'national' in orientation, including in the areas of curriculum, teaching and assessment.

This emergent, quasi-national schooling policy assemblage (Lingard, 2018) is perhaps best exemplified by the development of a national testing system – National Assessment Program – Literacy and Numeracy (NAPLAN). NAPLAN is a standardized, census-style assessment program first introduced in 2008. Unlike the

National Assessment of Educational Progress (NAEP) in the US, or the Pan-Canadian Assessment Program (PCAP), which are sample tests, NAPLAN seeks to test the whole student population. Every year in May, students in Years 3, 5, 7 and 9 sit the test across the country. Interestingly, even as there are constant pressures and tensions between the federal government and the individual states over schooling, the state and territory ministers at the time advocated national tests prior to the election of a federal government supportive of such reforms in 2007 (Lingard, Thompson & Sellar, 2016).

This support for national testing has been further complemented by the introduction of national teaching standards, supported through a limited liability company – Australian Institute for Teaching and School Leadership (AITSL) – established by the federal government in 2010. Work commenced on the Australian Professional Standards for Teachers through the Ministerial Council for Education, Early Childhood Development and Youth Affairs (MCEECDYA) (which later became the Education Council) in 2009. The Standards were endorsed by federal and state Ministers of Education in December 2010, and came into effect in January 2011.

From 2009, and in response to an agreement by state, territory and federal Ministers of Education to establish a national curriculum as part of the 2008 *Melbourne Declaration on Educational Goals for Young Australians,* the Australian Curriculum, the first national curriculum in Australia, was developed. Support for a national curriculum has characterized schooling provision in Australia at different times since federation (1901), and there was something of a more serious push during the early 1990s in the context of concerns about Australia's economic competitiveness internationally, and a felt-need to adopt a more 'national' approach to ensure enhanced skill provision across the country (Seddon, 2001). However, a serious and concerted effort to establish a national curriculum did not occur again until a change in federal government in 2007 led to the push towards a more national approach that was eventually ratified by Ministers in 2008. The Australian Curriculum development process commenced around this time, and was first implemented in 2012.

Schooling reform in Queensland

These reforms played out in significant ways in Queensland. In 2012, Queensland was one of the first states to adopt the Australian Curriculum. This occurred in the context of concern about education provision in the state, particularly in light of poor results in the inaugural NAPLAN test in 2008, especially in comparison with the other most populous and influential states in the Australian context – New South Wales and Victoria. Lingard (2010) argues that the way in which schools and systems have responded to NAPLAN results has led to the test taking on a more high-stakes status in some contexts than others. In Queensland, concerns about relatively low results in 2008 resulted in increased scrutiny of educational provision. This included the commissioning of an external review by the premier at the time,

Anna Bligh. As a result, Professor Geoff Masters, CEO of the Australian Council for Educational Research, was appointed to review the literacy, numeracy and science performance of Queensland primary schools.

The subsequent report – *A shared challenge: Improving literacy, numeracy and science learning in Queensland primary schools* – made several recommendations, including the need for increased test preparation in the state (Masters, 2009). The 'Masters' Report', as it became known, also led to the implementation of state-wide literacy and numeracy audits of literacy and numeracy practices in schools throughout the state, and the increased collection and engagement with various forms of standardized literacy and numeracy data, as well as the establishment of state-wide targets for improvement on NAPLAN.

An increased focus on NAPLAN test outcomes at the national level in Australia also resulted in increased concern about educational provision, leading to sometimes perverse effects; this included NAPLAN data serving as a catalyst for media and systemic scrutiny and critique, as well as serving to 'dissolve' the authority of state and territory education authorities/systems (Lingard & Sellar, 2013). This further enabled the development of a more 'national' system of education in the Australian context – and one even more amenable to greater intervention at the federal level.

In this context, the state educational authority in Queensland, Education Queensland, supported and intensively resourced the development of detailed lesson plans, resources and assessments for Queensland teachers to implement as part of the enactment of the Australian Curriculum. In Queensland, these resources were known as the 'Curriculum into the Classroom', or 'C2C', and came to be seen by teachers throughout the state as synonymous with the Australian Curriculum.

How these policy and political responses exerted influence in Queensland is of the utmost importance for understanding how educational accountabilities actually affected practice in the state. It is the consequences of these policy and political processes, how policies and politics actually play out in practice – what Ball, Maguire and Braun (2012) describe as 'enactment' – where the logics of accountability are actually realized. This is the focus of attention of the following chapters, which situate the Queensland case and analysis in relation to broader literature and research about accountability practices as these pertain to curriculum, teaching and assessment practices in different national and 'global' policy settings more broadly.

Conclusion

This chapter has sought to provide an overview of the significance of educational policy and politics, with a focus on policy research, including in relation to educational accountabilities in schooling. This policy provision is also revealed as contested. The chapter also included information about the Queensland educational policy context to exemplify the complexity and increasingly 'national' character of education provision in Australia. This material frames subsequent chapters, with their focus on the nature of accountability logics that have played out in this policy context, and in relation to the three key message systems of schooling – curriculum, teaching and assessment (Bernstein, 1971). To help ground these practices empirically, the subsequent chapters not only focus on enactment of curriculum, teaching and assessment in a Queensland context of increased audit and accountability, but do so in light of international literature on these practices more broadly. As indicated in the introductory chapter, the empirical data collected for the Queensland case was undertaken between 2012 and 2017 – a time of significant reform in the state. Queensland educators' experiences help exemplify how these broader accountability logics evident in policy and politics more broadly are actually enacted in practice, and how alternatives to more performative logics of accountability also arise.

Notes

1 The National Assessment Program – Literacy and Numeracy (NAPLAN) is an annual standardized test of students' literacy and numeracy capacities, undertaken by all students in Australian schools in Years 3, 5, 7 and 9. The results are reported publicly through the *MySchool* website.
2 An example of this focus on productivity, in the Australian context, is the Australian government's advocacy for the work of the 'Productivity Commission' – a government-supported advisory group that provides research and policy advice. The work of the group focuses on public inquiries into all avenues of economic and social life, and, through this work, substantially shapes the policy landscape in all public policy arena, including schooling.
3 It is important to note that the term 'state' is used in this sentence in relation to broader conceptions of the state as nationally based i.e. the nation-state. This conception of 'state' differs from how the term is typically used in the Australian context (as outlined at the beginning of the next section) to refer to the individual states that constitute the Australian federation.

References

Appadurai, A. (2006). The right to research. *Globalisation, Societies and Education*, 4(2), 167–177.

Bacchi, C. (2009). *Analysing policy: What's the problem represented to be?* Frenchs Forest: Pearson Education.

Ball, S. (2012). *Global Education Inc.: New policy networks and the neoliberal imaginary*. Abingdon: Routledge.

Ball, S. J (2017). *The education debate*. Third edition. Bristol: Policy Press.

Ball, S., Maguire, M., & Braun, A. (2012). *How schools do policy: Policy enactments in secondary schools*. London: Routledge.

Beilharz, P. (1987). Reading politics: Social theory and social policy. *Australian and New Zealand Journal of Social Policy*, 23(3), 388–406.

Bernstein, B. (1971). On the classification and framing of educational knowledge. In M.F.D. Young (Ed.), *Knowledge and control: New directions for the sociology of education* (pp. 47–69). London: Collier-Macmillan.

Burch, P. (2009). *Hidden markets: The new education privatization*. New York: Routledge.

Clark, M., Gleason, P., Clark Tuttle, C., & Silverberg, M. (2015). Do charter schools improve student achievement? *Educational Evaluation and Policy Analysis*, 37(4), 419–436.

Connell, R. (2010). Understanding neoliberalism. In S. Braedley & M. Luxton (Eds), *Neo-libearlism and everyday life*. Montreal & Kingston: McGill-Queen's University Press.

Degeling, P. (1996). Health planning as context-dependent language play. *International Journal of Health Planning and Management*, 11, 101–117.

DiMartino, C., & Jessen, S. (2018). *Selling school: The marketing of public education*. New York: Teachers College Press.

Easton, D. (1981/1953). *The political system: An inquiry into the state of political science*. Chicago: University of Chicago Press.

Gleason, P. (2017). What's the secret ingredient? Searching for policies and practices that make charter schools successful. *Journal of School Choice: International Research and Reform*, 11(4), 559–584.

Hardy, I. (2013). Education as a 'risky business': Theorising student and teacher learning in complex times. *British Journal of Sociology of Education*, doi:10.1080/01425692.2013.829746.

Harman, G. (1984). Conceptual and theoretical issues. In J.R. Hough (Ed.), *Educational policy: An international survey* (pp. 13–29). London: Croom Helm.

Hursh, D. (2016). *The end of public schools: The corporate reform agenda to privatize education*. New York: Routledge.

Jessop, B. (2002). *The future of the capitalist state*. Cambridge: Polity.

Lingard, B. (2010). Policy borrowing, policy learning: Testing times in Australian schools. *Critical Studies in Education*, 51(2), 129–147.

Lingard, B. (2018). The Australian curriculum: A critical interrogation of why, what and where to. *Curriculum Perspectives*. doi:10.1007/s41297-017-0033-7

Lingard, B., & Sellar, S. (2013). 'Catalyst data': Perverse systemic effects of audit and accountability in Australian schooling. *Journal of Education Policy*, 28(5), 634–656.

Lingard, R., Sellar, S., Hogan, A., and Thompson, G. (2017). *Commercialisation in Public Schooling (CIPS)*. Sydney, NSW: New South Wales Teachers Federation.

Lingard, B., Thompson, G., & Sellar, S. (2016). National testing from an Australian perspective. In B. Lingard, G. Thompson & S. Sellar (Eds), *National testing in schools: An Australian assessment* (pp. 1–17). London: Routledge.

Luke, A. (2004). Teaching after the market: From commodity to cosmopolitanism. *Teachers College Record*, 106(7), 1422–1443.

Masters, G. (2009). *A shared challenge: Improving literacy, numeracy and science learning in Queensland primary schools*. Camberwell: Australian Council for Educational Research.

Mehta, J. (2013). The penetration of technocratic logic into the educational field: Rationalizing schooling from the progressives to the present. *Teachers College Record*, 115(5), 1–36.

Molnar, A. (1996). *Giving kids the business: The commercialization of America's schools*. New York: Routledge.

Nóvoa, A., & Yariv-Mashal, T. (2003). Comparative research in education: A mode of governance or a historical journey? *Comparative Education*, 39(4), 423–438.

Prunty, J. (1985). Signposts for a critical educational policy analysis. *Australian Journal of Education*, 29(2), 133–140.

Rhodes, R. (2012). Waves of governance. In D. Levi-Faur (Ed.), *The Oxford handbook of governance* (pp. 33–44). Oxford: Oxford University Press.

Rizvi, F. (2016). *Privatization in education: Trends and consequences*. Paris: UNESCO.

Rizvi, F., & Lingard, B. (2010). *Globalizing education policy*. London: Routledge.

Schön, D. (1979). Generative metaphor: A perspective on problem-setting in social policy. In A. Ortony (Ed.), *Metaphor and thought* (pp. 254–283). New York: Cambridge University Press.

Seddon, T. (2001). National curriculum in Australia? A matter of politics, powerful knowledge and the regulation of learning. *Pedagogy, Culture & Society*, 9(3), 307–331.

Stahl, G. (2018). *Ethnography of a neoliberal school: Building cultures of success*. New York: Routledge.

Stobart, G. (2008). *Testing times: The uses and abuses of assessment*. Abingdon: Routledge.

Suspitsyna, T. (2010). Accountability in American education as a rhetoric and technology of government. *Journal of Education Policy*, 25(5), 567–586.

Taylor, S., Rizvi, F., Lingard, B., & Henry, M. (1997). *Educational policy and the politics of change*. London: Routledge.

Tenbensel, T. (2002). Assessing the relative merits of policy commitments: Is it possible for policymakers to use 'rich' languages of rationality? *Administrative Theory & Praxis*, 24(2), 299–322.

The National Commission on Excellence in Education (1983). *A nation at risk: The imperative for educational reform*. Washington, DC: US Department of Education.

van Gestel, K., Willems, T., Verhoest, K., Voets, J., & van Garsse, S. (2014) Public–private partnerships in Flemish schools: A complex governance structure in a complex context. *Public Money & Management*, 34(5), 363–370.

Verger, A., Fontdevila, C., & Zancajo, A. (2016). *The privatization of education: A political economy of global education reform*. New York: Teachers College Press.

PART II

The politics of practice

In the push for ever increasing control of educational practice, the codification of schooling can be seen in advocacy for more standardized and prescriptive approaches to curriculum development, teaching and assessment. Part II of this volume reveals how curriculum, teaching and assessment reflect broader, more reductive accountability logics, even as these are always simultaneously open to challenge and critique by those to whom they are directed.

4

ACCOUNTING FOR CURRICULUM REFORM IN CONTEMPORARY TIMES

Standardized curriculum, accountability and contestation

Introduction

School curriculum reform has been a fraught area in relation to educational pro-vision. The contested nature of what constitutes curriculum, and ongoing debates and controversy around what to include in the curriculum, what to exclude, and how the curriculum is to be organized, all point to how curriculum development and implementation are deeply political undertakings, and always in a state of flux. This chapter commences with a brief history of curriculum reform, and the push for increased standardization of curriculum. Given the centrality of testing processes in contemporary schooling, it then focuses on the nature of the relationship between curriculum and testing, and the logics of accountability that are expressed through this relationship. The remainder of the chapter draws on the example of the enactment of the 'Curriculum into the Classroom' (C2C) in Queensland, as the Queensland manifestation of the Australian Curriculum, how this was inter-preted by the teachers and school-based administrators involved in this work, and what can be learned about policy enactment as this pertains to accountability pro-cesses more broadly.

A brief history of curriculum reform

In their overview of curriculum in the *Sage handbook of curriculum, pedagogy and assessment*, Jung and Pinar (2016) open their account of conceptions of curriculum as complex and understood in varying ways by different actors working in varied institutional contexts in different regions, and at different times. Within more rationalist traditions, curriculum may constitute a 'course of study, a syllabus, objectives and outcomes, guidelines and educational ideal', and may also 'stretch to represent and sometimes dictate what students study and teachers teach' (p. 29).

Furthermore, Jung and Pinar (2016) argue that even as they acknowledge the way in which assessment practices have become so prevalent 'over the last one hundred years' (p. 29), they also argue that curriculum remains a key component of national systems of education; curriculum represents 'a complicated conversation' in which various intellectual histories underwrite attempts to better comprehend current circumstances.

Some of the earliest conceptions of curriculum during the medieval period were characterized by a particular conception of 'method' as part of the emerging Enlightenment scientific tradition, and construed as a short-cut way of conveying desired knowledge and ends (Doll, 2002; Jung & Pinar, 2016). Reflecting the original Latin 'currere' – to run, or the running of a course – the term was adapted to educational settings where it implied not running or 'covering' a physical course, but a designated body of knowledge. Such an approach implied a more sequential ordering of material, that had not characterized earlier modes of study – such as those associated with the medieval university courses of the *trivium* (grammar, rhetoric and logic) and *quadrivium* (arithmetic, geometry, astronomy and music). The more dialogic approach adopted in the ancient world, from which these ideas were derived, and that reoccurred in medieval university courses, was challenged by efforts to organize knowledge into a particular 'order'. A broader codifying of knowledge ensued that sought to bring greater control and structure to how knowledge should be conveyed.

The adoption of Frederick Taylor's time and motion studies in the early 20th century to curriculum further ensured a 'tightening' of the notion of a 'course of study' that came to be associated with curriculum. In the field of education, this was supported by key protagonists, such as Cubberley (1916) and Bobbitt (1912) through their analogies between schools and factories, and conceptions of students as 'raw materials' that could be worked on to 'produce' particular kinds of desired 'products' (Jung & Pinar, 2016). Throughout, there was a strong focus on a 'scientific' approach, characterized by 'the imposition of goals, management, control, productivity, and evaluation' (Jung & Pinar, 2016, p. 32). What Biesta (2013) refers to as 'the beautiful risk of education' was to be expunged, and replaced with a sense of operability that was perhaps unprecedented. Tylerian notions (after Ralph W. Tyler; see Tyler, 1949) of identifying objectives, selecting and organizing experiences, and evaluating against objectives, dominated. Under such a regime, the more dialogic approach of the ancients, and of approaches to knowledge and education prior to these efforts to control, and particularly to order, knowledge, were under threat.

Importantly, in the subsequent conservative approach to curriculum development that has ensued since this time, there has not been as much of a focus on what should constitute the curriculum, as on how various forms of sedimented knowledges, largely determined by those beyond education (including in business, politics, interest groups), should be assessed: 'The focus shifted from the canonical curriculum question – *what knowledge is of most worth?* – to the assessment question – *have students learned what others have demanded?*' (Jung & Pinar, 2016, p. 32; emphasis original). The Tylerian, objective-oriented approach (Tyler, 1949) has contributed to this focus on assessing curriculum, rather than how to conceptualize curriculum. This has occurred alongside critiques of the 'hidden curriculum' (Apple, 1975), and what Aoki (2005) refers to as curriculum-as-plan versus curriculum-as-experience, and the tensions between the two; this latter work contrasts a more situated, praxis-oriented approach associated with how teachers engage with curriculum in schools, with a more instrumental approach that conceives of curriculum as planned elsewhere (beyond local school sites), and as simply 'implemented' by those in schools.

Standardizing curriculum

Processes of substantive curriculum reform in different state and national jurisdictions around the world also provide insights into the tensions that characterize curriculum development, including pressures for increased standardization. Given the multiple and contested pressures on the school curriculum, it is not surprising that contestation exists between conceptions of curriculum, including for citizenship development, and for more economic purposes:

> The school curriculum has a number of overlapping goals, from promoting the intellectual development of young people to the formation of a country's citizens, preparing them to contribute to a fast changing global economy. Each of these goals, their compatibility, the balance between them and how they are best realised by the school system, is the subject of wide debate in most countries.
>
> *(Yates & Young, 2010, p. 4)*

Such contestation gives rise to questions about the extent to which educators should be advocating for relative autonomy of the curriculum, or 'should we accept that the curriculum is increasingly used as an instrument of wider political, social and economic purposes?' (Yates & Young, 2010, p. 5). School curricula may be promoted for broadly humanistic purposes, for the development of social, emotional and political intelligence and engagement, for environmental sustainability, and for economic growth and development. In more recent times, contestation around curricular goals has increasingly taken the form of debates between those who advocate for education for economic purposes, and education for alternative purposes. Concerns about how to ensure educational practices contribute to the development of an economically competitive citizenry – perhaps the dominant articulation of citizens at present – have led to a focus on 'how to prepare students to be employable in an increasingly competitive economic environment' (Yates & Young, 2010, p. 4). At the same time, there are demands for increased control over education provision, often in the name of improving quality.

This emphasis on the economic, alongside concerns about educational 'quality', have very substantial effects on the nature of practices in schools. They privilege an instrumental view of education, focused on cultivating dispositions and knowledges seen as valued for economic growth and productivity, and processes of account-ability for keeping tabs on educational practices. Concerns about accountability also encourage a focus on more general outcomes-based approaches, and general cur-ricula capacities, rather than a strong focus on knowledge per se (Yates & Young, 2010). Pinar's (2011) notion of curriculum as a 'complicated conversation' becomes less difficult to prosecute under such conditions, as education becomes construed as increasingly the hand-maiden of economic prerogatives.

Also, the rise of more interdisciplinary approaches to knowledge are important in this regard. While some have argued that more interdisciplinary approaches lead to a lack of distinction between academic knowledge and everyday knowledge, and a problematic erasure of powerful forms of knowledge (Young & Muller, 2010), the broader issue of note seems to be why these shifts in relation to knowledge are occurring. Arguably, they have more to do with perceptions of the need to make curricula more 'relevant' for an economistically oriented 21st century world, than broader concerns around the framing of knowledge in curricula in ways which are designed to stimulate robust inquiry on the part of students. Relatedly, Whitty (2010) points to a focus on skills and away from concerns about knowledge in recent curriculum development. The development of courses around 'learning modules' and the focus of attention on qualifications frameworks also point to the commodification of education. The ways in which such courses are 'delivered' by teachers, and 'accessed' by students, point to a conception of education as discrete, and unencumbered by the contingencies and qualifications of a more productive learning disposition (Young, 2008a; 2008b).

This 'modularization' of curriculum is a complex process, however, and expres-sed differently in different contexts. Practices of standardization of curriculum may be evident even as foci on the domain of knowledges may be strong. This is evi-dent in the United States context, where the Common Core State Standards (CCSS; 'Common Core') for English Language Arts and mathematics, and Next Generation Science Standards (NGSS) have been variously taken up by different states. Even as there is variability in the way this has occurred, most states have adopted the Common Core, and many states are now engaging with NGSS (Richmond, Bartell & Dunn, 2016). Richmond et al. (2016) highlight how such standardized approaches to curriculum are broadly aligned with neoliberal approa-ches and foci, and how such approaches militate against the specificity of practice, including the lived realities of students, particularly from non-dominant back-grounds. This includes how NGSS do not adequately address the learning needs of students from ethnically and linguistically diverse communities (Rodriguez, 2015), even as these standards present a much more robust conception of scientific edu-cation than has previously been the case in the US (Hardy & Campbell, 2020). Prescriptive literacy programs have also become more dominant in the United States, with educators experiencing pressure to adopt district and state reading guides (Powell, Cantrell & Correll, 2017). Vaughn, Scales, Stevens, Kline, Barrett-Tatum, Van Wig, Yoder and Wellman (2019) reveal how schools and districts across multiple states in the United States have become increasingly pressured to adopt standardized literacy curricula in schools and how this is increasingly the case across diverse sites. Furthermore, across these sites, non-dominant students' needs are not adequately taken into account, with principals failing to mention the need for culturally responsive literacy approaches, and approaches that adequately address students' exceptionalities (Vaughn et al., 2019). Standardization of curricula have also been expressed in relation to students' values and dispositions; students in England, for example, experience a curriculum infused with 'British values' as a counter-terrorism measure (Winter & Mills, 2020).

These processes of curriculum standardization also create opportunities for profit-making on the part of large companies involved in provision of resources for these new curricula. That such curricula, and associated texts, tests and other resources, are taken up across state contexts means that significant economies of scale become possible. As with the *No Child Left Behind* and *Race to the Top* initiatives in the US, standardized curricula such as the Common Core and NGSS make it possible for companies to develop a plethora of resources for districts and schools to implement. Burch (2014) argues the Common Core builds out of earlier reform initiatives in similar ways, and encourages schools and districts to purchase various forms of technology to enact the program, and to continue to spend resources in maintaining this technology.

Also, various forms of computer-based tests are being generated to service accountability requirements associated with these curricula. Department of Education requirements that tests be computer-based, for both administration and reporting of results, means that increased investment is required in the establishment and ongoing maintenance of such technologies. Burch (2014) argues that because various companies involved in this testing are involved with multiple state educational authorities in setting the cut-off scores for proficiency, they exercise increased influence over all forms of educational practice. That such companies are involved in making decisions about the nature of assessment practices influences the nature of curriculum development processes, and subsequent teaching practices.

Hartong (2015) refers to forms of 'distributed' governance to describe the way in which a variety of government, non-government and private-for-profit companies and organizations intersect to produce a new form of regulatory policy ensemble associated with curriculum reform. The result is a process of 'governance through standards' as a form of reconstruction of regulatory practices. These governance processes are expressed through an 'enduring rescalation of education policy' (Hartong, 2015, p. 214) involving developing various heterarchical relations, characterized by reconstituted bureaucratic structures working in association with a variety of other policy actors, including private corporations. The result is a rearticulation of schooling. In the case of the Common Core State Standards, the regulatory framework in place shifted from more traditional hierarchical state-based relations to broader, more flexible, heterarchical relations of increased interaction and engagement between state and non-state actors.

The way in which curriculum has become a more politico-economic resource, rather than an educational 'roadmap', is also evident in the trend towards national curriculum making in Australia. Of course, approaches to curriculum have always been inherently political, even as this is perhaps most evident since early efforts during the late 1980s to develop and implement a national curriculum (Brennan 2011; Reid, 2005). While the states retained control over education after federation in 1901, the revelation of skill shortages during World War II, which also foregrounded the value of scientific knowledge capacity, led to increased involvement of the federal government in education, particularly responsibility for the tertiary sector. During the 1960s, community pressure for increased resourcing, including in response to technological developments in other parts of the world (most obviously scientific technologies arising out of the space programs in the USA and Russia) and concerns about Australia's capacity to keep abreast of scientific and technological change, led to further involvement by the Australian government in school education; this was most obvious in relation to tied grants for science laboratories, libraries and other infrastructure for schools.

The Dawkins reforms of the federal Labor Party in the late 1980s, particularly key policies such as *Skills for Australia* (Dawkins & Holding, 1987), *Strengthening Australia's Schools: A Consideration of the Focus and Content of Schooling* (Dawkins, 1988a) and *Higher Education: A Policy Statement* (Dawkins, 1988b), led to the increased push for a national curriculum and testing processes as part of a broader platform to provide evidence of how education was contributing to national economic growth and productivity. By 1993, however, concerns amongst coalition (liberal-national government) states about centralizing power with a Labor federal government scuppered efforts to bring a national curriculum to fruition. Outcomes-based, vocational-oriented, generic-skills and interdisciplinary curricula all characterized the 1990s – indicative of the influence of broader global discourses operating at state and national levels. Increased centralization through the Coalition of Australian Governments (COAG) during the Howard Government years (1996–2007) led to greater control of all aspects of government, including education, as a means of tightening control of dissent over public policy. Over time, governments have been characterized by an instrumental view of schooling, and there has been a strong focus on accreditation rather than the complexities of education provision. More recently, the push towards general and generic 'standards' has exacerbated pressures on teachers, as they seek to 'meet' these standards in relation to curriculum goals.

In both the USA and Australia, Savage and O'Connor (2015) explore the nature of more recent national curriculum policy reforms, particularly within increasingly globalized conditions. They reveal how in both the US and Australia, national curriculum policy-making has been reconstituted by global processes. Educational reforms since the 1980s have been forged in the crucible of concerns about national economic competitiveness in an increasingly global era. The result is the development of efforts to instigate increased national consistency in education provision – in the case of the US, through the Common Core, and in Australia, via

The Australian Curriculum. This provision is also associated with a conception of equity that has been rearticulated away from concerns about efforts to improve equity of educational outcomes, to a focus on the development of general and generic sets of knowledges to which all young people should have exposure and that are construed as essential for developing the sorts of skills to become competitive in this broader global context (Lingard, Sellar & Savage, 2014). Under these circumstances, the national is reconstituted to ensure increased alliance between the economy and education, with educational curriculum reform deeply implicated in economic productivity, even as issues of equity are recognized:

> National curriculum reforms have thus been envisaged by governments as serving dual educational and economic purposes: to improve student achievement and equity, particularly in the high-profile areas of literacy and numeracy, but also to standardize and exert control over what is taught in schools for the sake of ensuring young people are economically competitive.
>
> *(Savage & O'Connor, 2015, p. 610)*

It is this increased standardization of practice that is particularly interesting to explore as a result of these pressures and demands. Even as the history of curriculum reform in each country has been characterized by efforts to develop national goals in the 1980s, and failed attempts to facilitate national standards in the early 1990s, more recent efforts to facilitate national curricula statements and standards highlight the potency of efforts to foster more national reforms.

However, at the same time, and in spite of common federal structures in which education is provided through state governments, because of considerable local variation in the provision of schooling at the state and sub-state levels, local responses to broader global, competitive pressures are always situated in specific national contexts, reflecting local circumstances vis-à-vis broader demands. Varying systemic structures, different expectations of federal governments, varying levels of interaction and cooperation between the different levels of government, and different roles for non-government entities involved in educational reform all ensure considerable variation alongside various points of similarity and standardization (Savage & O'Connor, 2015).

Bounded autonomy

This expression of variation can be understood within what Burkhauser and Lesaux (2016) describe as 'bounded autonomy'. In the US context, Burkhauser and Lesaux (2016) reflect on how increased accountability for curriculum reform has shifted the way in which educational provision is understood and enacted:

> The No Child Left Behind Act of 2001 launched the US education sector into an unprecedented 'Age of Accountability', with states holding teachers and schools accountable for student performance through policy tools such as

learning standards, high-stakes standardized tests and teacher evaluation systems.

(p. 2)

In this context, while there was a push for increased use of theory-based curriculum materials, there was also a tendency to ensure that various district standards were being met. Decisions about the extent to which literacy reforms were enacted were reflected in how teachers perceived these reforms in light of accountability pressures emanating from the district. Even as some teachers felt able to engage with curricula reforms in light of district accountability standards and tests, others tended to take a more disparate approach to such reforms, treating the curriculum reforms as not necessarily aligned with district accountability demands, and how these demands were measured through standardized tests. Significantly, schools in high poverty settings exercised greater control over teachers' practices – in large part as a result of their efforts to respond to district pressure for improved outcomes as measured against various tests to prove attainment of district standards (Burkhauser & Lesaux, 2016).

National curricula exert varying degrees of influence, and the relationship between national prescription and local autonomy are constantly negotiated (Sinnema, 2016). While some curricula are heavily centralized at some points in time, at other moments, greater curricula autonomy is more evident. Furthermore, curricula centralization is an issue of concern for those in schools, as well as policymakers: 'Schools are asked to address the challenges inherent in designing and implementing a local curriculum in a manner that also ensures they give effect to a national curriculum' (Sinnema, 2016, p. 966).

Also, it is difficult to make judgements about the nature and extent of curricula centralization, given curriculum is subject to change on an ongoing basis. At present, curriculum policy in some jurisdictions appears to be tightening, including England and Australia, while other countries, including New Zealand and Scotland, appear to be advocating relatively more curriculum flexibility. However, and at the same time, critique of curriculum prescription is also evidence of continued contestation over curriculum making, with the review of the Australian Curriculum in 2014, for example, pointing out concerns about an overly detailed curriculum content that did not enable sufficient depth of inquiry to be undertaken into specific areas and issues (Department of Education, 2014).

Notions of curricula autonomy are also influenced by ideological positions that inform curriculum making and enactment. This includes: the scholar-academic, with her/his focus on specific disciplinary knowledge as most important for developing curricula; learner-centred approaches, with their focus on specific needs of students at particular moments in time; social efficiency foci, with their emphasis on curriculum as needing to be informed by what is required for adulthood; and more social reconstructionist approaches, with their emphasis on redressing entrenched social concerns and problems by developing progressive curricula (Schiro, 2013). Of these different foci, Sinnema (2016) argues the scholar-academic approach lends itself most readily to more prescriptive curriculum development approaches, with each of the other approaches demanding considerable autonomy on the part of teachers to ensure curriculum is relevant to students' particular needs, in context.

This theorizing of curriculum, and the need to ensure curricula are not prescriptive, and address the need for teacher autonomy, also have a rich history. For Schwab (2013),[1] curriculum must be, first and foremost, practical in orientation. Schwab (2013) argued that the way in which curriculum has come to be 'theorised', as exemplified by the categories to which Schiro (2013) refers, for example, has 'led to incoherence of curriculum and failure and discontinuity in actual schooling because theoretical constructions are ill-fitted and inappropriate to problems of actual teaching and learning' (p. 591). Schwab argues that efforts to engage curriculum theoretically have given rise to multiple concerns and problems, revealing various theories to be incomplete, doctrinaire or ill-suited to curriculum inquiry. Perhaps most significantly, theory cannot account for the multiplicity of influences – social, individual, ethical – that influence real teachers working with real students in real schools:

> Theory, by its very character, does not and cannot take account of all the matters which are crucial to questions of what, who and how to teach; that is, theories cannot be applied, as principles, to the solution of problems concerning what to do with or for real individuals, small groups or real institutions located in time and space—the subjects and clients of schooling and schools.
>
> *(p. 592)*

Importantly, and presaging substantive curriculum reform movements in the decades after the publication of Schwab's original ideas on the practice of curriculum, Schwab (2013) advocated 'the practical' as in opposition to more prescriptive, theory-driven approaches. On this rendering, 'the practical' is oriented towards making decisions, taking action under circumstances given and received at particular moments in time, responding as best one can to the given circumstances. A decision 'can be judged only comparatively, as probably better or worse than alternatives' (p. 593), but cannot be extrapolated from or elaborated to other circumstances in the same way as a more 'theoretic' conception. A decision 'applies unequivocally only to the case for which it was sought. Applications to other cases proceed only from analogy and turn out to be good ones mainly by chance' (p. 593). In this way, the practical is always grounded in practice. (This push for curricular autonomy was particularly influential during the 1970s and into the 1980s, immediately after Schwab's article was published (1969)). In the English context, the comprehensivization of schooling was seen as necessitating increased flexibility for how the curriculum was to be engaged at the local level. However, arguably, Schwab's (2013) arguments continue to resonate across the decades, as curriculum development and enactment become increasingly 'bounded' by the broader parameters in which curricula are developed, and within which 'autonomy' and agency on the part of educators are arguably more important than ever.

However, and again reflecting curriculum enactment as a contested practice, Sinnema (2016) also points out risks associated with curricular autonomy, including teachers' capacity and desire for autonomy in and of itself, and concerns to ensure that curricular frameworks are put in place so that every student has access to the curriculum to which they are entitled, as legislated. Curricula autonomy is also critiqued for its potential to limit the use of evidence to facilitate educational reform or to draw on successful interventions/approaches and expand these at scale.

Curriculum reform in the context of testing for accountability

The notion of 'bounded autonomy' is also apparent in the way in which those in schools might be accorded some freedom in curriculum decision-making, but are simultaneously restricted by the broader accountability conditions in which their work is undertaken. The influence of national testing regimes, in particular, have had a constraining impact on the apparent autonomy teachers and schools may be seen to be able to exercise.

The complexity of the relationship between curriculum and large-scale testing of students is brought to the fore in the way in which curriculum is understood as providing 'input', which can then be construed as the 'raw material' for various sorts of 'outputs', understood as test results. However, as Klieme (2013) argues, issues of time are crucial. Standardized test results cannot be construed as somehow the product of a particular curriculum undertaken at a particular point in time, but are instead a result of the accumulated learning experiences of students up to that time. It is students' specific, context-bound learning experiences that have most impact on their learning, and the nature of these experiences cannot be gauged from large-scale assessments. Such an understanding of curriculum resonates with broader conceptions of curriculum as a dialogue between those involved (teachers, students), over time, including with those no longer present (Jung & Pinar, 2016).

From a Japanese perspective, Takekawa (2016) provides insights into the effects of globalized assessment practices on local curricula. Such practices are undertaken in a context in which the state is construed as responsible for setting the parameters for people to participate in the market, while people themselves are expected to act as 'responsible' economic citizens who 'take measures on their own against risks from unseen power' (p. 946). Takekawa (2016) argues that declines in PISA results led to the introduction of standardized testing in Japan, resulting in a narrowing of teaching practice, and a reformulation of curriculum away from a focus on teaching content to teachers' practice as this related to performance against testing and accountability agenda. This resulted in heightened critique of more student-centred approaches, and a renewed and increasing focus on basic skills. Since 2007, the literacy and numeracy capacities of sixth grade elementary students, and third grade junior high school students, have been tested using a test that separates out students' basic skill and logical thinking capacities. The results of test scores are published and used to rank prefectures. While the publication of more localized regional and individual school results has been resisted, teachers work in an environment in which they are expected to ensure their children perform well on these tests, and consequently engage in standardized teaching practices in the national curriculum framework. Takekawa (2016) highlights the problematic situation in which assessment content is prepared prior to the educational content which is to be tested. The result is a form of 'front-ending' of assessment, and a curriculum development approach that actively encourages such 'front-ending'. Literacy is interpreted as comprising a set of basic knowledge and thinking skills; the result is a strong bias amongst teachers of emphasizing basic knowledge and skill development, particularly in lower performing schools. This focus on test-based curriculum has been further exacerbated by the explicit use of the national tests as an indicator of educational improvement by the Ministry of Education, Culture, Sports, Science and Technology in its advocacy for an 'educational curriculum and learning guidance' (Takekawa, 2016).

As part of this process, a 'Plan–Do–Check–Action' (PDCA) approach is encouraged by the Japanese government to foster educational improvement and reform. This entails a four-step process in which the government exerts strong influence in setting the agenda for what constitutes valid educational outcomes, for checking these have been achieved through national tests, and for influencing subsequent school improvement agendas:

(1) the central government determines the objectives to be achieved in compulsory education;
(2) local boards of education and schools are tasked with meeting these targets;
(3) the national government assesses the extent to which the objectives are being met; and
(4) based on this assessment, the state encourages local communities and schools to improve as necessary.

(Takekawa, 2016, p. 952)

Consequently, 'whilst trumpeting local autonomy and devolution to schools, in reality, the test-accountability system conditions schools and teachers to "voluntarily" accept an excessive burden' (p. 952). The consequence is pressure to improve on rankings in these tests, and to engage in forms of test preparation, particularly in lower performing schools. Various learning standards are established at the level of prefecture school boards, and tests developed, based on the national tests, to measure the extent to which these standards have been attained. Takekawa (2016) claims that the end result is an increasingly performative climate in which 'what was originally a means for assessing educational content has become the end in itself, with educational activities currently being designed to fulfil all assessment criteria' (p. 952–953). Classrooms have become increasingly streamed to try to maximize student performance against these measures, and teachers focus much time and attention on the tests 'and they feel powerless in planning a curriculum on their own' (p. 953).

The problem with the competency and skills-based approach to curricula advocated by PISA, and these kinds of national standardized tests, is that they foreground economic competencies and skills, and are devoid of a knowledge-based conception of the content that should inform curriculum development practices (cf. Young, 2008a). Such an approach ignores the knowledges that have actually been deployed in different contexts and circumstances, including differing family situations and settings, and that influence the extent to which students can make sense of the sorts of 'competency'/'skill' questions that comprise standardized tests. The result is the constitution of a system that fails to monitor more substantive factors, but instead measures the actual knowledges and understandings that students bring with them from their own familial circumstances, and not necessarily the kinds of intellectually powerful knowledges that students need to engage substantively in society more broadly.

Contextualizing curriculum reform: Standardized testing in Australia

Curriculum development and enactment in Australia have also been heavily influenced by testing practices, particularly the use of standardized national tests for accountability purposes. Since 2008, the National Assessment Program – Literacy and Numeracy (NAPLAN) has been undertaken by all students in Years 3, 5, 7 and 9, and the results published on the *MySchool* website by the Australian Federal government.

Given the focus on literacy and numeracy outcomes in NAPLAN, there is an increasing emphasis on these areas of the curriculum, often to the detriment of other domains. The consequence of increased attention and focus on testing for accountability purposes is a narrowing of the curriculum for enhanced outcomes. Klenowski and Carter (2016) refer to how some secondary schools in Queensland have shifted the focus of their curriculum to emphasize literacy (English) and numeracy (mathematics) for several weeks prior to NAPLAN, while others dedicate one or more lessons each week specifically for those students designated as struggling in these areas, and as requiring remediation; such practices are all oriented towards improved outcomes on subsequent NAPLAN tests. These approaches mean that the students to whom they are directed experience a narrowing of the curriculum, as elective subjects, such as those related to languages, performance arts and forms of manual and technical education, are all restricted.

Polesel, Rice and Dulfer (2014) also provide evidence of the reductive nature of these tests in their survey results of 8000 teachers, who were asked to reflected on the impact of NAPLAN as a form of high-stakes testing on students, their families and schools. Their results revealed that almost half of teachers involved engaged in some form of practice for NAPLAN at least once a week in the five months prior to the test (from the commencement of the school year (in January) in the Australian context, until almost the middle of the year (May) when the test was held).

Approximately 80% of teachers claimed to have taught to the test in some fashion as part of their teaching practice, and that their teaching had altered to take into account NAPLAN (Polesel et al., 2014).

Capitulating to and contesting curricula standardization: The Australian Curriculum and the C2C in Queensland

Consequently, under these more standardized policy conditions, it is important to ask how is curriculum understood and interpreted by teachers and other school-based personnel? Do such interpretations accord with current understandings in the literature? To what extent are such interpretations contested under current policy conditions, including increased pressure of standardized tests on curriculum reform? This section draws upon empirical data collected in the Queensland context from 2012 to 2017 (as elaborated in Chapter 1). These data comprised interviews with more than 400 teachers and school-based administrators in 14 schools located in geographic/administrative regions spread throughout the state. This was a significant period, given the introduction of a new curriculum, 'Curriculum into the Classroom' (C2C) – the Queensland manifestation of the Australian Curriculum – in 2012.

Practices of curriculum standardization, but also critique, were evident in the ways in which teachers made sense of the C2C. The remainder of the chapter provides insights into educators' experiences of increased pressures to implement the C2C as a manifestation of curriculum accountability in response to recent curriculum reform. Key themes relate to how teachers grappled with the C2C under broader policy conditions of standardization, how they engaged in processes of streaming, including as a way to managing workload, and how teachers responded to simultaneous processes of governing through curriculum and assessment.

Grappling with the C2C

When it was first implemented, the C2C was construed as challenging for teachers charged with its enactment. Engaging with the curriculum was seen as an ongoing activity, and entailing considerable dexterity on the part of teachers. The sheer volume of documents associated with the curriculum was seen as challenging, including for identifying the actual intent of units:

> The big change is the C2C, the national curriculum, and that has taken quite a while to get our heads around. … I think at the moment I've worked out how to get through, how to get around the units and know my way around all the documentation but it's still – every unit has so much in it and to know – to work out the real intent of the unit, and make sure you backward map and cover everything.
>
> *(Lillian, Year 6 Teacher, Tropical City School)*

While teachers sought to make sense of – interpret – the C2C on their own terms, there was also clear evidence of how they were governed by broader pressures to engage with the curriculum. The sheer volume of documentation meant they struggled to respond proactively to the new curriculum. The sense in which they sought to 'cover everything' also reveals how engaging with the C2C as a form of policy enactment exhibited elements of a more traditional approach whereby teachers were expected to comply with policy provisions; there was a sense in which teachers and others in schools were essentially 'written out of the policy process or rendered simply as ciphers who "implement"' (Ball, Maguire & Braun, 2012, p. 2). In those schools where results were poorest, such as in the northern regions of the state, reflecting the relative lack of autonomy amongst teachers in similar contexts (Burkhauser & Lesaux, 2016), there was a particularly strong sense in which teachers felt they had little flexibility:

> C2C is the national curriculum that Education Queensland has altered to match up with Queensland schools ... At the start of the year we were told that we need to teach exactly what is on those pieces of paper.
>
> *(Felicity, Year 7–8 Teacher, North West Rural School)*

This was a difficult situation, given teachers felt they were grappling with a curriculum over which they felt they had little ownership:

> The other thing I find that's hard is somebody else has written it 'in their head', and you're not the same person. So, you can't always see where they're coming from – how they're approaching something – or why they're approaching it that way.
>
> *(Elizabeth, Home Economics and Hospitality Teacher, North West Rural School)*

Even as the practicalities of teaching a large complex curriculum meant fidelity to the lesson plans as written was not possible, there was still a sense of loss about the work students were producing:

> For me it was a massive sense of loss in that I didn't have the ability any more to create my own units. ... So what I did was I've taken the most relevant parts of C2C, and our admin. [principal and deputy-principal] have been very supportive of that as well. I think at the start of the year, they were very much of the mind frame that, 'This is what you must do'. But I guess as time's gone on, they've also realized that there's a big difference between what you must do and what you are capable of doing ... I really felt like I'd lost a fairly large amount of job satisfaction because even what my kids were producing at the end – I felt like I had no ownership over that at all because I was teaching someone else's lesson, someone else's work.
>
> *(Felicity, Year 7–8 Teacher, North West Rural School)*

Teachers were also struggling to navigate the materials as presented, and finding the relevant information in the plethora of resources, as part of 'somebody else's lessons':

> A lot of it would be scrambling to interpret somebody else's lessons, somebody else's planning, and then trying to implement it.
>
> *(Desleigh, Year 2 Teacher, Tropical City School)*

There was also a sense in which teachers struggled to adapt to the C2C in light of students' needs *in situ*. The site-based nature that characterizes any given social practice (Schatzki, 2002) appeared to be much reduced in the minds of teachers as they grappled with the reforms. In one school serving a predominantly Aboriginal community in the far northern regions of the state, the C2C was not seen as responsive to these remote Indigenous children's needs, but as more relevant to a 'city-centric' understanding of the world. For a relatively new teacher, there was a sense in which the curriculum was a form of 'official knowledge' (Apple, 2014) that was remote from these children's needs, and did not reflect the specific experiences they had in their part of the world:

> It's horrible! … Because my children come with pretty much no background experience in [formal] learning, so I've got – yeah, some kids have been to day care, been to Kindy,[2] know some letters – that kind of thing. But I've got children that have never opened a book before – don't know what a book is! And to get my kids ready for Grade 1, and to give them the best start in learning, I have to spend so much time on looking at letters and numbers, and learning to count, and learning to recognize. Whereas C2C, I think, is written from a – I don't know – a 'Brisbane[3] perspective', where kids come to Prep, and they already know all their letters, and they can write their name. So, for me, it was almost too hard for my children. I had to try and squash that in, and cater to the C2C with the assessment and stuff, but still try and teach all the basics. Like I said, I've got a kid that still doesn't know 'the same' and 'different'.
>
> *(Dianne, Preparatory Teacher, North West Rural School)*

In this circumstance, Schwab's (2013) notion of the curriculum as needing to be 'practical' in light of students' circumstances seemed far removed from the reality of these students' and teachers' needs and experiences.

At the same time, a critical disposition, and more agentic capacity, was evident amongst teachers in another school serving a coastal city in the northern regions of the state. This was evident in how a teacher questioned why there was no opportunity to provide feedback about the C2C at a systemic level, and how some examples of assessment clearly weren't relevant or accurate to the year levels to which they pertained:

> The frustrating thing – I just said to [Head of Curriculum], is where's the spot that we can go into the C2C and say, 'Hey, this exemplar doesn't work!' …

The one we were doing on – very strange books – on one of the Grade 2 biography. When you looked at the framework of what they were telling us about, their exemplar didn't match it! Just wasn't even in the same ballpark! So, we're sort of writing our own exemplar on the framework because the one they've got is rubbish!

(Bella, Year 2 Teacher, Tropical City School)

Such critique was clearly evident in concerns about the disjunctive nature of resources provided as examples, and students' capacities at pertinent year levels:

The one I really particularly absolutely like is they do an oral presentation, which is very difficult when you haven't been doing it; the kids aren't used to it. … And they have a Grade 5 student giving you the speech! So, they don't have a Grade 2 kid doing a speech; they don't have a Grade 2 kid doing it: they have a Grade 5 kid! Now you don't tell me he's Grade 2 because he isn't! He's also standing up there with a teleprompter and you can see it's been 'cut!' Sorry, I find that really rather insulting if they think that my Grade 2s can do that when I know it's an older student, it's a teleprompter and it's an edited speech! And I can't get into it when it doesn't work.

(Bella, Year 2 Teacher, Tropical City School)

The opportunity to engage in a 'curriculum as conversation' (Pinar, 2011) – in this case, between teachers and Education Queensland as the relevant educational authority – was lacking. Furthermore, a 'richer' form of accountability (Lingard, Sellar & Lewis, 2017), involving systems as accountable to teachers for the resources they were expected to engage with, was similarly absent.

However, and reflecting the multiple interpretations of the curriculum, there was also a sense in which the prescriptive detail provided in the C2C could be beneficial, as it enabled transient students – a substantial proportion of the local population in schools in the northern and far northern regions of the state – to engage more substantively with the curriculum as they moved from school to school:

Yeah, I really think that up here in our region, because we do have a very transient population up here, you've got kids going from here to Doomadgee to Croydon to Mount Isa to Cairns, to Townsville, almost like a show circle.[4] And eventually they come back to here, or they don't. I think the delivery of the curriculum, if it's uniform in our district, then it'll be a real benefit to the kids.

(Les, Year 5 Teacher, North West Rural School)

The beauty of it's going to be, once it's taken up nationally, that kids that are swapping schools can just slot right in.

(Mirabella, Year 2 Teacher, Northern Mountains School)

In a sense, the C2C had the capacity to offer potentially powerful knowledges (Young, 2008a) that were recognized beyond the communities in which students lived and worked, and which could serve to propel some of these students from more problematic circumstances that characterized their lives in some communities in which meaningful jobs were not always plentiful, and transience disrupted the continuity of students' schooling experiences.

At the same time, for one predominantly Indigenous community, there was also the capacity for the curriculum to provide the scope for the development of culturally relevant pedagogies:

> Culturally with the C2C, there's a lot of Indigenous perspectives in there, already inbuilt. And we, as a school, with 85% aboriginal kids, we really cater for that: we implement it in the classroom. I had to make sure of that last term because I was on long-service leave. That other teacher who had my class – one of the units we did was on aboriginal culture, and looking at traditions. So, I organized for her to have the mayor in town to go in and speak to the class about the traditional areas, because he's aboriginal ... He came in, spoke to the kids about traditions, about the culture, about the 3 tribal groups here ... and that fed really well into the C2C. So, I think the C2C gives you that; there's that flexibility in there, to do things like that.
>
> *(Les, Year 5 Teacher, North West Rural School)*

At the same time, even as teachers struggled with the curriculum initially, there was a sense in which teachers took 'creative licence' to shape the curriculum for their students' needs, and to make the curriculum more 'workable' in the contexts in which it was being taught. A Prep teacher at a school in a large regional coastal city in northern Queensland expressed hesitations about engaging with the sheer volume of resources provided through the C2C because of the incoherence of some parts of the curriculum. However, she also indicated how it was important to engage with the curriculum in light of the particular needs of students in her school context:

> It was hard to get the head wrapped around it all. We felt, especially as Prep teachers, there were a lot of things that were left out and there were a lot of things that were moving too soon ... I think in Term One, they had them writing a postcard and a letter! And we were still trying to teach them letters and sounds! ... So we sort of took creative licence and added things in. ... we're sort of still taking bits [from the C2C resources], looking through going, 'That's good; that's helpful; that's a great resource; that's a great idea', but also implementing our own professional opinion as well as that ... Yeah a bit of compromise between the C2C and the school I suppose.
>
> *(Cecily, Prep Teacher, Tropical City School)*

Such an approach reflects a more site-based, praxis-oriented approach to educational change (Kemmis et al, 2014). Teachers engaged in different strategies to ensure the C2C was more manageable.

In her role of gaining an overview of teachers' practices, the head of curriculum in this school put in place a strategy of supporting teachers to learn about the curriculum in a distributed manner. Even if this did not always have the desired effect, it did serve as a useful stimulus to decide on future reforms:

> For me in this role it's been good learning to see where we're at, because I know now that I need to give an overview for the teachers so they can actually put the puzzle together. Because, at the moment, they're just getting a piece of the puzzle at a time, so that makes it even more confusing.
>
> *(Dympha, Head of Curriculum, Tropical City School)*

At the same time teachers grappled with the C2C, they believed the C2C, as a more rigorous curriculum, was necessary, and would have beneficial effects for students into the future. The way in which teachers construed the C2C as encouraging the teaching of 'proper skills' reflected advocacy for the rigour associated with the curriculum. Similarly, the way in which the curriculum emphasized deeper analysis of why texts were structured as they were was seen as beneficial:

> I actually like it, I actually do like the national curriculum. I think it's a great goal to achieve. It'd be very, very good in a few years' time, when especially the lower school kids come through to us – the kids that are in Grade 2 and 3 – that have been exposed to a younger age, when they come through to us ... They're proper skills. In the past we haven't actually talked about why language features are [used]; we've written stories, we've written stories and we know we use noun groups, we use these wonderful words, [but] we've never talked about why we do anything. So this national curriculum, a lot of it is about the 'why', the background, and knowledge and things like that ... So I think, I think it's actually quite good – the way it's all laid out.
>
> *(Desleigh, Year 6 Teacher, Tropical City School)*

There were also benefits in this regard for newer teachers, as evident in the reflections of a more experienced teacher:

> I think, once it's consistently established, it's going to be a good thing – especially when I started teaching, I wish we had the C2C then. It would have made my first years of teaching so much easier, because it's there; it's very explicit, the resources are there ... We can still individualize it, teach it how we want to, but it's there – I know what I've got to teach.
>
> *(Mirabella, Year 2 Teacher, Northern Mountains School)*

Again, the C2C seemed to provide at least a foundation of sorts for something closer to the kinds of more powerful disciplinary knowledges that should characterize curriculum reform (Young, 2008a), even as it could simultaneously be a source of angst in this regard.

Streaming learning and managing workload

That teachers' practices were governed by a more standardized curriculum was also evident in how streaming practices became more dominant in schools. Such streaming practices were, arguably, part of a set of 'exclusionary' practices that have come to characterize schooling more broadly. In an effort to capture the broader political predilection to exclude, Slee (2013) asks the question: 'How do we make inclusive education happen when exclusion is a political predisposition?' (p. 895).

However, this 'predisposition' is not simply evident in the wider political realm, but is also a much more 'pedestrian' practice at the level of individual schools. Rather than seeking to challenge the inherent discriminatory logics associated with streaming students by ability – to try to cultivate something of an 'irregular' school (Slee, 2011) in relation to inclusive practices – there was instead a taken-for-granted acceptance in many schools that such streaming was a necessary part of educational practices to respond to students' needs, including students struggling to access the C2C. This was occurring at all levels, including amongst teachers of the youngest students:

> And for my group, because I'm currently with the C2C, three of the Prep teachers are streaming for the C2C ... So, we do that twice a week on a Wednesday and a Friday for an hour. And I've got that middle group that's working at C2C level. Josie's got the group that are working above C2C levels, so they're getting extended, and Lou has those groups that are struggling to access the C2C.
>
> *(Cecily, Prep Teacher, Tropical City School)*

For a colleague at this same school, streaming was also construed as a way to manage teachers' workloads in relation to the C2C, and based on students' needs:

> Within maths, we've streamed our children which makes it easier with the C2C because we've got some children who obviously can cope reasonably well with it, and then we've got children who are really struggling. So, we've got four streamed maths groups.
>
> *(Lillian, Year 6 Teacher, Tropical City School)*

Streaming students was also seen as a way to provide more targeted learning support for those poorest performing students.

These streaming practices also constituted an important part of teachers' practices across diverse school settings. In a prosperous school community on the eastern edge of the urban conurbation in the south-east corner of the state, streaming was also conflated with notions of differentiation. There was a sense in which by dividing students into different ability groupings, teachers could more readily provide learning opportunities pitched at students' particular needs. This was an involved process, entailing constant revision of students' learning outcomes, particularly against standardized measures, including 'running records' of students' reading comprehension based on various 'levelled readers':

> We've streamed all our [Year] Threes and we're constantly reviewing back through standardized testing and running records, and all that kind of stuff. And we're about to review our groups at the end of this week. We've just finished a whole heap of running records to see: Are the kids still where they are? Who needs to move up and who needs to go back?
>
> *(Gretchen, Year 3 Teacher, South East Urban School)*

In a large school in the southern regions of the state, differentiation entailed a process of removing those students considered the most 'gifted' and able, and providing separate learning experiences to 'extend' these students. Described as the 'Strive' program, this entailed providing students with their own teacher for one session (approximately 1–2 hours) per week, away from other students:

> Yeah, those kids have been selected, they have – you know, the highest scoring kids, and they do lots of different ways of thinking and different things to stimulate them. They come out of class once a week and do specific programs.
>
> *(Alasdair, Year 4 Teacher, Southern School)*

However, and reflecting a sense of accountability for all students – more 'authentic accountabilities' – streaming was also questioned, including whether it provided the best circumstances for students' learning. For another teacher at this school, the benefits of streaming were questionable, particularly for those students identified as lower performing:

> In Maths last year, a couple of teachers tried streaming our kids. I had the lower level kids, and she [year level partner teacher] took the higher level. I don't know that it was tremendously successful; it was good in that the kids – the kids, actually got a lot out of it in that they thought that we were catering for their own ability levels. But what I found is that sometimes those kids, particularly in my level, they had this feeling that that's as good as they could get.
>
> *(Simon, Year 7 Teacher, Southern School)*

A logic of 'managing learning' was also clearly evident in the way students were split up amongst the teachers and taught different subjects by different teachers.

This was seen as less personal, and leading to more exclusionary practices, but necessary for managing the workload around the new curriculum:

> Zoe teaches SOSE. Once a week, all the classes go there. And the Maths streamed teacher will take – Zoe has got the 'B group' and things like that. So, she's got some of my kids and I've got some of her kids ... It's not like a primary school class in a way that you don't have your own kids most of the time, which is a bit sad in a way. But it's management, and trying to keep on top of things. And we find we've got such a big difference now between the top achieving kids and the kids that are the lowest achieving; we've got kids who are working at a grade 1 level reading wise, so they can't – they really can't access the mainstream curriculum.
>
> *(Lillian, Year 6 Teacher, Tropical City School)*

However, there were still concerns expressed about time to teach the curriculum, and this was seen as adversely affecting those students who struggled the most:

> [The curriculum is] very much [disjointed] so and it doesn't give you a good flow for the week in terms of covering multiple areas in a week ... You don't actually get to revisit stuff for too long because then you're just swapping on to the next thing. And the kids just don't have enough time to absorb it. Your good kids do but your – I call them the 'dog paddlers' – the 'D-plusses', who are just trying to keep their noses above water who need that little bit of extra time and revisiting, just don't get it. So, it's kind of 'grasp it and go', or you drown ... It is very quick.
>
> *(Desleigh, Year 2 Teacher, Tropical City School)*

Such a response reflects an active interrogation of the curriculum, and a desire to foster a more authentic sense of curriculum reform, oriented towards student learning. It also reflects a sense of accountability to these struggling students, and not simply to performative logics encouraging course coverage rather than substantive learning. This was a very different logic from the sorts of triage practices exercised in some settings, where those students who were deemed most likely to contribute to enhanced outcomes for more performative accountability purposes were provided extra assistance, while those who were not were marginalized (Booher-Jennings, 2005).

Nevertheless, more performative practices were evident in other ways. The time required to understand and implement the curriculum was a focus of attention as teachers struggled to make sense of the C2C in a context in which there was little systemic learning about the new initiative:

> C2C is the major one. And there's been no PD [professional development] on that at all. So that's just been trying to work it out yourself in your own time. That's probably the main one.
>
> *(Brittany, Year 4 Teacher, Tropical City School)*

Again, there seemed to be a lack of more systemic accountability for the needs of teachers – a form of 'rich' accountabilities (Lingard et al. 2017) – at least in relation to more formalized professional learning around the new curriculum.

This logic of managing learning was also expressed in relation to managing other reforms occurring alongside the C2C, including the focus on 'explicit teaching' (see Chapter 5), and in a context in which other subject areas were still to be implemented. While some support was acknowledged, this was still a struggle for many teachers:

> Yes, we have got support but I … it's time – the time factor is the biggest challenge for us … I think that's very overwhelming for a lot of teachers. And I think the stress levels have definitely been raised this year trying to cope with everything plus regional initiatives like 'explicit teaching' … Oh and I guess the daunting thing is we're only introducing 2, 3 [English; maths; science] C2C learning areas, we've still got the others to go, so that's a bit scary!
>
> *(Lillian, Year 6 Teacher, Tropical City School)*

This situation of pressure to enact the curriculum was further exacerbated during the initial year of the curriculum enactment (2012), at a period when many resources were not developed, and those that were present seemed to be developed 'on the run':

> What happens is you no sooner get into teaching one [unit] and they're four to five weeks, and all of a sudden you realize you've got to start teaching something else! And it's only just come up onto the web [C2C portal through Education Queensland] – I know our maths unit – we had a planning session before school started for Unit 1, and it wasn't even on there! We sort of started school and it only just popped up in that first couple of days, so teachers don't have enough time to actually do the learning around it.
>
> *(Desleigh, Year 2 Teacher, Tropical City School)*

However, this situation was also fluid. By September 2013, almost two years since the beginning of the enactment of the C2C, teachers were seeking to more actively interrogate and interpret the C2C for how it could be utilized to enhance student learning. This included developing much greater clarity around the nature of what was being asked of students, including the specific 'content descriptors' that summarized the key learnings to be developed in each unit:

> So when we have a planning day for our next unit, so at the end of this term we'll have half a day planning with [school curriculum co-ordinator] in our cohorts [year level groups]. And we've gone from looking at the unit to the content descriptors that are in that unit [and] looking at what's going to be assessed … And collecting some evidence of how the kids are going on that particular descriptor. And then sort of working – really working backwards

from the assessment; what do the kids need to know and do to be able to achieve that assessment piece? And then sort of do our own plan and then go, 'Okay, what do the C2C lessons have in them that we can use to support them [students]?' Instead of going, 'Lesson one, lesson 2, lesson 3, lesson 4!'

(Elspeth, Year 4–5 Teacher, Western City School)

These teachers were seeking to more actively interrogate the C2C resources in relation to their students' needs, rather than simply being dominated by the C2C. Such responses clearly reveal curriculum reform as contested, including how those teachers with greater capacity and capital for engaging authoritatively with the new curriculum, such as this teacher, were in a better position to be able to respond more proactively to the demands of the C2C, even as those with less capital struggled to do so (Hardy, 2015).

In these ways, again, a sense of accountability to themselves, and to their students was evident, even as the conditions under which the new curriculum was being taught sometimes made it difficult for teachers to engage more fully with the curriculum, and indicated a lack of systemic accountability to teachers themselves. Such responses not only reflect the lack of various forms of 'rich' accountabilities, involving responsibility of the system to teachers, rather than simply the other way around (Lingard et al., 2016), but also a sense of concern for the learning of students and a desire to be as well prepared as possible. A sense of genuine concern for their work, and for their students' learning in all its complexity – authenticity – was evident in how teachers strived to engage with the C2C, even as time and technical constraints inhibited such engagement.

Governing teachers through curriculum and assessment

At the same time, issues of assessment also exercised considerable influence in relation to curriculum reform. Torrance (2011) refers to 'the chimera of a perfectly integrated and functioning curriculum and assessment system' (p. 459) to describe the push to use assessment practices and processes to try to foster curriculum reform. This push for more seamless curriculum and assessment reform was evident in the Queensland context. At the same time curriculum resources had been developed that provided detailed information and resources about how teachers should teach, similar detail was provided in relation to assessment.

While issues of assessment were interpreted variously by teachers and school administrators, and there was evidence of contestation surrounding the curriculum reform process and how this reflected variations in the forms of capital possessed and accessed by some teachers (Hardy, 2015), some teachers were grateful for the direction provided by a national curriculum, and the assistance provided in the school to help teachers make sense of the curriculum as they implemented it, including the focus on assessment. Reflecting the influence of assessment more broadly on curriculum, there was also a sense in which teachers sought to 'filter' the curriculum to retain its intent, but to do so within the parameters of their classroom and time constraints, necessitating attention to the assessment task to be completed by the end of each unit:

> We decided to adopt C2C as it was presented with the lesson plans. Now to start with, the teachers were overawed, but there is a lot of information in the units. But I think every one of them that I have spoken with have said that now that we're at the end of Term 2, they now know how to look at it, and look at the assessment item at the end, and filter it. And work it so that it fits in with what they're doing, and take pieces out. So that it's [C2C] still, it's still there, but it suits best their classroom and it suits the time space that they've got.
>
> *(Mel, Deputy-Principal, North West Rural School)*

That the C2C was not followed blindly was also evident in how it was construed critically by teachers. The way in which the administration team in this school systematically analysed the units of work and assisted teachers to interpret – indeed, interrogate – what they needed to teach in the unit was recognized by teachers, and enabled these teachers in turn to engage with the curriculum. This also involved critically engaging with the assessment instruments:

> Okay I'm grateful to our admin. team … I'm grateful to them because what they've done is with our language leader here, Beverly, is gone through and drawn out all the ideas, put them into a plan that we can work with. Set up the assessments so at the end of each of the units – the assessment is there and you apply what you know is needed. You don't have to apply every single thing, which is good, because some of the assessment pieces that I've seen on there are ridiculous, absolutely ridiculous; how can anyone do that? I love the layout but if you think for a minute that's taken the load off teachers – if anything it's made the planning process – I wouldn't say harder, but more thorough I suppose is the word. And that I appreciate. Alright; I think that you can [plan better to teach better], if you know how to teach and you have your curriculum there; and it's really thorough, alright. Everyone's going to learn a lot. Yeah, yeah it makes sense.
>
> *(Les, Year 5 Teacher, North West Rural School)*

Again, a sense of more authentic accountability seemed to be evident, as teachers recognized the value of a more robust 'thorough' curriculum structure, even as some of the assessment tasks were construed as problematic, and difficult to understand in a curriculum being developed as it was being taught for the first time. Further critique was evident in the way in which the timing of the assessment instruments in the curriculum was seen as a challenge to teachers. The assessment tasks were seen as unduly difficult because of the compressed timeframes in which they had to be completed (five weeks):

> C2C. Cool. Actually the units are really good. They are really, really good units but the assessment every five weeks is driving me insane. Because I have

done six week units, I have done eight week units and I've never had to do an assessment piece – a strong, heavy, really complicated assessment piece – every five weeks … And from my point of view looking at it, the actual unit's wonderful, the assessment piece is complicated and they don't actually match. It's like I'm running two things beside [one another].

(Bella, Year 2 Teacher, Tropical City School)

Reflecting a critically reflective approach to teaching (Brookfield, 2017), while the curriculum was seen as potentially beneficial, the assessment instruments themselves were problematic as they did not always appear to align fully with the objectives of the unit, or the individual lesson plans that comprised the C2C. The backward mapping from exemplar assessment items (sample responses to assessment tasks to exemplify how students might respond) provided as part of the units of work seemed appropriate for building teachers' assessment literacy capacity, but only if the exemplars reflected the objectives of the unit:

Which would be fine if the assessment, the exemplar, matched the objective of the unit! But we're doing a persuasive piece of writing, which sounds very interesting but all of the language in the lesson, the sequence of lessons doesn't match what's come out – so you can't really use that exemplar to backward map because it really isn't any good! It's a piece of crap! Just not good.

(Bella, Year 2 Teacher, Tropical City School)

While there was evidence of how teachers' practices were influenced by this more prescriptive level of curriculum detail, teachers also interrogated this supposedly 'seamless' and 'perfectly integrated and functioning curriculum and assessment system' (Torrance, 2011, p. 459), revealing a form of interpretive governance that reflected concerns about the importance of ensuring a genuine relationship between what students were required to do as part of the curriculum and the assessment that formed part of the unit. Again, a level of authenticity was prevalent that challenged more performative logics associated with the push to enact a curriculum that, while detailed, clearly had not been fully edited and evaluated to remove substantial inaccuracies and inconsistencies prior to release.

These more authentic accountabilities were also evident in the way teachers were concerned about how to engage with assessment beyond the C2C – including NAPLAN. Even as teachers were concerned about how to engage with the unit plans in their entirety, particularly leading up to NAPLAN, they also sought to manage the assessment load, and the discord between multiple demands and a curriculum which could not be taught in its entirety:

We sat down with looking at the overall – looking at the lessons throughout the term. I guess a lot of them, we had the problem with how are we going to fit everything in leading up to NAPLAN, as well as trying to get the unit taught, plus all the extra little bits that needed to be included that weren't.

So it was kind of looking at that and condensing what we could condense down, and what we needed to spend the time on. And also adjusting assessment pieces and looking at exemplars and everything like that.

(Wilma, Year 5 Teacher, Tropical City School)

Such a response could be construed as evidence of concerns to make the preparations for the national testing productive for students' learning, and a desire to ensure coherence in relation to assessment practices in the curriculum more broadly.

Nevertheless, more performative pressures around standardization of curricula practices were also clearly evident in relation to national testing. That NAPLAN practice was governing schooling was apparent in how teachers sought to 'compress' the new curriculum to make room for test preparation activities, and this was even recognized by teachers not involved directly with teaching students who would sit NAPLAN:

It's not an impact on Year 1 at all. We don't need to look at compressing our C2C to fit in NAPLAN practice; we're so removed from that in Grade 1. I know that the rest of the school have a lot of pressure ... And they need to compress their C2C to fit in NAPLAN prep ... Having done it myself, I don't – it's just a given that it's going to happen

(Rachel, Year 1 Teacher, South West Urban School).

There was hope in one school, where teachers took varying approaches to preparing for NAPLAN, that the year level in which 'teaching to the test' occurred least would be most successful, but also fear that this might not be the case. Even as standardization practices in relation to curriculum (C2C) and assessment (NAPLAN) exerted influence contemporaneously, it was standardized assessment practices that were construed as more problematic. That teachers' practices were heavily governed by such standardized testing practices (cf. Takekawa, 2016) was evident in concerns in one school that if the year level that spent least time preparing for NAPLAN (Year 7) did more poorly than the other year levels that spent more time preparing for NAPLAN (particularly Year 3), this would be seen as vindication of those teachers who had suspended the regular curriculum to explicitly teach in preparation for NAPLAN:

ADY: It will be interesting to see our NAPLAN results this year; we had different approaches with a different year. They've all – the Year 7 teachers went, 'We haven't got time to drop everything and do NAPLAN. We will teach, we will then' – because their first units were persuasive speeches – 'We will hope that we will do a week of NAPLAN preparation. But it's got to fit in around all these other things. And then we will do NAPLAN.' The Year 3 teachers were very stressed about NAPLAN and dropped a lot–

PATTY: To do it.

ADY: Which probably reflects in their attitude towards C2C and the Australian Curriculum in the first term. Because they were so stressed about preparing the kids for NAPLAN that they maybe didn't give it a fair chance. The Year 5 teachers took the middle way. I really, really hope that when the data from NAPLAN comes back that it reflects that the [Year] 7s did the right thing. And that we are not, then, such a NAPLAN-driven school. I don't know whether then people will say, if it's not the case, …'Well we need to drop everything for NAPLAN!'

(Ady, Curriculum Coach, and Patty, Reading Coach, Southern School).

In these circumstances, even as standardized test results are not simply the product of a particular curriculum undertaken at a particular point in time (Klieme, 2013), some teachers appeared to be taking no chances to try to ensure that their students' results were as high as possible. In these circumstances, processes of curriculum narrowing were evident, with teachers teaching towards the test in some fashion (Polesel et al, 2014). Notions of curriculum as a dialogue between those involved (teachers, students), over time, including with those no longer present (Jung & Pinar, 2016), seemed somewhat attenuated.

Even as it was expressed in varied ways in different year levels in the schools, there was strong evidence of standardized testing influencing curriculum practices. As in the Japanese context in which pressures of standardized testing exerted influence on curriculum (Takekawa, 2016), the impact of NAPLAN on the curriculum was also evident in concerns expressed more broadly about the nature of students' learning experiences as they progressed through school, and the relative lack of variety of exposure to different genres, because of pressure to ensure adequate NAPLAN results. This was seen as heavily limiting the curriculum, and students' learning experiences:

> NAPLAN says that we are going to be doing persuasive language. And those poor bloody kids, after two terms of persuasive language, are all persuasive out! I talked to one lot of kids one day and said, 'Oh, you know, this is narrative; can you remember when you wrote a narrative?' 'Oh yes, that would be way back in Year Three.' I'm going, 'My God!'
>
> (Michelle, Literacy & Numeracy Support Teacher, Central Mining School)

For this teacher, more authentic accountabilities to students were evident in concerns to ensure a breadth of coverage of other genres which were important for students' holistic literacy and numeracy development, including in relation to what students needed to know to engage as members of the wider community on an ongoing basis:

> I really think that there's lots and lots of different types of writing that are far more important than persuasive writing. When you look at what is necessary for that child, the skills for that child, to take out there into the wider

community. That is what they should be focussing upon, not just the ability to say you know how to put a point of view across strongly or something like that. And argue a point. That's good, that's fine; that is one part of writing, but it's not the be all and end all of writing! And you should be able to judge the child's writing on what they are capable across a whole lot of different genres, rather than just the one.

(*Michelle, Literacy & Numeracy Support Teacher, Central Mining School*).

While curriculum development may be understood as characterized by processes of 'bounded autonomy' in educational settings in which greater control is exerted over teachers' work by standardized test results (Burkhauser & Lesaux, 2016), this focus on NAPLAN seemed the anthesis of the attainment of more substantive, expansive academic goals in schooling. Such a strong focus on a specific and limited set of academic goals also meant a devaluing of other necessary activities in schools. This was evident in how a guidance officer at another school lamented the decline of social and emotional goal attainment with the increased focus on academic goals in her school:

I think it is that just the teachers want to do well; it's an academic goal. But sometimes our goals are social, like just being in the class, sitting with the kids, being able to interact. And so, changing the goals as well. Because teachers are feeling that it's all academic ... It's all academic goals and we're not looking – we don't place as much value on the social goals as we do on the academic goals. And their self-esteem – because we should be educating the whole person, not just the academic self. But don't get me started ... And I think that that's really hard. And I think that teachers go into teaching because they care about kids, and intrinsically they know what they need to do to care for a kid. But the conflicting academic pressures, the academic goals – and it's all academic, academic.

(*Clarissa, Guidance Officer, Tropical City School*)

The 'scholar-academic' tradition was certainly in evidence in the school, and conflicted with desires to develop more locally responsive curriculum to address specific students' needs (Sinnema, 2016). For this guidance officer, working in a school with complex family and material circumstances, including relatively high rates of poverty, that the school was calm was important, and strong relationships with teachers for some students were a crucial constant in their lives:

Then, you're talking about working with a kid that may not have a constant adult in their life because they can be in a share house with different people. So the only constant relationship with one adult for the day is the class teacher, the one constant adult. So, and then I link back to 'relationships are the site of the repair and pathways [to better life experiences]'.

(*Clarissa, Guidance Officer, Tropical City School*).

In this way, there was clear advocacy for a broader conception of education, including 'beyond measurement' (Biesta, 2010) associated with academic goals, and particularly academic goals attached to more standardized curricula and testing. Teachers' interrogation of the curriculum, and advocacy for a more well-rounded curriculum reflected not only a form of interrogative governance on the part of teachers, but also evidence of more authentic accountabilities to students, as they sought to ensure as wide an array of experiences as possible, including crucial social experiences beyond the academic domain alone, and particularly for the most marginalized students.

Conclusion: Beyond standardized curricula

The research presented in this chapter reveals a complex amalgam of influences on enactment of curriculum policy in the Queensland context. While the governing of teachers' curriculum practices through more standardized forms, such as the detailed lesson plans associated with the C2C, were clearly in evidence, more student-centric, 'authentic' teacher logics were also apparent, at least some of the time. The way in which teachers struggled with the prescriptive detail of the individual lesson plans, and the plethora of resources associated with the C2C, reveals how more performative, instrumental logics exerted influence. This was also evident in the challenges associated with streaming students, and managing workload. However, that teachers also found the C2C resources beneficial, including to ensure substantive student learning on the part of more transient students – and to ensure provision of potentially powerful knowledges (Young, 2008a) – also reflects the more productive possibilities that attended C2C development and enactment. Also, while processes of streaming were clearly exclusionary (Slee, 2011), efforts to try to foster students' learning through more targeted interventions represent a more hopeful 'flipside' to efforts to attend to individual student difference. That assessment practices were also interpreted in varied ways by teachers also revealed the complexity that attended issues of assessment, and particularly standardized assessment, in relation to curriculum development reform. There was clear evidence of how assessment governed curriculum decisions, including the influence of standardized national testing. However, again, that more performative assessment logics could be challenged by more active interrogation on the part of teachers also reflects potentially productive points of intervention and pathways forward.

In what he describes as a 'critical turn in study of curriculum content', Takekawa (2016, p. 957) provides an alternative approach to the individualization of risk that characterizes standardized curriculum and testing approaches. Using the example of the Great East Japan Earthquake of 11 March 2011, which generated a tsunami that devastated coastal regions of Japan, including destroying the Fukushima Daii-chi nuclear power plant, Takekawa (2016) advocates for an approach to curriculum that embraces more pluralist and overtly political approaches to knowledge development and understanding. Such an approach entails a form of governance quite different from the standardized logics that characterize so much schooling at present, and entails openness to more community-centric resources and dispositions. In the case of the city of Kamaishi, collaboration between the schools and the local community resulted in the development and teaching of a disaster preparedness curriculum to enable students to respond to such an event. The result was the protection of 99.8% of its 3000 students through rapid evacuation approaches (Takekawa, 2016). A more integrated approach was taken across the whole curriculum, including incorporating disaster-related topics in specific subjects, across all year levels. While there was some evidence of curriculum relevance for students in Queensland schools through the C2C, there was also clearly a need for continued interrogation of the nature of the common Queensland curriculum, and whether and how it was providing a substantive, holistic education for all students.

As an alternative to standardized approaches, Takekawa (2016) argues that a process of 'unlearning' is necessary, such that it becomes possible to recognize that one's learning has led to increased understanding and knowledge in one domain, but that, subsequently, the development of alternative knowledges and understandings have not been possible. Such 'unlearning' in the Queensland context would enable a more constructive framing of curriculum reform more broadly, and more context-responsive approaches at the local level. Recognizing this gap then makes it possible to reconceptualize understanding around current knowledge domains to open these up to critique and/or augmentation, so as to further develop important insights into particular knowledges and ways of being. It is through such active interrogation that the expression of more authentic accountabilities becomes possible.

Notes

1 The 2013 article referred to here was originally published by Schwab in 1969 in *The School Review*. Schwab, J. (1969). The practical: A language for curriculum. *The School Review, 78*(1), 1–23.
2 Kindergarten – a pre-preparatory year in the Queensland context.
3 The capital city in the state of Queensland; approximately 2000 kilometres away from this school.
4 A reference to the predominantly agricultural shows/fairs that characterized the 'show circuit' in which performers and other personnel moved between each town and city as part of the annual display of local produce and activities.

References

Aoki, T. (2005). Teaching as in-dwelling between curriculum worlds. In W. Pinar & R. Irwin (Eds), *Curriculum in a new key: The collected works of Ted A. Aoki* (pp. 159–166). Mahwah, NJ: Lawrence Erlbaum.

Apple, M. (1975). The hidden curriculum and the nature of conflict. In W. Pinar (Ed.), *Curriculum theorizing: The reconceptualists* (pp. 95–199). Berkeley, CA: McCutchan.

Apple, M. (2014). *Official knowledge: Democratic education in a conservative age*. 3rd edition. New York: Routledge.

Ball, S., Maguire, M., & Braun, A. (2012). *How schools do policy: Policy enactments in secondary schools*. London: Routledge.

Biesta, G. (2010). *Good education in an age of measurement: Ethics, politics, democracy*. Boulder, CO: Paradigm Publishers.

Biesta, G. (2013). *The beautiful risk of education*. Boulder, CO: Paradigm.

Bobbitt, J. (1912). The elimination of waste in education. *The Elementary School Teacher*, 12(6), 259–271.

Booher-Jennings, J. (2005). Below the bubble: 'Educational triage' and the Texas accountability system. *American Educational Research Journal*, 42(2), 231–268.

Brennan, M. (2011). National curriculum: A political-educational tangle. *Australian Journal of Education*, 55(3), 259–280.

Brookfield, S. (2017). *Becoming a critically reflective teacher*. San Francisco: Jossey-Bass.

Burch, P. (2014) The role of vendors in the implementation and effects of CCSS: A first look. *Journal of Curriculum and Pedagogy*, 11(1), 37–40.

Burkhauser, M., & Lesaux, N. (2016) Exercising a bounded autonomy: Novice and experienced teachers' adaptations to curriculum materials in an age of accountability. *Journal of Curriculum Studies*. doi:10.1080/00220272.2015.1088065

Cubberley, E. (1916) *Public school administration*. Boston, MA: Houghton Mifflin.

Dawkins, J.S. (1988a). *Strengthening Australia's schools: A consideration of the focus and content of schooling*. Canberra: Australian Government Publishing Service.

Dawkins, J.S. (1988b). *Higher education: A policy statement*. Canberra: Australian Government Publishing Service.

Dawkins, J.S., & Holding, A.C. (1987). *Skills for Australia*. Canberra: Australian Government Publishing Service.

Department of Education (2014). *Review of the Australian Curriculum: Initial Australian Government response*. Canberra: Australian Government.

DollJr, W. (2002). Ghosts and the curriculum. In W.DollJr and N. Gough (Eds), *Curriculum visions* (pp. 23–70) New York, NY: Peter Lang.

Hardy, I. (2015). Curriculum reform as contested: An analysis of curriculum policy enactment in Queensland, Australia. *International Journal of Educational Research*, 74, 70–81.

Hardy, I., & Campbell, T. (2020). Developing and supporting the Next Generation Science Standards: The role of policy entrepreneurs. *Science Education*. doi:10.1002/sce.21566

Hartong, S. (2015). New structures of power and regulation within 'distributed' education policy – the example of the US Common Core State Standards Initiative. *Journal of Education Policy*, 31(2), 213–225.

Jung, J-H., & Pinar, W. (2016). Conceptions of curriculum. In D. Wyse, L. Hayward & J. Pandya (Eds), *The Sage handbook of curriculum, pedagogy and assessment* (pp. 29–46). Los Angeles, CA: Sage.

Kemmis, S., Wilkinson, J., Edwards-Groves, C., Hardy, I., Grootenboer, P., & Bristol, L. (2014). *Changing practices, changing education*. Singapore: Springer.

Klenowski, V., & Carter, M. (2016) Curriculum reform in testing and accountability contexts. In D. Wyse, L. Hayward & J. Pandya (Eds), *The Sage handbook of curriculum, pedagogy and assessment* (pp. 790–804). Los Angeles, CA: Sage.

Klieme, E. (2013). The role of large-scale assessment in research on educational effectiveness and school development. In M. von Davier, E. Gonzalez, I. Kirsch & K. Yamamoto (Eds), *The role of international large-scale assessments: Perspectives from technology, economy, and educational research* (pp. 115–147). Dordrecht: Springer.

Lingard, B., Martino, W., Rezai-Rashti, G., & Sellar, S. (2016). *Globalising educational accountabilities*. New York: Routledge.

Lingard, B., Sellar, S., & Savage, G. C. (2014). Re-articulating social justice as equity in schooling policy: The effects of testing and data infrastructures. *British Journal of Sociology of Education*, 35(5), 710–730.

Lingard, B., Sellar, S., & Lewis, S. (2017). Accountabilities in schools and school systems. In G. Noblit (Ed.), *Oxford Research Encyclopedia of Education*. doi:10.1093/acrefore/9780190264093.013.74.

Pinar, W. (2011). *The character of curriculum studies: Bildung, currere, and the recurring question of the subject*. New York, NY: Palgrave Macmillan.

Polesel, J., Rice, S., & Dulfer, N. (2014). The impact of high-stakes testing on curriculum and pedagogy: A teacher perspective from Australia. *Journal of Education Policy*, 29(5), 640–657.

Powell, R., Cantrell, S., & Correll, P. (2017). Power and agency in a high poverty elementary school: How teachers experienced a scripted reading program. *Journal of Language and Literacy Education*, 13(1), 93–124.

Reid, A. (2005). *Rethinking national curriculum collaboration towards an Australian curriculum*. Canberra: Department of Education, Science and Training.

Richmond, G., Bartell, T., & Dunn, A. (2016). Beyond 'tinkering': Enacting the imperative for change in teacher education in a climate of standards and accountability. *Journal of Teacher Education*, 67(2), 102–104.

Rodriguez, A. (2015). What about a dimension of engagement, equity, and diversity practices. A critique of the Next Generation Science Standards. *Journal of Research in Science Teaching*, 57(2), 1031–1051.

Savage G., & O'Connor, K. (2015). National agendas in global times: Curriculum reforms in Australia and the USA since the 1980s. *Journal of Education Policy*, 30(5), 609–630.

Schatzki, T. (2002). *The site of the social: A philosophical account of the constitution of social life and change*. University Park, PA: The Pennsylvania State University Press.

Schiro, M. (2013). *Curriculum theory: Conflicting visions and enduring concerns*. Second edition. Thousand Oaks, CA: Sage.

Schwab, J. (2013). The practical: a language for curriculum. *Journal of Curriculum Studies*, 45(5), 591–621.

Sinnema, C. (2016). The ebb and flow of curricular autonomy: Balance between local freedom and national prescription in curricular. In D. Wyse, L. Hayward & J. Pandya (Eds), *The Sage handbook of curriculum, pedagogy and assessment* (pp. 965–983). Los Angeles, CA: Sage.

Slee, R. (2011). *The irregular school: Exclusion, schooling and inclusive education*. London: Routledge.

Slee, R. (2013). How do we make inclusive education happen when exclusion is a political predisposition? *International Journal of Inclusive Education*, 17(8), 895–907.

Takekawa, S. (2016). Effects of globalised assessment on local curricula: What Japanese teachers face and how they challenge it. In D. Wyse, L. Hayward & J. Pandya (Eds), *The Sage handbook of curriculum, pedagogy and assessment* (pp. 946–965). Los Angeles, CA: Sage.

Torrance, H. (2011). Using assessment to drive the reform of schooling: Time to stop pursuing the chimera. *British Journal of Educational Studies*, 59(4), 459–485.

Tyler, R. (1949). *Basic principles of curriculum and instruction*. Chicago: The University of Chicago Press.

Vaughn, M., Scales, R., Stevens, E., Kline, S., Barrett-Tatum, J., Van Wig, A., Yoder, K., & Wellman, D. (2019). Understanding literacy adoption policies across contexts: A multi-state examination of literacy curriculum decision-making. *Journal of Curriculum Studies*. doi:10.1080/00220272.2019.1683233

Winter, C., & Mills, C. (2020). The Psy-Security-Curriculum ensemble: British values curriculum policy in English schools. *Journal of Education Policy.* doi.org/10.1080/02680939.2018.1493621

Whitty, G. (2010). Revisiting school knowledge: Some sociological perspectives on new school curricula. *European Journal of Education,* 45(1), 28–44.

Yates, L., & Young, M. (2010) Editorial: Globalisation, knowledge and the curriculum. *European Journal of Education,* 45(1), 4–10.

Young, M. (2008a). *Bringing knowledge back in: From social constructivism to social realism in the sociology of education.* London: Routledge.

Young, M. (2008b). From constructivism to realism in the sociology of the curriculum. *Review of Research in Education,* 32(1), 1–28.

Young, M., & Muller, J. (2010). Three educational scenarios for the future: Lessons from the sociology of knowledge. *European Journal of Education,* 45(1), 11–27.

5

TEACHING IN AND BEYOND AN AGE OF ACCOUNTABILITY

> The pursuit of explicitness must always be the servant of practice, not its master.
>
> *(Green, 2013, p. 142)*

Introduction: Teaching in an age of accountability

More standardized approaches to accountability have also significantly influenced teaching practices in schooling settings, and have attracted increased attention in recent times. Such standardization has entailed greater focus on the role of the teacher as an individual, with concomitant attention to 'teacher quality' as an individual responsibility. This emphasis on teaching, the work of teachers more broadly, and teacher quality as an individuated entity in particular, are construed as increasingly vital for educational reform, including from the beginning of teachers' careers (Hardy, Jakhelln & Smit, 2020), and in multiple contexts (e.g. see Mizala & Schneider (2019) for discussions about the nature of teacher quality in the Chilean context). Even as there is recognition that student learning is perhaps more heavily influenced by broader social conditions and the backgrounds and circumstances of students, the nature of teachers and teaching is construed as vital for effecting in-school improvements in practice, and subsequent student learning. Influential research and policy reports have fostered this focus on 'teacher quality' in particular. John Hattie's (2009) *Visible Learning,* for example, has had considerable take-up in schooling systems around the world, with its attention to the specific practices on which teachers and those in schools are purported to have most impact. The OECD's (2005) earlier report *Teachers Matter: Attracting, Developing and Retaining Effective Teachers* is similarly iconic in its advocacy for increased attention and focus to the nature of teachers' work, and the impact of this work. While both volumes refer to the influence of broader factors on student learning, they are also

emphatic in their assertion, in the words of the OECD (2005) report, 'that "teacher quality" is the single most important school variable influencing student
achievement' (p. 2). The work of teaching has been foregrounded in this chapter,
and reflects both the individuation of teaching, as well as the broader context and
conditions for teaching.

Contextualizing current teaching practices

In large measure, standardization in relation to teaching has occurred alongside
broader processes of the privatization of education, and been fuelled by increased
pressures of accountability. In a context in which public schooling has become
increasingly subject to privatization processes at micro and macro levels – in terms
of the practices that are undertaken in public schools more specifically, and how
public schooling is provided for more generally in society, or what Walford (2013)
refers to as 'the privatisation in and of education' (p. 421) – it is also evident that
these standardization processes have been accompanied by the implementation (or
more accurately, 'enactment') of specific programs and initiatives at the school level
that are deemed appropriate for take-up in schools. Indeed, there is an increasing
market for (and marketing of) such programs, and these programs are often targeted at informing both teachers' learning for improved teaching practice, as well
as student learning more directly.

This chapter focuses specifically on teachers' teaching practice, and makes the
case for how and why particular approaches to teaching have governed teachers'
teaching practice in recent times. As outlined in the policy chapter, more neoliberal
pressures have influenced all aspects of educational policy, including policies targeting teaching practice. This includes advocacy for particular initiatives, approaches and programs to inform teachers' teaching practice. Such 'pre-packaged'
programs are examples of what Luke (2004) refers to as the 'commodification of
education', part of what Ball (2004) questions as 'the commodification of everything?' In a more measured approach, Ball (2004) calls for the interrogation of the
extent to which privatized practices are appropriate in relation to public service
provision, such as in education:

> It is, I hope, a timely reminder of the need to bring a critical gaze to bear
> equally upon the two forms of provision – private and bureau-professional.
> I also hope to highlight the need for proper debate about the necessity or
> validity of defending some boundaries between public and private – in other
> words to ask whether there are places where the market form is just
> inappropriate.
>
> *(p. 3)*

Of course, in the intervening period since Ball made these comments, much has
happened in the English educational system to which he was primarily referring.
Alongside particular teaching programs and approaches, a plethora of schooling

types has also been promulgated, which influence the nature of teaching practice being supported. Many of these schools have arisen in response to calls for increased 'choice' in educational provision. Some of these schools are operated by bodies other than the traditional local authorities/councils, including directly by the national government, with ever increasing numbers of schools operating with an increasingly 'independent' status. The majority of secondary schools, for example, are now run as academies, and various 'Free Schools'; such schools are funded by government, but not operated by local councils (United Kingdom Government, 2016). These schools are also not required to follow the national curriculum, but have much greater influence over how they orchestrate teaching and learning experiences for students. The dramatic rise in secondary schools accorded academy status is one particularly prescient example of how privatization techniques have exerted significant influence in schooling.

Such governing practices have substantial effects on broader educational goals and foci, including the erosion of democracy in relation to education as a professional field. Biesta (2016) reflects on how the democratic dimension of professionalism has become distorted in the wake of increasing neoliberal demands, and how this reconstitutes professional knowledge away from making judgements about teaching in context, and pressure to conform to what is identified as evidence-based approaches seen 'to work'. Necessary professional judgement about the most effective teaching for particular students, in particular contexts, becomes marginalized by generic approaches and foci identified via the reified 'gold standard' of randomized controlled experiments (Biesta, 2020).

However, teaching is a challenging undertaking, and there are always multiple factors at play that influence the nature of teaching practice in context. This includes the extent to which teaching is sufficiently creative to adequately address the needs of students. In response to the rhetorical question 'Why, when one listens for teaching for creativity, does one hear only the sounds of silence?' (p. 115), Sternberg (2015) provides three key points as to why teaching practice can sometimes seem to be so pedestrian: 1) 'fads and fashions'; 2) 'standardized teaching'; and 3) 'teacher education'. Fads and fashions refers to the way in which teaching is characterized by the take-up of various approaches and foci at different points in time without detailed consideration of their potential benefits or otherwise; in relation to creativity, this has included dramatic swings from an absence of more creative approaches during an earlier era focused on content knowledge, towards various 'thinking skills' approaches which seemed to occur in the absence of sufficient understanding of the knowledge base to which these skills were to be applied. Edward de Bono's (1985) 'six thinking hats' and Howard Gardner's (1983) 'multiple intelligences' are emblematic of these latter approaches. Secondly, and speaking from a United States perspective, Sternberg (2015) makes the point that 'standardized testing has been a powerful force in U.S. society for a long time' (p. 116). However, as he also points out, the difference between previous approaches and current approaches is the way in which legislation was formulated in the early 2000s – specifically through the authorization of the *No Child Left Behind* Act – and how this has led to a high-stakes environment in which standardized test results have become the focus of attention, rather than more creative approaches to teaching. Such tests, generally in multiple-choice format, do not lend themselves to more creative approaches and foci. Instead, what is valued are various forms of general knowledge as the product of convergent thinking. Thirdly, Sternberg (2015) also critiques teacher education for what he describes as its generally conservative approach to teaching practice, and relative lack of applications of new and innovative approaches and foci; while technological innovation means change does occur, this does not necessarily equate to substantive emphasis on creative thinking and teaching:

> Teaching does change over time – technology forces it to, at least in some degree. But teaching for creativity is hard and contrary to traditional ways of thinking, leaving many teachers in higher education utilizing some new technology, but not necessarily in ways that foster creative thinking. Until this problem is solved, we are unlikely to see much spontaneous teaching for creativity in the schools.
>
> *(p. 116)*

Already entrenched approaches make it unlikely new approaches can be actively cultivated.

Test-focused teaching

Various test-focused teaching practices are particularly salient in relation to standardized teaching approaches, and have the most visceral effects for those students deemed failing. Anagnostopoulos (2003) revealed how teachers dedicated significant amounts of time to test preparation and skill development activities on district standards-based tests, and particularly in the lowest performing schools. In English lessons, recitations of key themes and questions likely to be tested, and various kinds of reading aloud activities dominated teaching practices. Furthermore, in keeping with conservative approaches to teaching more broadly, such practices also often reflect more typical instructional routines. Under these circumstances, and perhaps reflecting earlier critiques of the 'conservatism' that characterizes teachers' practices more broadly (Lortie, 1975), more creative teaching approaches and foci become further diminished. Such diminution is also encouraged by reductive foci on various kinds of standardized data – often standardized test data, but also data derived from various standardized readers for literacy learning. Lewis and Holloway (2019) refer to the datafication of the teaching profession to try to capture these more reductive approaches. This further reflects the New Taylorist (Au, 2011) principles and practices that have characterized educational provision in the context of increased standardization created through high-stakes testing and increasingly scripted curricula.

Under these circumstances, the reconstitution of teaching means that the nature of students' learning becomes recalibrated as a positional good, and one which is construed as somehow value-neutral. Biesta (2010) refers to the focus on learning as a good as the 'learnification of education'. This approach assumes that any form of learning on the part of students is valid, regardless of the nature of that learning. As Biesta (2010) argues, 'while learning obviously is one of the central concerns of education, a language of learning makes it particularly difficult to grapple with questions of purpose – and also with questions of content and relationships' (p. 5). This is all part of processes of 'remaking teaching' (Smyth & Shacklock, 1998), and of limiting the conception of teaching that is afforded most attention in policy, and, ultimately, practice. Given the more reductive focus of test-centric policies in the context of globalizing educational accountabilities (Lingard, Martino, Rezai-Rashti & Sellar, 2016), it is not surprising that key contradictions exist in relation to policies that support varied conceptions of learning, and the teaching to enable such learning.

Standardization of teaching in Australia

In the Australian policy context, standardization of teaching is perhaps most clearly expressed in the push for uniform professional teaching standards. This is manifest at the national level through support for the development of The Australian Professional Standards for Teachers (APST). Such standards represent part of a broader push towards more 'national' approaches to teaching and teacher development. During the 2000s, through the *National Partnership Agreement on Improving Teacher Quality*, and more recently through ongoing work of the Education Council – the intergovernmental body comprising the federal and state Ministers of Education – the federal government has sought to provide incentives to the states to adopt a more national approach to teacher professional standards. Even as Savage and Lewis (2018) argue national standards, such as these, represent something of a 'phantom' national construct that is difficult to delineate, and that simultaneously reflect various disjunctive logics, including more transnational traits and impulses, arguably both this push towards the national, and to address transnational disjunctures, reflect efforts to foster more homogenized practices more broadly. Such standards also represent something of a global techno-scientific enterprise even as these are always expressed in context-specific ways (Lewis, Savage & Holloway, 2019). Even as educational policies, such as those associated with the push for national standards, are always 'incomplete insofar as they relate to or map on to the "wild profusion" of local practice' (Ball, 1994, p. 10), they are also significant tools for governing these local practices.

However, it is through actual teaching practices that the influence of these broader national and state policy processes can be better understood. At the level of practice, such advocacy of standardization is reflected through the adoption of particular programs and initiatives, the origins of which may not always be immediately apparent, but that reflect policy processes of homogenization and standardization more broadly. This is apparent in relation to teaching practices in the state of Queensland, Australia, which are presented in this chapter as an example of how standardization pressures have influenced teaching. This includes the nuanced and multiple ways in which such standardization practices and the accountability logics that underpin them have actually been enacted in teachers' teaching practices. Such responses also reflect how teachers have sought to contest more standardized practices, and to 'reclaim' teaching as part of their professional practice, even as this is a challenging undertaking. As in the previous chapter, the data presented here were collected from more than 400 teachers and school-based administrators throughout the state of Queensland between 2012 and 2017, across 14 diverse school settings. These responses reflect the broader policy conditions that governed teachers' practices, even as they were simultaneously evidence of teachers' own efforts to interpret these conditions.

Explicit teaching

In the state of Queensland, standardization processes have been expressed in myriad ways, but perhaps most obviously in relation to what is described as 'explicit teaching'. Notions of 'explicit teaching' were not only seen to permeate the policy discourses in Education Queensland, but expressed in particular ways at the individual school level. Reflecting the commodification of education more broadly (Ball, 2004; Luke, 2004), the concept was clearly manifest in relation to advocacy for several educational consultants whose work was drawn upon in schools to reform teachers' pedagogical practices. This included the work of John Fleming, an educator from the Australian state of Victoria who advocated a version of explicit teaching/instruction emphasizing a three-step process of individual teacher instruction ('I do'), followed by whole class activity ('We do') and individual student engagement ('You do'). This focus on explicit instruction resonated strongly with the work of other theorists taken up in the Queensland context, particularly Anita Archer and Charles Hughes' (2011) work on explicit instruction and effective teaching, and Robert Marzano's (2003) research into 'what works' in instruction.

While the work of Archer, Hughes and Marzano were referred to explicitly by teachers and principals in schools in Queensland, the work of John Fleming seemed to have been taken up particularly strongly in the specific schools informing the research presented in this chapter. This particular iteration of explicit instruction governed teacher practice in Queensland for a variety of reasons, but most overtly as a result of poor NAPLAN (National Assessment Program – Literacy and Numeracy) results in Queensland. Consequently, there was a perception that what was required was much more 'explicit teaching' of key concepts across the board.

Policy support for explicit teaching

This emphasis on models of explicit teaching elicited a variety of responses from teachers. Explicit teaching was openly recognized as an initiative which had regional and state support, and which was seen to have been adopted in response to poor national test results on NAPLAN:

> It's taken up because our reading results and NAPLAN are so poor in the [Central Queensland] region. They're like some of the poorest in the state and we're just not getting the improvement that EQ (Education Queensland) would like.
>
> *(Valmae, Principal, Central Mining School)*

That the explicit teaching approach governed teachers' practices was also reflected in the way teachers recognized the substantial investment in these reforms, and how they were even supported to visit the elite private school in Melbourne where John Fleming was based. This was the case particularly in the more northern regions of the state, where his ideas attracted much interest:

> This region [in northern Queensland] is really pushing explicit teaching because of course our NAPLAN results have been probably amongst the poorest in the state in this region … we had put a lot of money into it – John Fleming … And he's acting as an advisor for several schools in this area, like Valley Way … etc, Linton Fields maybe, so not all schools in this region, but probably the schools that are struggling the most … And also, he goes up to places like Lyrapili. So he's been a big investment and he doesn't come cheaply! Also, several of us have been to his school [in Melbourne]. I went down last year
>
> *(Lillian, Year 6 Teacher, Tropical City School).*

The support at the regional level directly governed what occurred in the schools, with the Fleming approach becoming a priority across regions (particularly in the northern and central areas of the state), and stimulated by the focus on NAPLAN results:

> We've got that big umbrella picture that says because Queensland, with the lower level of literacy and numeracy through the NAPLAN test, the region has said, 'Okay, how do we increase those student outcomes?' And then the region has said, 'Okay, let's look at research'. And what they've actually linked into is the … John Fleming research, around some of the work he's done … the explicit teaching model. And because the region has done that, that's filtered down into the schools. So that's now become a priority within the region. The pressure is on the principals to deliver that, and as a school, we've said, 'How is the best way for us to do that?'
>
> *(Lynagh, Literacy Coach, Tropical City School)*

In this sense, this responsiveness to performative pressures around NAPLAN reflects how more external indicators have increasingly influenced schooling practices, potentially limiting the nature of the practices most valued. While the terrors of performativity (Ball, 2003) varied across school sites, teachers were certainly cognizant of the demands for improved results, and the need to achieve such improvements; in this sense, teachers' practices were interrogated through the governance processes at play in relation to testing. Such responses also reflect how metrics have become increasingly significant, with material effects on teaching practice (Priestley, Biesta, Philippou & Robinson, 2016).

That explicit teaching governed schooling practices so emphatically was also evident in how the John Fleming approach was construed as overtly beneficial by the principals at the school sites. This approach was also linked with other foci and emphases in schools, and as endorsed by the broader education system. For one principal, explicit teaching was a core part of a strategic initiative aimed at improving students' writing skills, and in response to federal support through the *National Partnerships* scheme, and in the context of a state supported literacy strategy:

> For about the last three years we've been on a bit of a mission across the school to develop an explicit teaching framework and explicit instruction … and so part of our *National Partnerships* money that we had around coaching was around developing writing skills with kids. So, we worked extensively with teachers in Grade 4 and 5 specifically in developing an explicit teaching model based on writing. And a lot of that centred out of EQ's literacy strategy around functional grammar. So, it was around coaching the teachers to actually be better teachers at teaching functional grammar.
>
> *(Harry, Principal, Deep North School)*

There was a strong sense that explicit teaching was a key policy initiative of the state, and that principals and teachers were expected to respond accordingly.

Responding to the focus on explicit teaching

This take-up, however, was expressed in multiple ways on the ground. Given the broader context of concern about test results, the focus on explicit teaching was also appropriated by teachers for more educational purposes, even as it was recognized as having the potential to foster more reductive responses. For a Prep teacher at a school in the northern regions of the state, the explicit teaching model, together with higher expectations through the new curriculum (C2C; see Chapter 4), enabled her students to progress at a much more substantial rate than expected. This was in spite of initial hesitations about how different the approach was to more conventional 'play-based' approaches employed in Prep:

> I've loved it. I guess it was a big thing in terms of Preps because it definitely was not the approach that was ever designed, implemented, intended for Prep when it was the old 'play-based' and very kind of student initiated … So

> I think it's definitely changed the face of a lot of grades, so to speak. I personally have loved it. I know that last year I had a lot of people going to me, 'But you can't do that in Prep!' But then you see how amazingly 80% of them, 90% of them could kind of rise to that and do it. So I guess that it shows that in some sense we were probably under-selling them sometimes, just keeping them to a certain standard.
>
> *(Mildred, Prep Teacher, Tropical City School)*

At the same time, the Prep students' levels of learning were also seen as more amenable to the explicit teaching approach per se, with its emphasis on memorization:

> And I think it's probably easier for the Preps because, I guess, we are that foundational level, so we are really focused on the basics ... It used to be the expectation for Preps that they could recognize the numbers to 10 by the end of the year. Our kids go to 50 if not 100 now ... The explicit teaching model and the warm-ups and stuff, which is repetitive and really about moving those skills from short term to long term memory, has definitely shown that they can.
>
> *(Mildred, Prep Teacher, Tropical City School)*

This analysis of teachers' practices was also interpreted as beneficial for encouraging teachers to interrogate their practices more carefully. Again, for a Prep teacher in the same region, the explicit teaching approach represented not so much a restriction and instance of scripted curriculum and standardization more broadly (Au, 2011) on her practice, as an opportunity to look more closely at what she was actually teaching, and how she was going about teaching it:

> It does make you think about what you're doing and you do really – they want you to do your lesson plans, it's really like going back to Uni[1] and writing those types of involved lesson plans you had for your final year prac.[2] And while, initially, you think, 'Oh, what have I got to do this for?' it really does make you pull a lesson apart and think about what you're going to do and what you're going to say and how you're going to say it. And, at the start of the year with the C2C, I couldn't get my head around it and I'm thinking what exactly are they wanting me to teach here? And I went and I broke it down and I did an explicit teaching write up.
>
> *(Ruth, Prep Teacher, Deep North School)*

For these teachers of students in the early years of schooling, the explicit teaching approach seemed to provide more substantive opportunities for students. Teachers seemed to display a sense of authentic accountability to their students through their efforts to raise standards, and to realize prior standards for the youngest students (Prep) in particular may have been limiting the learning of these students.

At the same time, there was recognition that the explicit teaching approach involved following a particular series of steps, as evident in the well-rehearsed way teachers reiterated how the program unfolded:

> That's where we've got the 'warm-up' which is basically, I suppose to 'switch the kids on' and keep them remembering things that they've already learnt – keep them fresh in their heads. And you've got the 'I do', which is the teacher explaining and showing what they need to know. The 'we do', where we do it together jointly. And then the 'you do', where the kids could have a go at the work by themselves.
>
> *(Winsome, Year 3 Teacher, Deep North School)*

That the explicit teaching approach governed teachers' practices was evident in how the formulaic approach around explicit teaching was seen as part of the success of the initiative.

However, there was also realization that teachers actually needed to be more explicit about what they were requiring of their students to enhance their learning. While references to the more formulaic nature of the explicit teaching approach gesture towards more problematic effects of standardization of schooling practices (Ball, 2003; Au, 2011), explicit teaching approaches were also interpreted as governing teachers' practices in more substantive and necessary ways to ensure student understanding of particular tasks and foci. The explicit teaching approach was a 'formula' but one which could contribute to developing more explicit understanding amongst teachers of what was required of students:

> So what we did – probably by the end of 2010 we had finally come to the realization that we actually needed to be a lot more explicit in what we were doing. We were developing a formula. The formula was around you introduce a lesson; the lesson starts – what's the KLA[3] we are working on? It's English. What's the text type we are working with in that KLA? It's narrative. What are the key features of narrative? And we were kind of going through those steps. And then we were into the key features that we were teaching. And so on like that.
>
> *(Harry, Principal, Deep North School)*

In a school in the south-east corner of the state, explicit teaching was also seen as particularly powerful for providing necessary structure and routine to students' learning:

> Yeah that's huge for me – just that structure, and the kids know that as well. We do a lot of PowerPoint presentations when it comes to maths and English and it always says, 'Okay, this is going to be the "I do stage"'. So, they know to listen. And then they'll come up with a 'we do', so they know it's going to be 50–50, so they know. That routine and structure again has worked well.
>
> *(Tony, Year 5 Teacher, South West Urban Primary)*

There was also a sense in which teachers were expected to follow the model, to be 'checked off' for having done so. This was evident in how one of the deputy-principals at one school visited teachers' classrooms:

> He definitely had a set of guidelines – I don't know if it was from John Fleming. He had like a checklist he had to tick off to make sure I was doing what he expected
>
> *(Sadie, Year 7 Teacher, Tropical City School).*

In a sense, such explicit teaching approaches reflect something of a consensus about how to teach a relatively well-defined body of content, or clearly delineated skills, and there is certainly value in such structured approaches, as reflected in educators' interpretations of such foci. Such an approach can be 'a systematic method for presenting material in small steps, pausing to check for student understanding, and eliciting active and successful participation from all students' (Rosenshine, 1986, p. 60). Such an approach is considered useful for teaching mastery of particular skills and knowledges, and often associated with the teaching of 'mathematical procedures and computations, reading decoding, explicit reading procedures such as distinguishing fact from opinion, science facts and concepts, social studies facts and concepts, map skills, grammatical concepts and rules, and foreign language vocabulary and grammar' (Rosenshine, 1986, p. 60). In this sense, more explicit approaches have considerable value.

However, Rosenshine's (1986) earlier research into explicit teaching also reveals such approaches:

> are less relevant for teaching in areas that are less well-structured, that is, where the skills do not follow explicit steps or the concepts are fuzzier and entangled. Thus, the results of this research are less relevant for teaching composition, writing of term papers, reading comprehension, analysing literature or historical trends, for the discussion of social issues or for teaching entangled concepts such as 'liberal' or 'modernism'.
>
> *(p. 60)*

There is a danger, therefore, that something akin to a lower order, basic-skills curriculum – a pedagogy for fulfilling basic tasks and responding to orders directed by others, a 'pedagogy of the oppressed' (Freire, 1972) – may be promulgated over more 'authentic' and substantive educational practices.

However, even as this more formulaic approach was clearly underway, efforts were also made to cultivate a broader sense of pedagogic practices for active engagement and for fostering students' capabilities. Part of this involved a recognition and valuing of students' experiences, and the challenging of any sense of deficit or denigration of students because of their particular circumstances:

> We were also looking at what we call a school-wide pedagogy and some people call it a 'signature pedagogy'. If you're going to be a great teacher at

Deep North State School for this particular group of kids – what have you actually got to be as a teacher? Because one of the mythologies – one of the negative mythologies that I have really worked on … is to break the mythology amongst a lot of teaching staff that these kids don't do their homework; their parents are unloving so they don't send them to school – all those types of things; to say that actually between 9 o'clock and 3 o'clock we've got no excuse. They're our kids – they might come from – Dad might be a 'druggo' – whatever like that – it doesn't matter. But [between] 9 and 3, they are still our kids. So what do we need to be doing to be able to – between 9 and 3; let's forget about what's happening – just forget about [penalizing] the kid that doesn't do their homework because some kids will never do their homework – between 9 and 3.

(Harry, Principal, Deep North School)

Such a response reflects multiple discourses at play. On the one hand, that 'we've got no excuse' could be construed as not taking students' circumstances into account and simply 'blaming' teachers for students' difficulties. However, there are also elements of a more inclusive approach to schooling, whereby students' circumstances were not used to penalize students. On this latter reading, the focus of the 'signature' or 'school-wide' pedagogy could be understood as a more socially just and equitable approach – in this case, in relation to challenging sedimented practices and perceptions that reinforced deficit accounts about particular students in the school. These more site-specific practices (Schatzki, 2002) have the potential to facilitate more responsive pedagogies, enabling teachers to ensure they are more authentically accountable for their particular students' needs. Such responses are not reflective of a restrictive conception of explicit teaching, but seem to fold such approaches into a broader, more responsive set of pedagogies that are deeply reflective and responsive to the needs of the particular students in question. Such an approach reflects a much more 'authentic' response on the part of this principal to the students in his care, characterized by a need for teachers to be responsive to students' learning needs and not to simply blame students or their parents for the sometimes traumatizing circumstances that characterized some students' lives, and that mitigated against their learning. However, such a position also needs to be proffered cautiously, in the knowledge that the broader circumstances within which some children were living and learning were beyond what could be reasonably compensated for by teachers, and that broader social conditions needed to be challenged and responded to more substantively, beyond school sites, including at a broader political level.

Structural support for explicit teaching

That the explicit teaching approach governed educators' practices was also evident in how considerable resourcing was provided, including, as mentioned earlier, sending teachers to the school where the external consultant (John Fleming) supporting explicit teaching was based. This was not simply taken at face value, however, but seen as a resource to stimulate teachers' learning vis-à-vis how to enhance their existing practices:

> I am actually a teacher who's been to Haileybury [College, Melbourne] … it's really good to, actually watch teachers who know what they're doing do it – that, as a learning process is invaluable. And that's not to say that that person's perfect, but it gives you ideas on what you could do. And then it gets your brain moving.
>
> *(Alice, Prep Teacher, Tropical School)*

Teachers also visited one another's schools locally to learn more about the approach. This was the case for schools in the south-western regions of the state:

> I went with [Year 6 Teacher] to school at [neighbouring town] which was using Fleming's approach very strongly, and came back here and just became more explicit with what we were doing really.
>
> *(Laverne, Year 5 Teacher, South West Rural School)*

This resourcing as a form of governance was also evident in how a dedicated numeracy specialist role was reassigned in one school to focus on explicit teaching. This was construed as beneficial as a vehicle to inform teacher learning:

> The focus at the moment is on warm-ups, and I've been working with Flora Jones, who works for Ed-Queensland in a numeracy role. She originally came to our school as a numeracy coach, and she was actually the woman I went to Melbourne with, funnily enough. And we just chatted the whole way there and the whole way back. And we were brainstorming about how she shouldn't really be a math coach, she should be an explicit teaching coach; that's her role now. It's changed since then, since Melbourne, to explicit teaching, which has been great. So, I'm still taking a math focus with her when she comes in and we work on warm-ups for math and explicit teaching lessons for math. So, she's come in and watched me teach, and then she will feed me back some ideas.
>
> *(Alice, Prep Teacher, Tropical City School)*

Structural support was also evident in the form of advocacy for explicit teaching by principals, in the context of a broader educational reform agenda. This support did not arise in isolation, but was explicitly recognized as a response to concerns about students' data, including NAPLAN data, and concerns that in spite of teachers working hard in the school, 'our data still wasn't moving':

> And then at the end of 2010 after looking at all our data, the teachers here worked incredibly hard but we still weren't hitting the mark. We felt that we

were working hard; we were making a lot of headway but our data still wasn't moving.

(Harry, Principal, Deep North School)

While such datafication of the early and primary years of schooling could be reductive in focus (Bradbury & Roberts-Holmes, 2018), and while more reductive approaches to testing were certainly apparent (see Chapter 6), there was also evidence of efforts to utilize data for more educative purposes, and not simply in ways reflective of more performative logics.

In response, this focus on explicit teaching was not the only approach adopted in schools. More inquiry-based approaches were also adopted as well as more overtly 'direct instruction' approaches:

So we are scratching our head – so the end of 2010 we came up with an hypothesis that a strategic balance between explicit teaching, direct instruction and inquiry-based practices will improve our student data at Deep North State School, and that was the hypothesis that we came up with. And we wanted to keep refining that until we actually hit that mark.

(Harry, Principal, Deep North School)

Even as the focus here seemed to be on 'improv[ing] out student data', the school was not simply engaged in data-centric work for its own sake, and a broader conception of education seemed to inform the work of this principal at this site. There was a sense in which, even as teachers' practices were heavily governed by more explicit teaching approaches, this was recognized as not the only influence, and that what was needed was a 'strategic balance' between more explicit teaching approaches, and more inquiry-based approaches. However, even as these efforts to strike a 'strategic balance' give confidence that the support for explicit teaching was not just undertaken in response to broader governing logics supporting more reductive approaches to explicit teaching for its own sake, that student data were part of this discourse also reveals the power of potential datafication processes in relation to the work of teachers more broadly. Teachers were still often the subjects of policy, even as they sought to exert influence over their circumstances (Ball, Maguire & Braun, 2012).

For another principal, structural support was expressed through a three-tiered approach designed to address students' needs, particularly for those students who struggled the most. There was a particular focus on explicit teaching but this time inspired by a different source. Anita Archer and Charles Hughes' (2011) work on 'explicit instruction', with its focus on all students, including students with special needs, was seen as particularly influential, and applied in conjunction with the three-tiered program:

So the work of Archer and Hughes and those sort of things are the things that we are focusing on. We run a 3-level program at our school in terms of expectations of teachers. And one is they do an excellent job in the classroom, and that's around modelled practice, guided practice, independent practice and review. ... As a second tier of intervention we run an 'Academic Success Program'. Now the Academic Success Program is ... we take the bottom cohort of kids, from Prep to Year 3 ... and what they do is they get an extra hour of explicit instruction 4 days a week, which equates to 40 hours a term, which equates to 80 hours a semester which equates to 160 hours [per year]. So, for that extra hour what we've done, we take the bottom 25–30 kids; we take one of the year level cohort teachers. And the other kids are spread out. Because we're taking a group out, so the cohort remains the same size ... And the third level of intervention is case management ... we have a special education program here as well, so we do have kids with disabilities, both intellectual and physical.

(Cameron, Principal, Tropical City School)

However, this focus on 'tak[ing] the bottom cohort of kids' as part of the 'Academic Success Program' also reflects more exclusive rather than inclusive schooling practices (Slee, 2013), with these students focusing on literacy and numeracy rather than other curriculum areas (see also Chapter 4 in this regard re streaming). In this way, the focus on explicit teaching could be potentially limiting, even as it was construed as providing additional support for those students whose literacy and numeracy capabilities were weakest.

Observing teaching, surveilling teaching?

That specific explicit teaching approaches, particularly that advocated by John Fleming, governed teachers' teaching practices was also apparent in other ways. Practices of classroom observation of explicit teaching were a common occurrence in some schools in the research. Observations provided clear evidence of the governance of teachers' work and learning, and served to interrogate teachers' work, even as such practices were simultaneously interrogated by teachers.

Such observations may be educative in function, or evaluative. Cohen and Goldhaber (2016) argue observations for teacher evaluations have much higher face validity than other forms of 'value-added measures' (VAM) that have been used to evaluate teachers more recently. Kupermintz (2003) reveals concerns about the validity of test-based teacher evaluation systems in the Tennessee (USA) context, and the need for greater scrutiny of such tests and alternatives to teacher accountability. Updated research in this context also reveals mixed views about the purpose and validity of the VAM model as used in Tennessee (Davis, Lampley & Foley, 2016). Konstantopoulos (2014) argues there is a need to develop more comprehensive systems for teacher evaluation rather than relying on various value-added models. Pivovarova, Amrein-Beardsley & Broatch (2015) also flag the limitations of value-added measures as vehicles for the evaluation of teachers, and that their limitations mean such measures should not be used for high-stakes decision-making.

In such contexts, classroom observations have been construed as useful vehicles to both address concerns about accountability, and to serve as vehicles to enhance teacher learning for student learning. Classroom observations are construed by teachers themselves to have much higher levels of face validity because they evaluate practices that teachers perceive themselves as observable (Cohen & Goldhaber, 2016).

Of course, this is not to suggest that observations of teachers should not themselves be open to scrutiny and inquiry. Observations are typically undertaken using various protocols which are themselves often seen as insufficiently discriminating to be of substantive value (Cohen & Goldhaber, 2016). Lynch, Chin and Blazar (2017) reveal inconsistencies between classroom observation scores and student achievement scores on standardized assessments, with considerable variation across school districts in the United States. On the basis of such inconsistencies, Cohen and Grossman (2017) argue school characteristics and student demographics may influence the relationship between student outcomes and teaching variables on more standardized tests, and observation protocols. Good and Lavigne (2015) reveal how some teacher observation systems have been developed to be undertaken rapidly, but do not have the conceptual validity and integrity to actually inform teachers about their practice. Other research shows how observations reveal the overwhelming majority of teachers are rated highly in evaluations of their performance; 98% of teachers in Michigan, 97% of teachers in Florida and 98% of teachers in Tennessee, for example, were rated 'effective' or higher in various evaluation metrics, causing concern about the validity of the observation process, particularly where principals are loathe to critique teachers (Anderson, 2013).

In spite of such concerns, observations of teachers' classroom practices are a key part of the technical apparatus that governs educators' work in schools. Principals and deputy-principals, in particular, are integral to fostering this work, and construe this opening up of teachers' classrooms as an important means of improving practice. Such advocacy is evident alongside broader accountability demands (Zavala & Valenta, 2017). Senior administrators' presence, together with technologies such as explicit lesson plans, serve as mechanisms for constructing observations as important sites of intervention. Structured practices are construed as needing to be put in place to support more critical reflection on practice (Zavala & Valenta, 2017).

In Queensland, and in the context of support for explicit teaching, there was clear evidence of observations as governing technologies. For the principal of one school, observations were construed as essential for more critical reflection about how to introduce new knowledge as part of an explicit lesson plan, and this was not something that could be left to teachers alone:

> My goal about that was to build teacher effectiveness by helping teachers to reflect on their learning and teaching. And so, you can't leave teachers alone to do that because whilst we have 31 teachers, probably 3 of them are 'best-practice'. So, if they're reflecting on their own teaching and learning, they're not improving, are they? So, we've introduced – we scanned the teachers

around what they thought they needed help with, and it was about the introduction of new knowledge. Then we came up with an explicit lesson plan. And so that's what we focused on. So, the introduction of new knowledge is done in a consistent way across the school. And so, our strategic team then does this feedback – we go and watch a teacher.

(Theresa, Principal, South West Urban Primary)

This attention by the leadership team was overtly recognized by teachers. These observations were directly focused on the explicit teaching approach, with an emphasis upon the lesson intent at the beginning of classes, and were understood by teachers as demanding their attention:

The teaching and learning model is where at the moment, we are going under observations. And it's two members from admin. that come and watch. And our lesson structure – we're looking at, at the moment, is the 'I do', 'you do', 'we do'. And are just really focusing on that, because we'd found, or admin had found, that we weren't making our intent at the start of the lesson clear.

(Anne-Maree, Year 2 Teacher, South West Urban Primary)

In this way, observations were themselves explicit, and rendered as necessary because of the need to focus more strongly on lesson intents at the start of classes. Such responses also leave open questions about whether individual administrators were more or less accurate in their evaluations of teachers; while relatively accurate overall, individual principals display considerable variability in their capacity to effectively rate teachers through classroom observations (Bergin, Wind, Grajeda & Tsai, 2017). Either way, teachers were construed as more passive subjects in this process (Ball et al., 2011), even as the principal initially indicated that teachers themselves had identified the introduction of lessons/identification of lesson intent as requiring more attention.

Such was the embedded nature of these observations that they could also be enacted in ways that teachers were unaware of them as a form of surveillance:

She [Deputy-Principal] sits at the back of the class; you don't know she's there …You just do your thing and then you get a time to be released and you come back and she goes through everything with you – how you think it went; what you could have done better; what went well.

(Molly, Year 3 Teacher, Deep North School)

Such was the dominance of these observation protocols that some teachers seemed to simply accept the observations without question.

This work was assisted by drawing on the technology of lesson templates, sometimes dependent on particular approaches and/or commercial products, and sometimes developed in the respective schools. The 'John Fleming' model of explicit teaching informed observation protocols in schools, particularly in regional areas in northern and central Queensland. In one school, the principal saw himself observing teachers as integral to the process of focusing attention on the specific pedagogical approach of explicit teaching employed in the school. However, at the same time, and reflecting the need for trusting relations as a key component of leadership practices (Tschannen-Moran, 2014), the focus on 'social processes' as part of this work was also recognized as important:

> For the first part of this year, we've been focusing on the 'warm-ups'. What are the 'warm-ups' and what needs to go into the 'warm-ups'? So, we're developing a better understanding around our explicit teaching model with 'warm-ups'. We're focusing on that particular area. So that's what I do and that's across the school. And that's how I get into the classrooms. And now the way that I actually – the social processes that we need to do this is really important. And I don't know that it will capture on here or anything like that and I don't want to make it sound like I'm a super hero in social process, but understanding what is a good teacher [is important].
>
> *(Harry, Principal, Deep North School)*

There was a sense in which this principal felt that teachers needed to have a clear and shared understanding about the nature of the explicit teaching approach adopted in the school, and what this should look like, and that much work had occurred collaboratively to this end in the school:

> I think teachers have got to have a shared understanding of that. They've got to know what I'm looking for in the classroom. They've got to have an in-depth understanding of the methodology that we're looking at. So we're an explicit teaching school, and this is how we do explicit teaching. So we have done a heap of work around what is explicit teaching, not only with Fleming but ourselves. We've done a stack of work; we've developed collaborative [understandings]. We've developed warm-up exercises; we've developed lessons.
>
> *(Harry, Principal, Deep North School)*

These governance processes extended to compiling an extensive array of resources that could be provided to ensure new teachers were immediately aware of the nature of explicit teaching as practised in the school, and that there were a set of teaching practices that were expected as part of this work, and that these would be scrutinized by the principal:

> I don't have it here but later on we'll get on the computer and I will just show you the file that we have in there. So if you're a new teacher in the school I would say 'We're doing explicit teaching in the school; I'm going to come and see you teach in a couple of weeks' time but I need a lesson plan' – you can actually go onto that part [file on computer] and there's a lesson plan.

> This is what it looks like; this is how we do it; this is what we mean by each of the areas. Go into the Year 4 section and you will see all the Year 4 'warm-ups'.
>
> *(Harry, Principal, Deep North School)*

Such was the effect of this process that the principal reported a high level of homogeneity in the classrooms as a result of teachers' engagement with this school-wide explicit teaching approach: 'There was a lot of shared understanding and work around that that we did. So that when I walked in there, it's like everything is familiar' (Harry, Principal, Deep North School). Such shared resourcing and understanding is perhaps one response to the 'wicked problem' of teacher evaluation, and concerns about tensions between observations for more typically evaluative purposes, and formative purposes (Lillejord, Elstad & Kavli, 2018).

The governance of teachers' practices was also evident in how teachers described being observed by members of the senior administration team in their school, and how they needed to provide these administrators with their lesson plans, following the 'I do, we do, you do' lesson structure. Feedback was also provided as part of this process:

> So being a new teacher, I've had two [observations]. So I think everyone else had one this year. So yeah, they [members of school administration team] come into our class and we give them the lesson plan on the 'I do, we do, you do' structure. And then they provide us with feedback on how we can improve that. And, also, on Monday, sometimes we stay after school and they go through that process as well.
>
> *(Jennifer, Year 4 Teacher, Deep North School)*

The governance of teaching practice was evident in how teachers followed a pre-scribed structure with their students, explicitly outlining lesson objectives to students at the start of lessons, and how they would be enacted during the lesson. Students were required to write down what they had learned at the end of each lesson as part of this structured process, and this was seen as guiding teachers' teaching practice as well. Reflecting how principals need to and can develop effective environments to support ongoing teacher learning (Pitton, 2016), there was also a sense in which the principal was supportive of teachers, and observations were more developmental than evaluative:

> Normally we start with lesson objectives, telling kids today we're going to learn this and you talk about it, what it means. So, they come and observe that, and how we do it. At the moment Theresa [Principal] is very good about how we deliver our lessons. We follow the model 'I do, we do, you do', and the reflection at the end. The kids have to write in their books or sometimes we ask them, 'What have you learnt today?' Or, 'What did you learn in maths and is there anything more you want to learn?' Things like that, so that helps us with the teaching as well.
>
> *(Elsa, Year 5 Teacher, South West Urban Primary)*

Arguably, the more developmental aspects reflect efforts on the part of school administrators to display a more authentic form of accountability towards teachers – providing support for the development of more structured approaches to students' learning for educative purposes – rather than simply being dominated by more performative logics. However, more performative logics clearly exert influence in schooling settings (Lillejord, Elstad & Kavli, 2018), and reductive approaches to the use of explicit teaching templates in these schools certainly reflect more performative logics.

That observations in schools often followed a rigid standardized protocol was still readily apparent in this particular school site. The senior members of staff sat in on lessons but did not interact in any way, and followed up these observations with a feedback session at the conclusion of the lesson:

> They [observations] started Term 3 this year. And I believe it's an EQ initiative, not just for this school. So basically we get two of the, I suppose two of the team leaders or the head people in the school. And they come around and they observe our lesson … They're not allowed to interrupt the lesson; they're not allowed to jump in and help out. And so it's basically they come in, sit down, watch and walk out. And then we get feedback at the end of that.
>
> *(Zita, Year 1 Teacher, South West Urban Primary)*

In this school, Robert Marzano's work endorsing more systematic and explicit instructional planning constituted an important part of the apparatus governing teachers' practices. Marzano's (2003) research and resources were drawn on to develop a lesson planning format that was cultivated across the school. This shared many common features with the Fleming approach, and involved explicitly stating the goals for the lesson, engaging in some sort of 'warm-up' or revision, followed by the 'I do, we do, you do' sequence:

> They [school administrators] got the ideas out of Marzano and just sort of tried to focus on a few things and just made a lesson format … So the first thing you do is you state the goals for each lesson to the children. And then you have some sort of 'warm-up' or revision or overview of where they're – what they were doing in their last lesson on that subject. And then you sort of do some modelling – like the 'I do' part of the lesson the teacher models. And then you do a bit where the children are all working together and with the teacher and you're saying well, 'I might do it like this, what do you think?' And so, they're all bouncing ideas off each other. And then you have the next bit – the 'you dos'; the children's have to do something more independently. And then you have at the end the reflection; you asked the children, 'What did you learn?' 'Does it help you?' 'How will you use it in the future?'
>
> *(Bonnie, Learning Support Teacher, South West Urban School)*

The take-up of such approaches reflect how syntheses of 'what works' in teaching, and of a broad base of literature, have come to dominate discourses about what constitutes effective teaching in many school settings in different parts of the world. Marzano's (2003) *What works in schools: Translating research into action* epitomizes this push towards identifying key practices in schooling settings that are framed as able to be implemented – as what will 'work' in interactions between teachers and students. These approaches offer the hope of enhanced practice if practitioners are prepared to follow the guidance provided:

> My premise is that if we follow the guidance offered from 35 years of research, we can enter an era of unprecedented effectiveness for the public practice of education – one in which the vast majority of schools can be highly effective in promoting student learning.
>
> *(Marzano, 2003, p. 1)*

Such approaches serve to govern schooling practices, through advocacy for attention to particular domains identified as important in syntheses of more traditional research evidence. In Marzano's case, this pertains to identifying those school, teacher and student level factors construed as exerting positive influence on students' academic learning practices. Under such circumstances, more situated, site-based approaches associated with action research, for example, struggle to be taken up, even as they represent beneficial alternatives to more reductive standardized approaches (Hardy & Rönnerman, 2011).

That the teaching practices were more standardized was also evident in how the approach adopted at the school was overtly described as 'like a template', even as it was described as 'not prescriptive':

> It's like a template, yes, and you just kind of set the goals and then you go through. Like it doesn't, it's not prescriptive, but it gives you the 'I do, we do, you do' steps, and then reflection time. And that's it in a nutshell, but there's quite a few other steps in that. And so that came about. And then I guess the admin. decided, 'Well, okay, we've given the teachers this; is it in practice? What is happening actually in the classrooms?'
>
> *(Joy, Year 4 Teacher, South West Urban School)*

However, even as it was described as 'not prescriptive', reflecting the increased governance of educational practice more broadly, there was also a concern to ensure that teachers were indeed following the more explicit teaching approach as it had been introduced to them, including ensuring the objectives were outlined prior to the lesson, that the 'I do, we do, you do' approach was being followed, and that lesson consolidation was occurring:

> Well, at the moment, admin. are coming in and observing lessons being taught for the purpose of making sure that our lessons are being taught explicitly. So, making sure that we're following the 'I do, we do, you do' approach, making

sure you outline the objectives, and doing our reflections at the end to con-
solidate that learning for each lesson.

(Delloraine, Year 7 Teacher, South West Urban School)

Alongside this process of 'making sure' that what was occurring was what was
desired, there was also a sense in which these observational protocols had become
increasingly formalized over time, with increased attention to how teachers were
engaging with their students, whether students understood the intent of the lesson
and how explicitly that teaching was occurring:

It's actually timetabled so we know when our half-an-hour teaching time
observation will be. We've been asked not to start teaching our lesson until
the observers actually enter the room. It's so structured in that we've got very
clear guidelines about how we operate. And admin. will be walking through
and we continue teaching a lesson,

'We're not expecting you to stop and say good morning.' So, now it's very
clear, 'Right when we come in, this is what we expect; this is what we expect
to see; we are coming to look at this particular theme; making sure you are
stating your objectives; making sure you are teaching that content and then
doing the reflection at the end; looking at engagement of students.' Are they
getting it, basically? And it's been suggested that our teaching, and how
explicitly we teach, is what really matters.

(Delloraine, Year 7 Teacher, South West Urban School)

Such an approach seems to be associated with the development of a standardized
knowledge base for the teaching profession more broadly (Hiebert, Gallimore and
Stigler, 2002). Even as identifying such a knowledge base presents as a challenge,
more scripted approaches to teacher knowledge and development seemed to
underpin advocacy for more explicit teaching practices. This is challenging work
because teachers' knowledge is intimately associated with their everyday practice –
akin to a form of 'craft knowledge' focused on doing a job well (Sennett, 2009) –
which cannot be readily captured and distilled into a form of knowledge that can
then be somehow 'translated' into generalizable practices and principles. However,
this is exactly what more reductive approaches to explicit teaching seek to achieve.
Part of the challenge is that the 'craft' knowledge of teachers such as that advocated
in action research (cf. Hardy & Rönnerman, 2011) for example, is not scrutinized
in the same way that more 'public' research generated by educational researchers is,
such as through the journal review process. The result is a tendency to place
greater emphasis on syntheses of teaching knowledge, and 'template' approaches,
rather than more practitioner inquiry approaches, even as the latter are essential to
making sense of the former, in context.

That the governance of teachers' teaching practice was heavily regulated was also
evident in how it was not only teachers who were surveilled through the explicit

teaching process. The role and work of the senior administrative staff involved in undertaking the observations were also scrutinized. This process entailed the administrative team engaging in several identifiable steps that had to be followed in succession:

> So I might observe and then someone observes me giving the feedback. And then that person then gives me feedback on how I did that.
>
> *(Theresa, Principal, South West Urban School)*

The technology of a specific school-designed lesson format not only regulated the way in which teachers developed and delivered lessons, but also how administrative staff observed teachers:

> This South West Urban State School lesson format has started last term ... And that's partly for the teachers but it's partly for those people observing to become good leaders. So that they can give – they can learn to give the feedback in the right way.
>
> *(Bonnie, Learning Support Teacher, South West Urban School)*

Again, giving the feedback in the 'right way' reflects how teaching practices were heavily governed by such technologies. Such templates served as a tool to control practices in prescribed ways, and to foster a sense of the need for ongoing change and development. After Rose (1999), such a process entails a 'constant and never-ending *modulation* where the modulation occurs within the flows and transactions between the forces and capacities of the human subject and the practices in which he or she participates' (p. 234).

Indeed, that those engaged in providing feedback were just as regulated and modulated as those observed was evident in the way the principal of the school in the south-western part of the urban conurbation in south-east Queensland that was most heavily engaged in teacher observations critiqued how members of the 'strategic team' (administration team and literacy and numeracy coaches) gave feedback to teachers. This included the need to critically reflect on how feedback was provided by members of the strategic team to teachers at the end of each observation. Preconceived judgements about teachers' practices were seen as inhibiting the value of feedback provided to teachers:

> And the feedback session today that I'll be doing is around helping people understand that we're not doing our feedback loop well, because that's my observation. My other observation is that some of the strategic team are going into certain teachers with a prejudgment in their heads about the effectiveness or otherwise of that teacher and making excuses around what they see. And so that's all interesting stuff. Like to give honest feedback, you've got to lose all those prejudgements and all of those things that you go in there with. You've got to sit back and look at what you see and give feedback on that. ... I think

[deputy] and I, the deputy and I, are the only two effectively giving feedback to the feedback.

(Theresa, Principal, South West Urban School)

Even as it was heavily regulatory in orientation, this critique of members of the strategic team involved in providing feedback was also potentially emancipatory, influenced as it was by previous experiences of observation processes in which this principal had herself been a part as a teacher. She was concerned that the process could become too directive and draconian, involving treating teachers as though they were under close critical scrutiny about their practices, with members of the strategic team as sources of necessary knowledge and teachers as 'lacking'. Such an approach exemplifies how observations served as techniques for the disciplining of the self (Foucault, 1990) and how, in this case, such disciplining was oriented towards various forms of self-reflective capacities amongst teachers, including senses of responsibility and professional accountability:

And I don't want it to be – I mean as a teacher, I hated the principal or anyone coming in to watch me. I don't want it to be like 'we're the experts and you're the dummies and we're taking notes on you', kind of scenario. That's why I say it's about building tools of self-reflection and improvement in yourself – in teachers – and that responsibility and professional accountability around doing a better job.

(Theresa, Principal, South West Urban School)

Arguably, even as teachers and administrators were constituted by potentially reductive and performative practices, the cultivation of professional accountability though self-reflection and improvement were also a form of more 'authentic accountability' of teachers to themselves, and of the administrators to the teachers. The latter was evident through the efforts of these administrators to foster more self-reflective processes as a vehicle for improvement amongst teachers. This was evident in how this principal sought to cultivate such sensibilities amongst teachers in her school.

However, at the same time, and reflecting how observations could serve as oppressive techniques with problematic effects, the principal also sought to manage the nature of the information flow about the observations in order to ameliorate potential concerns amongst members of the leadership team, and subsequently, amongst the staff more widely:

And I mean I'm probably – in the interest of not putting too much terror out there amongst the strategic team, I've probably divulged information around it a little bit at a time. And so, we've done the whole, surveyed the staff through … designed questions. And got the area that they wanted help with, which was the introduction of new knowledge.

(Theresa, Principal, South West Urban School)

Arguably, this recognition about not 'putting too much terror out there' reflects the actual 'terrors of performativity' (Ball, 2003) that characterize these practices of surveillance, and ultimately of 'deliverology' – with their focus on 'delivering' results (Barber, 2007)[4] that so frequently underpin such terrors.

These governance processes could also be much more subtle on the part of those engaged in observations. Reflecting the importance of trusting relations amongst those in leadership positions in schools (Tschannen-Moran, 2014), for the head of curriculum in the northern Queensland school where observations were most evident, this sense of trust was pivotal to her capacity to observe teachers, so as to assist them in their literacy teaching practices. This was built out of prior relationships with teachers, and an already existing coaching culture:

> I like the literacy coaching because the focus has been on reading, so I've been able to get into classrooms and work with teachers; our school has a big coaching culture, so people are used to people coming in. But a part of that was this literacy coach role because, hopefully, they found it non-threatening, because they all knew me beforehand. As I said, I'm a reading recovery teacher, so I believe I know a fair bit about reading. So it was good to be able to get into a whole lot of classes and see what was happening, and then work with the teachers to improve their practice.
>
> *(Dulcie, Head of Curriculum/Literacy Coach/Acting Deputy, Deep North School)*

In this way, teachers' practices were open to scrutiny but in potentially less problematic ways than other schooling contexts in which such practices were not already part of shared practices. Again, more authentic accountabilities were at least partially evident in the efforts of this head of curriculum/coach to use the observations as a vehicle to work with teachers to enhance their practice, even as teachers were themselves were potentially positioned in more passive roles through such efforts.

Even as observing teaching was construed as beneficial, the way in which teachers made sense of such observations reflects the pressures that still attended such activities. For one relatively new teacher, being observed on a discrete part of her practice by the former head of curriculum/acting deputy was quite different from being observed for a full lesson (by the deputy or principal):

> Well with Dulcie [former Head of Curriculum/Literacy Coach/Acting Deputy], she's just watching a small group activity you know of reading groups which is something that's – you go through the book, you read the book, those sort of things. So, it's a lot less pressure, I guess. Whereas [having Deputy or Principal] watching a full lesson, and especially when you've never done the Fleming model before!
>
> *(Winsome, Year 3 Teacher, Deep North School)*

Consequently, the way in which teaching practices were scrutinized reflects broader concerns about accountability as productive of considerable anxiety, including the anxiety that attends new teachers' practices more broadly (Prilleltensky, Neff & Bessell, 2016), even as observations could also be construed as beneficial.

That teaching practices were being governed through explicit teaching strategies was also evident in the way some teachers enjoyed having someone come into their class, and complimenting them on their work:

> They've been really useful, I suppose, because they've had some new teachers arrive recently for them to see where we are and what we're doing and what skills we have. And it's useful getting the feedback as well. Then the new teacher models what they're trying to use – the I, we, you do – and just make sure that the whole school is being consistent. And I think it's really good and it makes you, not that you wouldn't work hard anyway, but it's nice having somebody come in and compliment you on the hard work that you're doing.
>
> *(Cassie, Year 2 Teacher, South West Urban School)*

Indeed, for some teachers, at the same time they were nervous about being observed and evaluated, there was also a sense in which they were being validated in their work, and how the observations of them engaging in the explicit teaching sequences constituted an important part of this validation. This was the case amongst experienced teachers, who were anxious about the experience, even as they found it affirming:

> Yeah, I was nervous, the first time … there's high expectations, 'Is he up to the task that we want him for in a very new environment?' But I took it as such a valuable thing because I needed to prove to myself, 'Have I got it'? Rather than assume that I have, I needed the validation. So, I'm certainly on the right track. And to me, that was really important. You can go along sort of thinking, 'Well, I think I've got it; it seems to be working; the kids are happy'. And then you find out you're miles off course! So this is an opportunity to sort of test that. And as it turned out, on both occasions, [the principal] was happy with me, and that's important because it does give you that sense of understanding where you're at.
>
> *(William, Year 5 Teacher, Deep North School)*

As well as revealing efforts to engage with teachers, and perhaps to help address issues of anxiety, loneliness and inadequacy that often attend new teachers (Hargreaves & Fullan, 2012), such responses also reflect efforts to overcome the compartmentalization that characterizes teachers' work in schools – part of the habituated practices that constitute the grammar of schooling more broadly (Tyack & Cuban, 1995). Validation of teachers' work by senior personnel was seen as important more broadly, and as a vehicle to help redress concerns about teachers feeling left to teach in isolation:

> We're doing these teaching and learning audits which are quite beneficial for teachers' learning and seeing how they're going. And having the senior staff

members come in and watch you and give you feedback. And, oh you can do reflections and things like that which is nice. I just like it because it's a 'touch base' situation. And we're not just left teaching in the classroom by ourselves all the time.

(*Nerida, Prep Teacher, South West Urban School*)

Through such engagement with teachers, school administrators were acknowledging and valuing teachers' work through their presence, and making themselves available – accountable – to these teachers, through engaging with them to try to foster enhanced practice. Again, potentially more authentic practices were enabled, even as more performative logics focused on observations for accountability purposes exerted influence.

This was not always a comfortable process, evident in how teachers supported the observations even as they simultaneously disliked the process:

I guess it's just to up-skill you, give you feedback on your teaching. I absolutely hate it, but it's very useful, so it's – yeah, it makes me sick the night before. But it is good to hear– It really does make you think about your teaching … Just getting that feedback is – has been really good.

(*Philomena, Year 2 Teacher, South West Urban School*)

Even as there was clear evidence of stress at play, and a visceral sense of the terrors of performativity (Ball, 2003), and of the governance of teachers' work in relation to their teaching practice, something of an appropriation of more performative accountability-oriented logics (cf. Hardy, 2014) also seemed to be in evidence. This was evident in the way in which some teachers sought to engage with administrators around the observation process for more educative purposes. This more authentic sense of accountability was apparent in how one very experienced teacher believed it was important that the principal observe her during a class in which she felt she needed to improve:

It's been a long time since I had someone come in and watch me. Yeah, it's always good to get feedback on the way that you teach. And I usually try to do stuff that I'm not overly confident with. I can do the explicit teaching very well with maths – that's just one of the things that I find quite easy to teach. But I was having trouble with English. So I've made him do that, so he gets something back on things like that.

(*Jenny-Lea, Year 4–5 Teacher, Deep North School*)

Through such an action, there was not only a sense in which this teacher was governed by processes of observation of explicit teaching, but also how such observations could be used as a vehicle to inform the principal about the nature of the explicit teaching program in particular, and teaching practices in the school more generally. There was a sense in which the principal was governed by not only a broader accountability logic that construes observations of teachers as important to 'keep track' of teachers' practices but also by a much 'richer' logic of accountability (Lingard, Martino, Rezai-Rashti & Sellar, 2016) that placed more substantive, collaborative teacher professional learning at the forefront of teachers' practices (Datnow, 2018), and that teachers could use as a vehicle to build understanding visa-vis the principal about actual teaching practice. Again, a more authentic sense of the nature of actual teaching practices was evident, reflecting more than a one-way accountability process.

In a similar vein, the support teacher for literacy and numeracy relayed how teachers appeared supportive of being observed, including a story about how a teacher had asked one of the senior administrators to visit her again because she was not happy with the class observed initially:

> But they're happy to have them because they enjoy the feedback. I think we even had one teacher that said, 'Look, I know that didn't work really well but I want you to come back again and watch me'. I mean, gosh, how powerful is that?
>
> *(Melanie, Support Teacher – Literacy and Numeracy, Deep North School)*

That teachers did not simply passively engage with more standardized teaching practices was also evident in how another experienced teacher construed disagreements between herself and members of the administration team over the nature of the lesson she presented as a valuable opportunity for professional conversation about the nature of the explicit teaching model:

> So, the 'I do' is – it's a different lesson, you know, completely. So they saw me do the 'I do'; I just did a revision of what we'd already done, quickly asking the children for feedback and that. And then we did the 'we do'; they didn't ever get to the 'you do'. And I said to them, if we're following the C2C lessons, then this is where I'm up to. So, yeah, so you had to explain; I actually had a debate with them over it. They thought it was the 'you do'; no – it was 'we do'. And I said to them, 'No, if you had a look at the model, then tick the things that we did, it's in the "we do"'. And then they realized that, 'Yes, that was a "we do" and not ["you do"]'. So, it's good in that regard that, you know – professional conversation coming out of your lesson, and you being able to know what actually part of the model that you were doing.
>
> *(Krystal, Year 7 Teacher, South West Urban School)*

In these ways, even as it may be difficult to gauge the quality of the senior administrator and principals' evaluative skills (Bergin et al., 2017), and even as the terrors of performativity did sometimes attend the observations of a potentially reductive teaching model, there was also a sense that the whole process could be useful for refining and enhancing teachers' practices. There was also a sense of acceptance in relation to the governance of teachers' work through the adoption of the explicit teaching regime, and how teachers came to accommodate the expectations that they would conduct themselves in particular ways in response to expectations around these regimes. While at times this reflected more performative logics, the way teachers also sought to orient the focus on explicit teaching to enhance their practice, and their own professional learning, reflects a more authentic sense of accountability in relation to the needs of their students, and their responsibilities to one another to try to provide the best possible teaching circumstances/conditions for their students.

Teaching observations as challenging and challenged

In spite of potential benefits to practice, the formal unfolding of the observations of teaching practice had been implemented in such a way that at times they were seen as an imposition in a busy teaching day. At times, there was a sense in which teachers had to alter their practices to accommodate being observed, and that this was problematic. That teachers were not just interpreting but interrogating their circumstances was evident in the way they were concerned about the reductive applications of the explicit teaching approach which required them to have to wait for the members of the administration team who were observing them to do this work:

> They can be kind of intimidating. And it's a bit annoying, because they start at awkward times. And especially for myself or the Grade 6 and 7s, our lessons run for an hour or just over, where they're [administrators] doing them [observations] in half-an-hour blocks. And we're expected to start our lesson when they get there! And there's different phases to the lesson plan – so you've got your reflection on the previous lesson, then the 'I do, we do, you do'. And sometimes it's a bit hard to delay the start of the lesson for half an hour at the start of the day or something when you've got a lot to get through.
>
> *(May, Year 6 Teacher, South West Urban School)*

Again, such reservations reveal more authentic concerns to avoid inhibiting student learning; even as teachers' practices were clearly heavily governed by more explicit teaching approaches, teachers resisted the performative aspects of the approach, such as having to undertake the lessons according to the scripted format (reflection on previous lesson; I do; we do; you do), and having to undertake specific aspects of the lesson to fit in with being observed. Such an approach was far removed from the substance – authenticity – of an actual, effective lesson.

These concerns resonate with how Green (2013) argues the push for explicitness in education is not necessarily oriented towards improvement of practice. In her aptly entitled work *Education, professionalism and the quest for accountability: Hitting the target but missing the point*, Green (2013) makes the case that the knowledge about how to respond appropriately to a given situation emerges in context, and in the enactment of practice under the specific conditions which characterize that practice. Such knowledge, sharing some resemblance with Polanyi's (1966) 'tacit knowledge', cannot be explicitly delineated, commanded or controlled. Rather, this knowledge arises under circumstances conducive to its development, and reflective of productive (or otherwise) experiences. While propositional knowledge can be useful, and assist practice, it is only through practice that appropriate decisions are made:

> [W]hen one learns from one's experience, one's state of perceptiveness, one's state of being, awareness, and sensibility is what changes. *That* is the basis on which one can say, 'I won't do that again … I should have …' Such propositional thought works dialectically with our practical experience.
>
> *(Green, 2013, p. 146; emphasis original)*

This practical basis of experience was challenged by the focus on explicit teaching, and the push by members of the administration team to observe teachers. Some teachers found the focus on specific aspects of their practice pertaining to explicit teaching relatively ineffectual for their learning, in light of their own experiences. That teachers interrogated their circumstances was evident in the way the focus on explicit teaching by one of the coaches in one teacher's school was not seen as a useful vehicle for her learning, even as the opportunity to reflect on her own practice was beneficial:

> Probably not … In terms of me reflecting on my own teaching, it's good to have time to actually do that, to actually have a little bit of time and just to specifically reflect on that lesson. Because I do that all the time, but I don't always record it and think purposefully about it. So, for me it was good. In terms of discussing what I was going to do in the lesson, I don't really think that [Head of Curriculum] had a great deal of input.
>
> *(Rosie-Lea, Year 7 Teacher, Deep North School)*

For this teacher, the emphasis on a specific aspect of the explicit teaching model, 'ploughing back' – involving reiterating the key points covered at the conclusion of a lesson – was seen as less beneficial, and as something that she undertook already as an integral part of her previous teaching experiences:

> And she [coach] was focusing, really on the 'ploughing back', which I've done forever. You know, it's something new to people in [northern] Queensland, I think … But in England, it was a key part of the lesson. It was always part of the numeracy, and it was always part of the literacy. And we called it something different, but I would never have done a lesson without having what I call a 'plenary'.
>
> *(Rosie-Lea, Year 7 Teacher, Deep North School)*

As well as actively critiquing the value of the focus on explicit teaching, observations were considered stressful, and identifying key elements of explicit teaching difficult to determine. For another teacher, and reflecting the stress that can attend teaching through decisions made at an organizational level (Prilleltensky, Neff & Bessell, 2016), the observations were seen as anxiety-provoking. Furthermore, the approach to observing teachers in a half hour period meant it was difficult to ascertain the value of such observations that attended the explicit teaching approach. On being asked the purpose of the observations, this teacher replied:

> To stress us out … It always is [stressful]. It brings you back to your prac. days. I can understand why we have it but − So, last time was to focus on the set up of the lesson and then just provide feedback … The 'we do'. I think that's probably hard to gauge in half an hour because it depends on what you're doing; it depends on what stage you're at; in terms of what subject you're doing. I mean I think it's good, and I think everyone does it, and I think it's an essential part of our lesson. I'm not saying anything about that, but I think as far as observations go, it's quite hard to gauge.
>
> *(Chazelle, Languages Other Than English (LOTE)/Special Needs Teacher, South West Urban School)*

While not averse to being explicit about what students were to learn, it was the way in which the observations were undertaken that was the particular source of angst. The regimentation that attended the observations seemed less 'educative' and reflective of more accountability logics. The critiques of such performative logics reflected more authentic sensibilities on the part of such teachers, as they struggled to engage productively with the explicit teaching model.

Reflecting the 'wicked problem' of tensions that attend more developmental versus evaluative logics of observations (Lillejord et al, 2018), and even while couched in terms of developmental processes, observations by school principals and deputy-principals, heads of curriculum, and sometimes literacy and numeracy coaches, were also construed as challenging. Their formality was seen as not enabling teachers to adapt their pedagogies 'in the moment' if a particular lesson was not working as effectively as hoped:

> And sometimes it's hard being observed because if you're there by yourself and a lesson's not going to plan, sometimes you might just scrap it and move on to something else. And then the next day you might reflect and do something differently. But if someone's there observing, you sort of have to try to make it work.
>
> *(Stella, Year 1 Teacher, South West Urban School)*

While the observations could be useful, and 'it's a good thing to be able to learn to think on your feet' (Stella, Year 1 Teacher, South West Urban Primary), they could also contribute to the cultivation of a more instrumental approach to such practices, whereby such observations become part of an apparatus of surveillance in which a managerial 'lifeworld' focused on monitoring various short-term targets are undertaken without necessary attention to the educational ideals that should characterize such work:

> So when, in the name of 'continuous improvement' ... educators comply with managerial requests to measure and report on their 'performance' in order to demonstrate the 'effectiveness' and 'quality' of their work, they should not really be surprised to find that such requests take them to a place where they really do not want to be ... Where is that? A managerial 'life-world' committed to monitoring 'short-term targets' or to recording data for 'assessment exercises', 'transparency reviews', 'standardized assessments', 'enterprise audits', 'strategic/development plans', 'marketing strategies', and so on. In that world there is no appeal to further standards that stand above or beside managerial ones. There is little room in such a 'lifeworld' to ask how the efforts of an educational institution relate to *educational* ideals. Here we have a form of Habermasian 'colonization', *par excellence*.
>
> *(Green, 2013, p. 154; emphasis original)*

However, and reflecting how teachers also sought to respond more proactively to these potentially problematic practices – to interrogate more performative logics of accountability – for a new teacher, the observations also reflected an opportunity to gain feedback about her teaching practice, and to enhance awareness of her practice:

> But from the start I just – since last year, since my first year, I take on absolutely any feedback I can and I've learnt to do that. I've just taken it as a positive thing. And even though you do a lesson, if they observe and it doesn't go to plan, they're not going to be giving you negative personal feedback. It's going to be stuff [that's] constructive, and how you can do things better. So, I think it's good. And I think it's making people more aware of their own teaching.
>
> *(Stella, Year 1 Teacher, South West Urban School)*

Even as the observations were seen as challenging, they were also construed as a vehicle to potentially enhance teachers' practices. At the same time, there was also recognition that excellent teaching practices were evident and occurring in schools:

> There's some fabulous, fabulous – and I haven't been in every classroom – but there is fabulous work happening out there.
>
> *(Kara, Deputy-Principal, South East Urban School)*

In this way, even as teachers' practices were governed by particular renderings of explicit teaching, there was a sense of achievement associated with teachers' work and a desire to reassure teachers about the good practice that was occurring, even as observations were simultaneously construed as necessary vehicles to try to enhance teachers' practice. Teachers were not simply being interrogated by practices of observation associated with explicit teaching; they were also interrogating the more performative logics, and seeking to extract more substantive learnings from educational aspects of such practices.

An alternative to explicit teaching: 'Watching others work'

Teaching was also governed by and through alternative approaches to informing teaching practice beyond various forms of established 'explicit teaching' approaches. In contrast to the more directive explicit teaching model, a 'watching others work' (WOW) approach was adopted in two schools involved in the research, and was seen as an effective means of encouraging teachers to develop alternative pedagogical practices, and to continually revise their own taken-for-granted assumptions. Such approaches focused on using observation skills to develop more effective teaching capacities, and required knowledge of requisite teaching content and methods, and the ability to be able to see the patterns and sequences of teaching practice that comprise the repertoire of effective teachers – to be able to see beyond the 'parts' to the 'whole' of effective teaching practices (Borich, 2016). In one school in which this approach was in its infancy, there was recognition of the potential value for the WOW initiative, but also hesitation about whether teachers would avail themselves sufficiently of the opportunity to watch others work. Teachers were also reluctant to promote themselves as engaging in productive practices from which others could learn:

> Some people although have started to visit other schools in the local area to have a look at some aspect of what they're doing. I don't know – probably the only person most of them watch work is me [as Head of Curriculum/Teacher-Librarian]! So I don't know how many people have taken up the opportunity in terms of actually going into somebody else's classroom and seeing what they're doing with their students. And I think that's a part of – people don't necessarily want to intrude on another classroom. And I think probably quite a few people aren't that comfortable with the idea of having somebody come in, or they don't feel they have something to offer. I've had the conversation with a couple of teachers about, 'Well, you're actually really good at this, this and this. And people can come and see you do this'. But, you know, we're teachers; we don't blow our trumpets, and not saying, 'Hey, I'm really good at giving feedback. Come and watch me do it!' And yet, some of them are brilliant at that. And I've said to them, 'People would come and see you do that!'
>
> *(Yvette, Head of Curriculum/Teacher-Librarian, South East Urban School)*

That this process of observing teaching was seen as potentially challenging was evident in hesitations to visit other teachers' classrooms. Long-standing cultural norms of teaching –individualism, conservatisim and presentism (Lortie, 1975) –

seemed to encourage isolation and worked against more meaningful, learning-oriented interactions amongst teachers. More established practices governed teachers' teaching even as various forms of observations served as alternatives.

This was slow work, with teachers taking time to become accustomed to having others in their classroom. For the new deputy-principal at this school, building trust over time was also considered an important part of the necessary leadership work which had to be undertaken (Tschannen-Moran, 2014). In this school, WOW was still in its infancy, and there was a sense that it would take time for teachers to feel comfortable allowing other teachers to watch their practices, even as many teachers were recognized as engaging in exemplary practice:

> From the beginning when it started, there weren't any takers for that. And it's built up now where [supply teacher] is booked. He's now booked the next term as well, working on the Mondays. So, the teachers are taking that, and it is baby steps looking at that. I have been watching some brilliant guided reading lessons from teachers that I would love other teachers to come and visit; just to see how it goes. But that's a little bit further down the track. And it's just, as I said, I'm still building that trust, I suppose.
>
> *(Kara, Deputy-Principal, South East Urban School)*

Issues of trust amongst members of the leadership team were construed as essential to further progressing and promoting observations for more professional learning purposes (Tschannen-Moran, 2014). Hesitation amongst teachers and cultural conservatism, inhibitions and lack of confidence about teachers' own capacities were evident in how some teachers expressed reservations about how other teachers might construe their practice, and governed access to classrooms:

> I mean [Principal] has been trying to get it going all year, I guess. The thought of someone coming in to watch you really didn't thrill people. I guess we all look at ourselves as, 'Well, I'm nothing special; why would anyone want to come and look at me?'
>
> *(Gretchen, Year 3 Teacher, South East Urban School)*

Some teachers argued that this sharing approach was already in practice amongst functioning teaching teams at particular year levels, as they engaged with one another on an ongoing basis:

> We're already doing it if you know what I mean; we're already watching each other, and they often help me. It's a really good year.
>
> *(Paul, Year 3 Teacher, South East Urban School)*

However, even as there were hesitations, and even as teachers down-played the nature of WOW time, working with a colleague was understood as beneficial. While some teachers may not have explicitly sought to watch other members of staff teach, when teachers worked well together in the same year level, they did have the opportunity to work closely with one another in ways that approximated WOW time:

> I've been involved when it comes to – I haven't gone to see anyone else teach. Ingrid [Year 5 teaching partner] and I do work fairly closely together, and we have opened the walls, and doors, between the classrooms. And we do work together that way.
>
> *(Peter, Year 5 Teacher, South East Urban School)*

Such a response implies evidence of more incidental learning as part of teachers' ongoing daily work, and a more open level of engagement than implied in more traditional accounts of the individualism that has traditionally characterized teaching (Lortie, 1975). It also suggests how the established schooling practices and interactions – the grammar of schooling (Tyack & Cuban, 1995) – continue to exert significant influence on teachers' practices, governing the nature of associations that are enabled and that have the opportunity to develop.

Perhaps this also helps explain why and how collaborative arrangements tended to be very localized, and involved colleagues working on a one-on-one basis. Nevertheless, this more local, individualistic attention was construed as beneficial for teachers' individual learning, and provided the opportunity to learn in what was perceived as a supportive environment:

> I went to Yvette [Head of Curriculum] for some WOW time and we looked at how to develop an Ed Studio[5] and how to set that up with my class. Yeah … It was useful. It got me started and got me understanding it a bit more, because I had just like no idea; I'm not very technical … I think we work well together when we're both over there [classroom space where Head of Curriculum often worked]. Like if she's got it on the big screen and that, and it is good learning, she does go over it in such a way that I can understand it.
>
> *(Sonya, Year 2 Teacher, South East Urban School)*

A second school in which the 'watching others work' approach had been in place for some time (the acting principal of the school mentioned above had previously been deputy-principal at this school) revealed the potential of such an approach, and how such an approach could become more normalized, even as it was still something that was being developed, and even as it still represented a more conservative approach to stimulating change in teachers' practice. In this inner-city primary school serving a more affluent community, this focus on 'watching others work' was more embedded into schooling practices, and was generally construed as beneficial by many teachers. For a relatively new ('graduate') teacher, WOW time entailed working closely with more experienced colleagues:

> I've done some mentoring with some of the other teachers. I've also had, because being a graduate teacher obviously, a bit more for me. [I] also have

had WOW time, 'watching others work' – for things like Big Book sessions. Sort of more working with my peers for that one.

(Valentine, Year 1 Teacher, City Urban School)

The opportunity to collaborate more intensively with a colleague enabled sharing ideas and the ability to request or give advice. It also seemed to involve a more substantive relationship that enabled this new teacher's learning, and not simply based on providing social support, or reducing workload (Hodkinson & Hodkinson, 2005). By doing so, it served as a more authentic form of accountability of teachers to their colleagues, themselves and their students, oriented to more substantive teacher learning for student learning.

This was recognized by the teacher whom this teacher visited to learn more about Big Books, and involved providing the opportunity for this teacher to learn about specific strategies that were becoming a more normalized part of practices in the new Prep curriculum. This process of enabling a less experienced teacher to watch a more experienced teacher was also seen as an important vehicle for fostering enhanced teaching practice for a relatively new teacher whose classroom was remote from her colleagues:

Yes, 'watching others work', I've done, I do a little bit of, in my first year here, peer modelling for Valentine; Valentine works next door to me now. She's a Year 1 teacher but in my first year here, it was her first year teaching. And she was on Year 1, but she was in a demountable [detached classroom], sort of by herself. And it made it hard. Because there were three Year 1 teachers, and because she was sort of by herself, she wasn't seeing a lot of what was going on – just location-wise – with what's going on in the classroom. So I would go to her class and do some modelling with Big Books and reading strategies and things like that.

(Narelle, Year 1 Teacher, City Urban Primary)

For a colleague, teachers visited to develop a sense about children's experiences to date, and to learn about specific curricula activities, such as guided reading. However, even as this was a more established practice at her school, and even as such collaboration had the potential to inspire teachers to engage in experimentation (Meirink, Meijer, Verloop & Bergen, 2009), this was still something that she had not yet had the opportunity to avail herself during the year:

Last year, so one [teacher] came just because she wanted to have a little general look at Prep. Because she was a Grade 1 teacher and was just really curious to know at the beginning of the year to know what Preppies really looked like, so she could compare to what she had in Grade 1. And she was gob-smacked and said, 'I'm never coming back again!' It was just so busy. And the other teacher came to look at guided reading time, so that was fine. This year, if I was to have WOW time, I would like to have it with technology, and see what some of the other teachers are doing with technology. But I haven't got to that yet.

(Meredith, Prep Teacher, City Urban Primary)

Reflecting respectful relations between teachers, and a more authentic sense of accountability for one another's learning – responsibility for one another's learning – the Year 1 teacher who came to watch this teacher corroborated the value of the opportunity to watch her colleague, and how this benefited her teaching. Interestingly, this was not undertaken within the parameters of formally allocated WOW time, but was instead the product of more informal interactions between the two teachers, and enabled by their close proximity to one another:

This year has been good; there's been some timetabled WOW time on Friday mornings but I haven't used any of that as yet. But I informally – our class-rooms have got a section that sort of folds back from the bookshelf to the wall, so I am always ducking my head around. Not always, but I ask Meredith every now and then if I can just pop in. And, fortunately, I don't do guided reading at the same time as she does. So, I've been in and watched some of the things that she does, which I've found useful. Because I've now got a bank of words that I can flick through, and have ready, so that we can do a 'word walk' rather than just a 'picture walk'. … And just her questioning [how she asked questions of students].

(Kelly, Prep Teacher, City Urban Primary)

In this way, even as teachers' work was governed by explicit teaching in some settings, in this school, there was less evidence of more directive governance practices at play, and more evidence of how teachers' practices were governed by more localized decision-making, and teachers' responses to such practices. This included 'taking an interest in what others do' as part of collaborative learning experiences (Hodkinson & Hodkinson, 2005, p. 116).

This governance of teachers' practices through interest in others' work was also evident in how another teacher from this school was able to undertake WOW time in another school setting. This teacher spoke about the opportunity to meet with a curriculum leader who was recognized as an exemplary practitioner in another region. Having worked in this region previously, and as a relatively new teacher to her current year level, this teacher was familiar with the work of this curriculum expert, and valued the opportunity to spend a full day watching her work with colleagues on curriculum development/planning at her school:

I said to [Principal] … 'Could I please [visit this school] – there's a teacher that had the Prep and the Year 1, and she's the Curriculum Leader within that school'.

(Cynthia, Prep Teacher, City Urban Primary)

For this teacher, the opportunity to meet with a senior colleague at another school was particularly valued. That this was guided by the teacher herself reflects a more agentic stance in relation to curriculum reform in Queensland at the time, and a genuine, authentic, desire to look beyond the immediacy of her own classroom to inform her teaching practice. More authentic accountabilities were also evident in the way this teacher sought out opportunities to work with other Prep teachers from this particular school site. The governing of teaching practices was not homogeneous, and through the WOW initiative, more directive approaches and foci could be open to challenge, interrogation and interpretation.

Finally, in a rural school in the north-western region of the state, WOW time was originally conceived as a way to help induct new teachers into the school. This was particularly important, given the school attracted a relatively large proportion of early-career teachers. However, this had also evolved into a more collaborative approach, and involved drawing on the expressed needs of staff, even as there was still a considerable focus on sharing information about particular, often technical matters associated with the running of the school (such as how to input data into the data management system 'OneSchool'):

> Well the intention initially was really for new teachers and teachers new to the school. And it was almost like an extended induction program in a lot of ways in that you made sure people were aware of different processes at the school. But then it became like we can share things and get ideas from each other. I always send it out to all teachers, the invitation, and say if you've never done this, come along. If you just want a refresher or you want to come and hear what others have to say, come along. So, basically everyone's welcome, and depending on what it is, you do get a range of different teachers that come along. I find some of our new-to-the-school teachers are regulars and they come to lots of different ones. But like [experienced teacher] that was there yesterday, she said I like to do the 'essential skills' [of classroom management] every year, so she comes along because I've run that a few times. So, she comes along each year, but she might not come to 'How do you open up OneSchool to do your report cards?' because she knows how to do that. So, it just varies, and I put it back out to the staff to go, 'Well, what else do you need to know?'
>
> *(Lucia, Support Teacher-Literacy and Numeracy, Western Border School)*

These opportunities were recognized as valuable by those participating, even as they were also recognized as entailing often more transmission-style activities, including in relation to reporting, and classroom management:

> One thing is that for all the new staff we have 'WOWsers' meetings which Lucia [Support Teacher-Literacy and Numeracy] organizes and they're on topics that we sort of identify as being something that we would like to get more information on and advice. I remember when report cards were due,

there was one on reports. There was one on – I think next week's on classroom management ... It is for the new people but it's sent out to whole
school email, and then if you are aware that that's an area that you'd like to
brush up your skills on, then you can go along.

(Charlene, Year 2 Teacher, Western Border School)

Such work is perhaps indicative of a more traditional conception of professional
accountability of experienced teachers to newer members of the profession.

Accountabilities to student learning were also clearly in evidence in the way a
teacher from the Special Education Early Childhood Development unit attached to
the school spoke of the importance of participating in such meetings as a means of
ensuring she was as well prepared as possible to assist her students in the lead-up to
Prep. This included in relation to language development:

We were just talking about the reading, actually, we were talking about – and
just knowing the different strategies like for oral language and things that
they're using up there [at primary school]. Because for my children, their
language is something I really, really need to develop. So just sort of knowing
what's going, what's being used up there [in Prep] so that if there's any part of
it I can take down and use.

(Irene, Special Education Early Childhood Teacher, Western Border School)

While such responses do not reflect the sorts of systemic accountabilities of the
system to schools (Lingard, Martino, Rezai-Rashti & Sellar, 2016), they do reflect
senses of accountability of teachers to their students, and efforts to try to draw on
such learning experiences to try to provide for the needs of all students, including
those most marginalized in the 'regular' school (Slee, 2011). This included these
very young students identified as requiring sometimes substantive additional needs
to maximize their potential.

Conclusion

More standardized approaches to teaching have clearly influenced pedagogical
practices, both within and beyond the Queensland context. This chapter has provided insights into a variety of ways in which such standardization occurs, including
through advocacy for particular approaches to 'explicit teaching', and how more
performative applications to such practices can diminish the possibility for productive reform. More performative practices were evident in more reductive conceptions of observations associated with such practices. The chapter has revealed how
explicit teaching practices govern teaching practice, and how such governance
processes have had significant, sometimes problematic effects on teachers' pedagogical practices.

However, and at the same time, the empirical data presented also reveal how
teachers seek to challenge the more reductive effects of accountability processes

associated with standardized teaching. There is also at least some evidence of how teachers seek to harness more performative foci for more educative effects. Concerns about the rigidity of explicit teaching practices served as stimuli for orchestrating alternative practices, and challenging more performative effects. Through making themselves accessible to colleagues, teachers can foster more authentic accountabilities – showing responsibility for one another's learning, not simply isolating themselves in relation to their colleagues, and engaging in teaching practices for substantive student learning. While productive change to teaching practice is difficult, it is possible, and possible without resort to more reductive conceptions of what constitutes 'effective' or 'explicit' teaching. The hope of alternative practices to more standardized approaches that govern teachers' teaching practice is echoed in Sternberg's (2015) calls to 'do differently' in relation to such practices, and to foster processes of creative rather than reductive teaching. Those more substantive instances of teachers' learning that occurred through the 'watching others work' initiative is just one example of alternative, potentially more productive practices. Such alternatives will create changed practices, and end the 'sounds of silence' (Sternberg, 2015, p. 117) in relation to more substantive, creative thinking and learning, and challenge more problematic relations. These alternatives will foster more substantive and 'authentic' sensibilities in relation to particular initiatives and directives, including those associated with various forms of 'explicit teaching'.

Notes

1 University.
2 Practicum – practical experience in schools during university studies.
3 Key Learning Area – a term used to describe individual subject domains in the Queensland context.
4 While the phrase 'deliverology' is attributed to Michael Barber, particularly in response to his work as the head of the UK Prime Minister's Delivery Unit (PMDU) focused on ensuring specific targets were met (such as in relation to hospital casualty waiting times, rates of street crime, and school results as measured against various league tables), the term has clear resonances here in relation to ensuring improved teaching outcomes as part of the focus on more explicit teaching in the schools described.
5 An online platform technology to assist teachers develop, collate and teach engaging e-learning experiences for students.

References

Anagnostopoulos, D. (2003). The new accountability, student failure, and teachers' work in urban high schools. *Educational Policy*, 17(3), 291–316.

Anderson, J. (2013). Curious grade for teachers: Nearly all pass. *New York Times*, A1. Downloaded 30 August 2018 from http://www.nytimes.com/2013/03/31/education/curious-grade-for-teachers-nearly-all-pass.html

Archer, A., & Hughes, C. (2011). *Explicit instruction: Effective and efficient teaching*. New York: Guilford Press.

Au, W. (2011). Teaching under the new Taylorism: High-stakes testing and the standardization of the 21st century curriculum. *Journal of Curriculum Studies*, 43(1), 25–45.

Ball, S. (1994). *Educational reform: A critical and post-structural approach.* Buckingham: Open University Press.

Ball, S.J. (2003). The teacher's soul and the terrors of performativity. *Journal of Education Policy,* 18, 215–228.

Ball, S. (2004). *Education for sale! The commodification of everything?*King's College Annual Education Lecture. King's College, University of London, 17 June. Downloaded 10 January 2019 from: nepc.colorado.edu/sites/default/files/CERU-0410-0253-OWI.pdf

Ball, S., Maguire, M., Braun, A., & Hoskins, K. (2011). Policy subjects and policy actors in schools: some necessary but insufficient analyses. *Discourse: Studies in the Cultural Politics of Education,* 32(4), 611–624.

Ball, S., Maguire, M., & Braun, A. (2012). *How schools do policy: Policy enactments in secondary schools.* London: Routledge.

Barber, M. (2007). *Instruction to deliver: Tony Blair, the public services and the challenge of delivery.* London: Methuen.

Bergin, C., Wind, S., Grajeda, S., & Tsai, C-L (2017). Teacher evaluation: Are principals classroom observations accurate at the conclusion of training? *Studies in Educational Evaluation,* 55, 19–26.

Biesta, G. (2010). *Good education in the age of measurement: Ethics, politics, democracy.* London: Routledge.

Biesta, G. (2016). Education, measurement and the professions: Reclaiming a space for democratic professionality in education. *Educational Philosophy and Theory,* 49(4), 315–330.

Biesta, G. (2020). *Educational research: An unorthodox introduction.* London: Bloomsbury.

Borich, G. (2016). *Observation skills for effective teaching: Research-based practice.* Seventh edition. London: Routledge.

Bradbury, A., & Roberts-Holmes, G. (2018). *The datafication of primary and early years education: Playing with numbers.* London: Routledge.

Cohen, J., & Goldhaber, D. (2016). Building a more complete understanding of teacher evaluation using classroom observations. *Educational Researcher,* 45(6), 378–387.

Cohen, J., & Grossman, P. (2017). Respecting complexity in measures of teaching: Keeping students and schools in focus. *Teaching and Teacher Education,* 55, 308–317.

Datnow, A. (2018). 'Time for change?' The emotions of teacher collaboration and reform. *Journal of Professional Capital and Community,* 3(3), 157–172.

Davis, J., Lampley, J., & Foley, V. (2016). The relationship between growth scores and the overall observation ratings for teachers in a public school system in Tennessee. *Journal of Learning in Higher Education,* 12(1), 45–51.

de Bono, E. (1985). *Six thinking hats.* New York, NY: Little, Brown & Co.

Foucault, M. (1990). *The history of sexuality: An introduction* Volume I. New York: Random House.

Freire, P. (1972). *The pedagogy of the oppressed.* Harmondsworth: Penguin.

Gardner, H. (1983). *Frames of mind: The theory of multiple intelligences.* New York, NY: Basic.

Good, T., & Lavigne, A. (2015). Rating teachers cheaper, faster, and better: Not so fast. *Journal of Teacher Education,* 66(3), 288–293.

Green, J. (2013). Return of the lure of the explicit: 'Making the implicit explicit'. In J. Green, *Education, professionalism and the quest for accountability: Hitting the target but missing the point.* New York: Routledge.

Hardy, I. (2014). A logic of appropriation: Enacting national testing in Australia. *Journal of Education Policy,* 29(1), 1–18.

Hardy, I., & Rönnerman, K. (2011). The value and valuing of continuing professional development: Current dilemmas, future directions and the case for action research. *Cambridge Journal of Education,* 41(4), 461–472.

Hardy, I., Jakhelln, R., & Smit, B. (2020). The policies and politics of teachers' initial learning: The complexity of national initial teacher education policies. *Teacher Development*. doi:10.1080/10476210.2020.1729115

Hargreaves, A., & Fullan, M. (2012). *Professional capital: Transforming teaching in every school*. New York: Teachers College Press.

Hattie, J. (2009). *Visible learning: A synthesis of over 800 meta-analyses relating to achievement*. London: Routledge.

Hiebert, J., Gallimore, R., & Stigler, J. (2002). A knowledge base for the teaching profession: What would it look like and how can we get one? *Educational Researcher*, 31(5), 3–15.

Hodkinson, H., & Hodkinson, P. (2005). Improving schoolteachers' workplace learning. *Research Papers in Education*, 20, 109–131.

Konstantopoulos, S. (2014). Teacher effects, value-added models, and accountability. *Teachers College Record*, 116(1).

Kupermintz, H. (2003). Teacher effects and teacher effectiveness: A validity investigation of the Tennessee Value Added Assessment System. *Educational Evaluation and Policy Analysis*, 25(3), 287–298.

Lewis, S., & Holloway, J. (2019). Datafying the teaching 'profession': Remaking the professional teacher in the image of data. *Cambridge Journal of Education*, 49(1), 35–51.

Lewis, S., Savage, G., & Holloway, J. (2019). Standards without standardisation? Assembling standards-based reforms in Australian and US schooling. *Journal of Education Policy*. doi:10.1080/02680939.2019.1636140

Lillejord, S., Elstad, E., & Kavli, H. (2018). Teacher evaluation as a wicked policy problem. *Assessment in Education: Principles, Policy and Practice*, 25(3), 291–309.

Lingard, B., Martino, W., Rezai-Rashti, G., & Sellar, S. (2016). *Globalising educational accountabilities*. New York: Routledge.

Lortie, D. (1975). *Schoolteacher: A sociological study*. Chicago: University of Chicago Press.

Luke, A. (2004). Teaching after the market: From commodity to cosmopolitanism. *Teachers College Record*, 106(7), 1422–1443.

Lynch, K., Chin, M., & Blazar, D. (2017). Relationships between observations of elementary mathematics instruction and student achievement: Exploring variability across districts. *American Journal of Education*, 123, 615–646.

Marzano, R. (2003). *What works in schools: Translating research into action*. Alexandria, VA: Association for Supervision and Curriculum Development.

Meirink, J., Meijer, P., Verloop, N., & Bergen, C. (2009). How do teachers learn in the workplace? An examination of teacher learning activities. *European Journal of Teacher Education*, 32, 209–227.

Mizala, A., & Schneider, B. (2019). Promotion quality education in Chile: The politics of reforming teacher careers. *Journal of Education Policy*. doi:10.1080/02680939.2019.1585577

OECD (2005). *Teachers matter: Attracting, developing and retaining effective teachers*. Paris: OECD Publications.

Pitton, D. (2016). *Supporting teacher development: New skills for principals in supervision and evaluation*. Lanham, MD: Rowman & Littlefield.

Pivovarova, M., Amrein-Beardsley, A., & Broatch, J. (2015). Value-added models (VAMs): Caveat emptor. *Statistics and Public Policy*, 3(1), 1–9.

Polanyi, M. (1966). *The tacit dimension*. Chicago: University of Chicago Press.

Prilleltensky, I., Neff, M., & Bessell, A. (2016). Teacher stress: What it is, why it's important, how it can be alleviated. *Theory into Practice*, 55(2), 104–111.

Priestley, M., Biesta, G.J.J., Philippou, S., & Robinson, S. (2016). The teacher and the curriculum: Exploring teacher agency. In D. Wyse, L. Hayward & J. Pandya (Eds), *The Sage handbook of curriculum, pedagogy and assessment* (pp. 78–91). London: Sage.

Rose, N. (1999). *Powers of freedom: Reframing political thought.* Cambridge: Cambridge University Press.

Rosenshine, B. (1986). Synthesis of research on explicit teaching. *Educational Leadership*, 43, 60–69.

Savage, G., & Lewis, S. (2018). The phantom national? Assembling national teaching standards in Australia's federal system. *Journal of Education Policy*, 33(1), 118–142.

Schatzki, T. (2002). *The site of the social: A philosophical account of the constitution of social life and change.* University Park, PA: The Pennsylvania State University Press.

Sennett, R. (2009). *The craftsman.* London: Penguin.

Slee, R. (2011). *The irregular school: Exclusion, schooling, and inclusive education.* London: Routledge.

Slee, R. (2013). How do we make inclusive education happen when exclusion is a political predisposition? *International Journal of Inclusive Education*, 17(8), 895–907.

Smyth, J., & Shacklock, G. (1998) *Re-making teaching: Ideology, policy and practice.* London: Routledge.

Sternberg, R. (2015). Teaching for creativity: The sounds of silence. *Psychology of Aesthetics, Creativity and the Arts*, 9(2), 115–117.

Tschannen-Moran, M. (2014). *Trust matters: Leadership for successful schools.* Second edition. San Francisco: Jossey-Bass.

Tyack, D., & Cuban, L. (1995). *Tinkering toward utopia: A century of public school reform.* Cambridge: Harvard University Press.

United Kingdom Government (2016). *Types of schools.* Downloaded 16 June 2016 from: http s://www.gov.uk/types-of-school/academies

Walford, G. (2013). Privatisation, education and social justice. *Oxford Review of Education*, 39(4), 421–425.

Zavala, J., & Valenta, V. (2017) Elementary school principals supporting the professional capacity of teachers. In D. Touchton, M. Rodriguez & I. Acker-Hocevar (Eds), *Quandaries of school leadership: Voices from principals in the field* (pp. 143–156). Cham: Palgrave Macmillan.

6

TESTING TIMES

Teaching to and beyond the test

Introduction: Governing through testing

Even as conceptions of curriculum and teaching have been increasingly governed through more standardized practices, perhaps the best example of standardization in schooling is in relation to assessment. Standardized assessment practices have exerted influence nationally and internationally. This chapter explores how assessment practices, particularly various forms of standardized tests at the national level, have sought to govern practices in schools, and acted as key mechanisms of and for accountability in schooling settings. The chapter begins with an overview of processes of governance through numbers and data more broadly. An account is then provided of governance processes through international large-scale assessments, particularly PISA, followed by a review of the nature and effects of standardized testing practices at varied national and subnational levels. This serves as a precursor to considering the example of assessment practices in Australia, specifically in the state of Queensland, where the National Assessment Program – Literacy and Numeracy (NAPLAN) has had particularly consequential effects. This includes evidence of how the measurement of students' learning has had detrimental effects – where 'what is measured is treasured' (Pederson, 2007) – even as the use of standardized tests for more performative purposes is challenged. Through the empirical evidence provided in the latter part of the chapter, notions of more performative and more authentic accountability practices are explicated. The chapter concludes with a call to challenge the use of various forms of numbers as technologies for more performative accountability purposes.

Governing the population through numbers and data

The focus on large-scale testing is a manifestation of the dominance of efforts to 'capture' the population – in this case, in relation to schooling – more broadly.

Foucault (2007) eruditely expressed this in his account of the various ways in which particular forms of 'territory', 'security' and 'population' were brought into being during the 19th century. Of particular interest were notions of 'population', and how these were to be understood. Foucault argued it was through the technology of various forms of 'state numbers', 'statistics', that particular populations became identifiable. Ever since, the development of statistics has been key to governing social practices, including schooling practices.

In his 'history of statistical reasoning',[1] Desrosières (1998) argues that the development of numbers as various forms of 'objective' measures of human practice and capacity are very much social constructs which are inherently reflective of the processes of their development. Such numbers constitute forms of 'facts', but facts which are always and everywhere reflective of the particular conditions in which they were generated; they are 'social facts'. Such facts as social constructs imply a conundrum; various numbers that pertain to any given population are important points of reference, and 'evidence' in broader debates, but, by virtue of their intrinsic sociality, are always very much subject to debate themselves:

> Unemployment, inflation, growth, poverty, fertility: these objective phenomena, and the statistics that measure them, support descriptions of economic situations, denunciations of social injustices, and justifications for political actions. They are inscribed in routinized practices that, by providing a stable and widely accepted language to give voice to the debate, help to establish the reality of the picture described. But this implies a paradox. As references, these objects must be perceived as indisputable, above the fray. How then should we conceive a debate that turns on precisely these objects? How can we dispute the undisputable? These questions are often raised in a critical context. Do statistics lie? How many people are really unemployed? What is the real rate of productivity? These measurements, which are reference points in the debate, are also subject to debate themselves.
>
> *(Desrosières, 1998, p. 1)*

Similarly, in his history of the origins of statistics, *The taming of chance*, Hacking (1990) captures this 'constructedness' of statistics, and the extent to which various forms of statistics can be seen as laws in themselves, and contribute to the development and promotion of a new form of 'objective knowledge'. These forms of knowledge were the result of new technologies for developing information about both physical and social phenomena. Chance 'became tamed' in Hacking's (1990, p. vii) words by the way in which statistical laws came to be used for not only describing but also understanding why circumstances transpired as they did: 'Chance became tamed, in the sense that it became the very stuff of the fundamental processes of nature and of society' (p. vii). Through 'an avalanche of printed numbers' (Hacking, 1982), practices came to be transformed in ways not previously possible. Notions of the 'norm' came to reconstitute what was considered appropriate, 'normal', within an 'acceptable' range of variety and variation. Such statistics, and classification and categorization to which they relate, have the effect of 'making up people' (Hacking, 1986). Indeed, this focus on the numbers was borne of a belief that 'one can improve – control – a deviant subpopulation by enumeration and classification' (Hacking, 1990, p. 3). Such tabulations and numbers are relentlessly collected and calculated, and have a long history that 'descends directly from the forgotten annals of nineteenth century information and control' (p. 5). Furthermore, '[t]his imperialism of probabilities could occur only as the world itself became numerical. We have gained a fundamentally quantitative feel for nature, how it is and how it ought to be' (p. 5).

The result of this capacity to enumerate was the ability to develop statistically significant measures of performance, including the 'norm', and distributions of normality. Populations in cities came be seen as 'a set of processes to be managed at the level and on the basis of what is natural in these processes' (Foucault, 2007, p. 70). It is this identification of 'what is natural' which is central to what becomes construed as 'normal' within any given population. National census-style test data help provide a picture of what is 'normal' and acceptable within a population, and what falls beyond these parameters.

Under these circumstances, forms of data are continuously generated and collected in relation to all aspects of life, including education, and may be utilized to develop ever fine-grained pictures of social practices. Such data include forms of 'big data' that can enable large-scale analyses and interpretations of human practices that would not otherwise be possible. Indeed, data is expanding at such a rate as to challenge our very capacity to recognize its growth and influence: 'the amount of data in the world is growing fast, outstripping not just our machines but our imaginations' (Cukier & Mayer-Schönberger, 2013, p. 8). Arguably, not only are our imaginations being 'outstripped', but what and how it is that we 'imagine' as important in this context is being radically reconfigured. Even as they may be deployed to foster sensible decision-making, such data may also be used against people, and may simply perpetuate or bolster existing inequalities, encouraging subservience to a 'dictatorship of data':

> We risk falling victim to a dictatorship of data, whereby we fetishize the information, the output of our analyses, and end up misusing it. Handled responsibly, big data is a useful tool of rational decision-making. Wielded unwisely, it can become an instrument of the powerful, who may turn it into a source of repression, either by simply frustrating customers and employees or, worse, by harming citizens.
>
> *(Cukier & Mayer-Schönberger, 2013, p. 151)*

When expressed numerically, the quality of such large data sets can be problematic, and simply fail to capture what they purport to understand. Under such circumstances, data can have more substantive effects upon people than may be recognized, and in problematic ways. This includes 'becom[ing] obsessed with collecting facts and figures for data's sake. Or that we will attribute a degree of truth to the data which it does not deserve' (Cukier & Mayer-Schönberger, 2013, pp. 165, 166).

Pointedly, and pointing to the potential limitations of the focus on data in relation to schooling, Cukier and Mayer-Schönberger (2013) make explicit reference to the potentially problematic use of standardized data, and how they may be utilized to criticize teachers and students, and limit their focus of attention:

> Education on the skids? Push standardized tests to measure performance and penalize teachers or schools that by this measure aren't up to snuff. Whether the tests actually capture the abilities of schoolchildren, the quality of teaching, or the needs of a creative, adaptable modern workforce is an open question – but one that the data does not admit.
>
> *(p. 166)*

There is a danger that we 'become so fixated on the data, and so obsessed with the power and the promise it offers, that we fail to appreciate its limitations' (Cukier & Mayer-Schönberger, 2013, p. 169). This is dangerous because 'in a world of big data, it is our most human traits that will need to be fostered – our creativity, intuition, and intellectual ambition – since our ingenuity is the source of our progress' (pp. 196, 197). Crucially, such data are always limited and limiting, and can only ever be 'a simulacrum of reality, like the shadows on the wall of Plato's cave' (p. 197). Data cannot capture the complexity of the practices to which they pertain.

Nevertheless, this has not prevented the rapid growth in various data sets associated with assessment practices in schooling, including not only at the national and sub-national levels, but internationally. The nature and effects of such international data are important to understand, given such data purport to enable comparisons at scales not previously possible, and insights into the 'quality' of national and sub-national schooling systems.

The push to internationalize assessment: The prominence of PISA

Some of the most significant examples of standardized assessment data occur in relation to international assessment regimes for schooling systems, with one of the most prominent pertaining to the Organisation for Economic Co-operation and Development's (OECD) Program for International School Assessment (PISA). PISA is the latest international measure to be deployed in the schooling space since the early 1960s. Such initiatives are construed by advocates, such as the OECD's Andreas Schleicher (Director of the Directorate of Education and Skills, and Special Advisor on Education Policy to the Secretary-General), as providing an additional means of interpreting national performance measures. They are construed as a sensible response to more performative conceptions of globalization by enabling constant comparison at an international rather than simply national level:

> Comparative international assessments can extend and enrich the national picture by providing a larger context within which to interpret national

performance. In a global context, where the yardsticks for educational improvement are no longer national standards alone but increasingly the best performing education systems internationally, that perspective is gaining prominence.

(Schleicher, 2016, p. 913)

One of the first international organizations to emerge from a more 'global' push to focus on educational attainment was the International Association for the Evaluation of Educational Achievement (IEA). Established in 1958, this body evolved from an initial meeting of several prominent researchers meeting as part of the UNESCO's International Institute of Education to explore whether and how it could be feasible to compare student performance internationally. The four-year Trends in Mathematics and Science Study (TIMSS) and the five-year Progress in Reading Literacy Study (PIRLS) initiatives emerged from this work, becoming some of the most prominent measures of international performance in these domains.

Following on from these initial 'international large-scale assessments' (typically referred to via the acronym 'ILSAs'), the OECD's PISA reforms represent the most recent prominent raft of international assessments. Since 2000, these tests have been undertaken every three years in the areas of reading, mathematics and science. They seek to provide insights into students' problem-solving capacities, as well as a variety of other non-academic outcomes.

Significantly, the OECD claims to 'ground' the data it generates by collecting a variety of context-specific information, including information pertaining to the respective national education systems as a whole, individual educational institutions/providers, classrooms/instructional settings, and individual learners themselves. Furthermore, the research approach adopted claims to be able to compare learning outcomes across these levels. It also provides insights into the specific policy levers that are seen as influencing these outcomes (including teacher working conditions; resourcing at school and system levels), and the socio-economic conditions in which students, schools and systems exist. A number of benefits are also constituted as arising from the investment of national governments in OECD PISA testing practices, including raising aspirations, identifying potentially significant points of similarity and difference between education systems to inform policy making and provision, and fostering long-term educational reform and gain:

- By describing student performance in the countries with the highest or most rapidly improving assessment results, international assessments can reveal what is possible in education.
- Although international assessments alone cannot identify cause-and-effect relationships between inputs, processes and educational outcomes, they can shed light on key features in which education systems show similarities and differences.

- International assessments are also increasingly used to set policy targets in terms of measurable goals achieved by other systems and to establish trajectories for reform.
- International assessments can assist with gauging the pace of educational progress and help review the reality of educational delivery at the frontline.
- Last but not least, international assessments can support the political economy of educational reform, which is a major issue in education where any pay-off to reform almost inevitably accrues to successive governments if not generations (Schleicher, 2016, p. 916).

This advocacy for such testing practices constitutes comparative logics as intrinsically beneficial for their capacity to facilitate improved practice by enabling educators and policy makers to compare different educational systems to 'learn' from these more 'successful' settings so as to improve schooling practices in their own jurisdiction. The identification of 'key features in which education systems show similarities and differences' reveals how such comparative logics are construed as powerful vehicles for ensuring constant engagement and interaction with other jurisdictions, even as the nature of these educational systems may be very different from one another (Nóvoa & Yariv-Mashal, 2003). These limitations are clearly not seen as sufficient to prevent the development of particular policy goals as 'measurable goals', the very establishment of which are construed as conducive to substantive reform. International assessments are also framed as useful for informing further decision-making about reform initiatives already under way. The way in which Andreas Schleicher construes international assessments as an important part of the political economy of educational reform at the national level also serves as a vehicle to tie broader international measures of assessment more tightly into national governments' efforts to promote reform. By framing international measures of assessment as valuable vehicles for justifying reform at the national level, governments are provided with an 'objective' means of rationalizing what might be seen as otherwise unpalatable or unnecessary reforms. It is this last characteristic of international assessments that is most overt in its recognition of the potential of such markers as vehicles for rationalizing the politics that surround nation-states' efforts to reform their educational systems. Schleicher (2016) refers to examples in Mexico in which students performed much more poorly on PISA assessment than might be expected from their parents' predominantly positive response about the quality of the education their children received. The result was the implementation of a 'PISA performance target' (p. 918) as part of reforms to education in Mexico, as a means of redressing the gap between what were perceived as 'national performance' and 'international standards'. In Japan, the comparative potential of PISA was deployed to incorporate more open-ended tasks into the national assessment regime as a response to students' relative lack of capacity to apply their knowledge to new and unfamiliar settings. Such approaches are construed as useful examples of how the educational political economy can be rethought at the local level in response to more 'global' influences.

The economy and education are also explicitly co-constituted within discourses of educational reform associated with international testing:

> International assessments have at times raised awareness that led to a public debate about education, with citizens recognising that their countries' educational performance will not simply need to match average performance, but that they will need to do better if their children want to justify above-average wages.
>
> *(Schleicher, 2016, p. 918)*

This focus on the economy is a form of disciplining of educational practice within the remit of economic prerogatives. Large-scale assessments of the more traditional variety, such as PISA, adopt an input-outcome model approach, which most closely approximates more economic models (Care & Beswick, 2016). While processes of comparison can foster new forms of information dissemination, and 'shed light on differences on which reform efforts can then capitalise' (Schleicher, 2016, p. 925), as Schleicher (2016) also acknowledges, focusing on particular features of educational performance can militate against sufficient attention to other approaches and initiatives that are potentially just as important. Inappropriately or narrowly defined benchmarks can focus attention to specific areas, and accentuating particular domains in public debates can potentially limit necessary attention to other important areas.

However, even as concerns are expressed about the difficulty of establishing international measures, and about the limitations of processes of comparability and the nature of comparative practices more broadly, such concerns are framed as secondary to broader global economic concerns – particularly 'given that the success of individuals and nations increasingly depends on their global competitiveness' (Schleicher, 2016, p. 926). Again, performative concerns about economic globalization dominate over empirical concerns about the value and validity of such comparative processes, and over broader socio-cultural conceptions of education. In a similar vein, such international tests are also valued because they are construed as providing important 'evidence' of the nature and effects of educational systems. Wiseman (2010) explores the key question of 'why use evidence in educational policymaking?' (p. 1), and argues there is a strong preference for a conception of evidence understood as 'what works', in conjunction with notions of 'evidence-based' practice (cf. Slavin, 2008). And, increasingly, the evidence considered of most value is that pertaining to averaged test scores on international assessments, particularly for their comparative potential. Robust critiques of 'what works' (e.g. Biesta, 2020) struggle to gain the ascendency under such circumstances.

Critiques of international testing

Such markers of comparison are valued even as there is evidence of the difficulty of using such data to actually compare educational systems within and across countries. Care and Beswick (2016) argue that comparative studies based on large-scale assessments gloss over the different curricula goals of countries involved in such studies, and fail to take into account the way in which these goals differ from the curriculum implied in international assessment tests. The concern is that 'agreement on desirable outcomes has not been achieved and predictability from inputs has not been established' (p. 930). Instead, local culture influences curriculum decision-making and large-scale international tests have very limited capacity to test such local prerogatives and approaches. Alternative, regional large-scale assessment programs exist, and operate in different parts of the world – including the UNESCO supported Southern and Eastern Africa Consortium for Monitoring Education Quality (SACMEQ), and UNICEF's Southeast Asia Primary Learning Metric program (Care & Beswick, 2016). These initiatives are construed as more regionally relevant, even as they are similarly premised on processes of comparison between individual countries that comprise these consortia, and that necessarily have varied approaches to curriculum, teaching and assessment.

Several critiques have been levelled at PISA, in particular. The focus on ranking countries' performance encourages a short-term approach to educational reform to promote their rankings. An 'Open letter to Andreas Schleicher' by prominent international educational researchers, published in *The Guardian* newspaper in May 2014, flagged this short-term assessment cycle approach, and lamented an increasing emphasis on standardized, commercialized lessons, deprofessionalization of the work of teachers, and narrowing of classroom teaching practice (Andrews et al., 2014). The key competencies approach to PISA was also recognized as privileging economic prerogatives over social, political and cultural values. Even as these social, political and cultural factors are recognized as valid and valuable within the broader OECD framework, economic considerations are given primacy. This is reflected in the way in which various national reports are explicit about how improved educational outcomes can be equated to improved economic output, even as the reports seek to overtly qualify any sort of simple input-output model.

The way in which PISA is framed in the OECD is also an example of what Takekawa (2016) points out, drawing on Beck's (1992) risk hypothesis, as the individualization of risk. In a 'risk society', in which various forms of risk are distributed differently, those who are most able to ameliorate the worst effects of risks generated through particular practices are the greatest beneficiaries. In more neo-liberal societies, this risk-management is increasingly the prerogative of individuals, and entrusting individuals to navigate these risks constitutes a form of 'individualizing risk'. International tests such as PISA, with their focus on generic competencies, encourage individualization and competition, leading to the marginalization of those least able to compete, and a construal of the individual as responsible for her/his circumstances, regardless of context. In this equation, the influence of broader social practices, processes and institutions become increasingly marginalized.

Managing and moderating pressures of test-based accountability: National and sub-national testing in schooling

Under such circumstances, testing (standardized testing in particular), has become a key meta-policy (Rizvi & Lingard, 2010) for steering schooling systems. It is now central to Bernstein's (1971) original message system of evaluation in schooling, and has enabled various top-down accountabilities tied to test performance. Rizvi & Lingard (2010) point out how educational systems utilize standardized testing to 'steer' practices in schools, with such tests serving as a potentially limiting and inhibiting vehicle for educational reform:

> Increasingly, systems of education around the world have begun to steer their systems using standardized testing regimes, both national and international. Indeed it could be argued that testing now constitutes a fourth message system, through which central policymakers seek to steer local practice through various demands and structures of accountability. Indeed, testing has become a central element in policy regimes. Such testing could be seen as a reductive version of the potentially broader evaluation message system.
>
> *(p. 94)*

Such reductive practices occur at a variety of levels, but are perhaps most overt in relation to national efforts to 'track' educational outcomes, and the governing practices instituted for this purpose.

These national efforts are also very much part of the broader international testing movement. Verger, Parcerisa and Fontdevila (2019) argue national large-scale assessments serve as the expression of broader 'global education reform movement' (GERM) principles of standards, accountability and school autonomy. Such is the power of these principles that they have begun to 'infect' countries that have traditionally resisted pressures of accountability associated with such standardized testing vehicles.

Under current conditions, various forms of national test data constitute forms of 'measurement, comparison and examination, numbers of many sorts ... [serving as] techniques to produce domination and responsibilization and construct "calculating selves"' and 'centres of calculation' (Ball, 2013, p. 59). Processes of measurement enable a 'grid of intelligibility' identifying responses within the 'norm', and those that transgress it, and enabling various forms of governance not previously possible. The shift towards governance is seen as tightly associated with the increased focus on the generation of data. As Ozga, Segerholm and Simola (2011) proclaim:

> We are making an argument that the shift towards governance rather than government in education (and in other areas of social and public policy) is intimately connected with the growth of data, and the increase in possibilities for monitoring, targeting and shifting cultures and behaviour that data apparently produce.
>
> *(p. 85)*

Test-based accountability implies that specific forms of 'objective' performance data provide the best means of assessing students' capacities or otherwise. The implication of such testing is that it provides the necessary information about students' abilities to make subsequent decisions in a timely manner. Under such conditions, teachers come to see themselves as constantly requiring intervention to address their shortcomings, and come to consider themselves 'perpetually imperfect' (Holloway, 2019). Teachers' very sense of self is reconstituted in light of constant processes of testing and evaluation.

At the same time, the way in which data are represented statistically hides the variability that attends the learning of specific groups of students, and how a strong focus on deleterious outcomes for schools, teachers and students absorbs so much of educators' attention (Gardner & Galanouli, 2016). Gardner and Galanouli (2016) refer to how the 2012 and 2013 STAR county-based results in California revealed different ethnic groups performing very differently in relation to one another, but how aggregated results tended to obscure and elide these differences. This makes it difficult to sustain arguments that such testing enables informed 'choice' about educational options for students and their families, even as standardized testing is construed as an important part of the apparatus of cultivating 'choice' in schooling:

> The notion that students and their families should choose between competing schools also provides a rationale for standardized testing; this implies provision of supposedly 'objective' data to enable selection of (and the development of) 'quality' schools.
>
> *(Hursh, 2016, p. 7)*

Also, improvements in national and sub-national standardized test results may simply indicate improved test-taking skills amongst students, rather than substantive educational improvements. Even as teachers deride the effects of teaching to the test, concerns about adverse outcomes on such tests, including loss of funding, lead to a skewing of attention to these tests, and of the outcomes of such tests as a principal focus of teachers' work:

> The phenomenon of teaching to the test is widely perceived by teachers to hinder classroom learning at best and, at worst, to corrupt the whole educational endeavour. Fearing the consequences of negative performance, which may involve the withdrawal of funds or even closure of schools ... it is not unreasonable to expect that teachers individually and collectively in schools will perceive their students' performance in national or state tests to be the paramount goal of their efforts, no matter how much they might also consider the potentially distorting effects on their students' learning.
>
> *(Gardner & Galanouli, 2016, p. 714)*

In the United States, such fears around test-based accountability were ratcheted up with the introduction of the *No Child Left Behind* legislation in 2001 as part of the reauthorization of the Elementary and Secondary Education Act (ESEA). While the more recent (2015) reauthorization of ESEA (*Every Student Succeeds Act* (ESSA)) has sought to reduce the influence of the federal government on educational provision in the individual states, the momentum built up around test-based accountability is difficult to dislodge, particularly in those districts and states where relatively lower performances have seen a continuation of more test-centric practices.

This focus on standardized test-centric results is a form of precision that does little to actually respond to the complexity and disadvantage that characterize some of the lowest performing schools and schooling systems. The performance measures of test-based accountability do little to redress class-based, racial or needs-based inequalities:

> While the sense of order, rationality, and utility that these [test-based accountability practices] possess is appealing, they distort the actual complexities and uncertainties of the educational enterprise and its core processes: teaching and learning. As large-scale information systems produce increasingly precise measurements of student, teacher, and school performance, they risk substituting precision for validity and distracting from important issues, such as educational equity, diversity, and social justice, that are not easily reduced to or redressed by standardized metrics.
>
> *(Anagnostopoulos, Rutledge & Jacobsen, 2013, p. 16)*

The irony of legislation such as *No Child Left Behind*, (and *Race to the Top* that later complemented this earlier Act), is that the very students to whom this legislation was most overtly directed – those in the most disadvantaged situations – were those most likely to be penalized through processes of potential school closures, and the adoption of punitive measures that encouraged increased focus and attention to results on state-sanctioned, standardized tests.

Furthermore, the focus on such national and sub-national tests means that context-specific, localized knowledge that characterizes actual teaching and learning situations is in danger of becoming increasingly effaced, even as such knowledge is essential for actually effecting productive change and development amongst students. The sorts of data that Anagnostopoulos et al. (2013) describe as constituting so much of the 'the infrastructure of accountability' is purely technical, and devoid of necessary contextual nuance and understanding.

And the close alignment between the use of numbers, the development of national systems of statistics, and various infrastructures of accountability associated with test data development and collation, all contribute towards the governance of education as a generic, rather than situated, site-specific, practice (cf. Kemmis et al., 2014; Schatzki, 2002).

Under these circumstances, test-based accountability policies influence school climate, which in turn affects teacher performance and well-being. Test-based accountability has been found to be generally negatively associated with teacher stress and school climate, and varied state accountability systems can lead to similar kinds of angst amongst teachers (Von der Embse, Pendergast, Segool, Saeki & Ryan, 2016). There is also evidence of connections between increased account-ability pressures and negative relationships between students, which, in turn, lead to increased stress on the part of teachers (Von der Embse et al., 2016).

Under such circumstances, assessment for learning becomes strained, even as it is important to acknowledge that it is less useful to construe 'assessment of learning' as somehow in opposition to practices of 'assessment for learning'. As Smith (2016) elaborates, assessment of learning is a useful means of developing preliminary understandings about students' capacities, and from which processes of assessment for learning can then be more meaningfully developed. However, even as there is an increased understanding of the complexity of assessment practices, and of a need for various forms of 'assessment of learning', as well as 'assessment for learning', the policies and politics that surround schooling practices in so many jurisdictions make it increasingly difficult to effect improved, more nuanced approaches to assessment.

Consequently, there is a need for what Henig (2012) describes as increased understanding of the politics of educational practice in relation to data use. It is crucial to have a clearer understanding of the politics that surround decision-making based on data, and how such decision-making reflects the interests of those engaged in this work. At the same time, it is also important to avoid more extreme modes of engagement that construe data use as simply manipulation; some sort of a 'middle ground' is perhaps most helpful for making decisions to help redress shortcomings about standardized approaches to testing, and to consider how they might be utilized for more educative purposes:

> Taken to an extreme, this perspective [data as manipulation] can seem cynical and unhelpful: If data are *nothing more* than political weaponry, there is little to say about how different structures and processes for utilizing data might improve the capacity of government to contribute to our collective well-being. In a more moderate dose, however, this perspective offers a valuable corrective to some of the more idealized and naïve portrayals of the potential for evidence-based decision-making in education, portrayals that – precisely because they are idealized and naïve – risk setting us up for two types of fail-ure. One type of failure stems from continual disappointment. Overselling the prospects for achieving better education through better use of data can lead to frustration when the results come up short, leading some to conclude that public education is hopelessly immune to sensible reform. A second type of failure stems from vulnerability to manipulation. Anticipating that data and their application will stir politically motivated responses can reduce the like-lihood that some individuals and groups will co-opt the process in ways that promote their interests at the cost of the broader good.
>
> *(Henig, 2012, pp. 6–7; emphasis original)*

Empirically examining whether and how a more 'middle ground' can be achieved in different contexts in which standardized tests have been used as a tool to generate data for accountability-oriented purposes is perhaps a more useful means of evaluating the nature and effects of such testing. To that end, the remainder of this chapter analyses the case of standardized testing practices in Queensland, Australia, to explore how such practices have exerted influence, with a focus on how such testing has governed teachers' work and learning, and how teachers have responded and interpreted these influences. As with the previous two chapters, the data drawn upon here were derived from more than 400 interviews with teachers and school-based administrators in 14 primary schools across the state from 2012 to 2017 – a period of significant educational reform across curriculum, teaching and assessment.

National testing in Australia

The empirical data presented in the remainder of this chapter reveal the contestation that surrounds teachers' engagement with data, particularly in relation to standardized national literacy and numeracy testing in Australian – more commonly known as 'NAPLAN' (National Assessment Program-Literacy and Numeracy). Given the way in which this test, and affiliated data, were expressed numerically, there is a particular emphasis on how the enumeration of education through such data served as a key vehicle to govern educators' practices. In the Australian context, Lingard, Creagh and Vass (2012) refer to 'education policy as numbers' as a key technology to direct educational practice, and such practices are clearly in evidence in this particular case. Such data feed into the broader emphasis on the need to provide 'evidence' as the justification for particular policy strategies. However, these are not the only logics at play, and the chapter seeks to indicate this variability, including how more problematic, performative logics can be contested within a broader field of schooling practices.

NAPLAN in Queensland: A state of constant comparison

The case of NAPLAN in Queensland is particularly interesting, given the strong public and political concern about Queensland's relatively poor (second lowest state/territory) performance in the inaugural national test in 2008. (See Chapter 3 for further contextual details about NAPLAN.) That national standardized testing governed schooling in Queensland was evident in the way in which NAPLAN testing was a constant reference for school-based administrators and teachers in schools across the state. The nature of these results was typically expressed numerically, and in relation to prior performances. In this context, in many parts of Queensland, NAPLAN was construed as problematic, but also improving over time.[2] Such improvement built upon what were construed as relatively poor results in many (often rural, regional and low socio-economic suburban) areas in 2008.

Reflecting the power of numbers as a technology governing educators' practices, the principal at a large school in a regional city in northern Queensland described how schools were expected to deliver a 3% annual improvement in NAPLAN results, year on year. Reflecting how a broader political logic influenced educators' practices, this target was also explicitly recognized as a political rather than an educational prerogative, particularly given relatively low NAPLAN results in Queensland schools as a whole, and in relation to the northern regions of Queensland in particular:

> So essentially what the system's asked us to do – the target has been a 3% improvement in terms of their results. And that's been a significant agenda, mainly because of the politics around it all. So, from [age] 9 to 11 – the expectation is that we improve 9% in terms of our raw scores around NAPLAN. If you look at the data across the nation, there's the nation's improvement, so you can see that it's been pretty stagnant. It's actually gone backwards in a couple of things, but it's pretty much remained around the same. Queensland's has improved significantly. I think one of the big things for us is that a lot of the Queensland improvement has been carried by the [region in northern half of state], and that's not because our results are necessarily good; it's because we've come from a very, very low base! So, if you looked at our NAPLAN data, we're still pretty much a 'sea of red'. However, I think we can prove that we have improved significantly.
>
> *(Cameron, Principal, Tropical City School)*

The metaphor of a 'sea of red' – referring to the bright red and pink graphics used to indicate those literacy and numeracy domains in which students in individual schools performed below the national average (and in comparison with 60 'like'/similar schools[3] across the nation) – caused some exasperation amongst educators. However, the relative improvement was also construed as a reason for celebration, even as teachers struggled to value results that were still below the national benchmark, and even as it was recognized these improvements were made from a very low base:

> We all love NAPLAN![4] It does give direction and it does show, for example everyone – as a school we get quite disappointed when the actual results come back and say our kids are all in red. There's a couple in green and a couple in blue, but you just can't look at that [out of context] – 'Look at that picture, you've got to look at the data behind it that says we were 3 times the state average improvement!' So what's happening is teachers get very disillusioned when those results come back but it's then saying to them, 'Hey guys; don't panic. We're actually showing 3 times the state improvement average. You are doing the right thing. It's just going to take a while for our kids actually to get up to that national benchmark'. And they keep saying, 'Yeah but the national benchmark keeps moving because everyone else is improving'. I said, 'Yeah, but 3 times the state average!' … That's a pretty – yeah you can't keep beating yourself up about that. It's just those types of messages, you get mixed messages. You look at that and you see all the kids – the majority in red – and the

immediate thing is, 'God we're doing a shit job!' And it's not that at all. Look
deeper!

(Lynagh, Literacy Coach, Tropical City School)

Such constant comparison reflects both a sense of disillusionment at times amongst
teachers, as well as efforts to recognize the improvements that had been made over
time, and how teachers were encouraged to be proud of these improvements. This
literacy coach sought to influence teachers positively and proactively, even as the
data clearly stimulated concern amongst her colleagues.

Such concerns around NAPLAN, and how teachers and educators in schools
responded, also reflect how comparative measures of attainment encouraged more
performative responses on the part of those affected – focused on student performance outcomes – rather than more educational aims. As a form of comparative
educational study, the constant comparison on the part of educators, and concerns
about these results, reveal how such practices were used as a mode of governance,
even as there were efforts to encourage reflection on the historical development or
journey of a particular educational initiative (Nóvoa & Yariv-Mashal, 2003).

Similarly, there was clear evidence about how the work occurring in a neigh-
bouring school in the same region was influenced by external, systemic pressures
for reform, and particularly in relation to enhanced NAPLAN results. For the
principal of this school, the focus on NAPLAN was productive for how it revealed
relatively high rates of improvement – an important marker of achievement in a
system construed as needing to dramatically improve performance as measured
against national test results. However, this did not diminish concerns about not
achieving national benchmarks and performing below the state average – again
reflected in the way NAPLAN was reported to schools through a visual representation of red bars:

Of course, from a systemic point of view, the stuff that they want to hear is
around NAPLAN. And I think NAPLAN – as much as people jump up and
down about it – I think it's actually good for us in the fact that our NAPLAN
data, fortunately for us, is improving. But it's not to the level where we want
it to go. Our 'relative gained' data is outstanding. It's well in front of our
district and in front of the state, but you're coming from a low base. So, let's
not think that we're doing [well] – we've come from a low base and we
really – we're not happy with it. As we say here, there's 'more reds than a
bottle shop'[5] in our NAPLAN data!

(Harry, Principal, Deep North School)

This focus on such comparative data reflect how '[d]ata production and management were and are essential to the new governance turn; constant comparison is its
symbolic feature, as well as a distinctive mode of operation' (Ozga, 2009, p. 149).
Such reflections about NAPLAN were reinforced amongst other teachers in the
schools. However, while there was clear recognition about school positioning in

relation to NAPLAN – that NAPLAN data had exerted influence – there was also recognition that the focus around NAPLAN data had also encouraged professional learning through various professional dialogues about pedagogical practices:

> Our NAPLAN results in [region] – are they the lowest in Australia? If not the lowest, they're very close to it! But our improvement is maybe the highest in Australia. I mean I know we've started at a very low place, but there are a lot of very, very good things happening in schools across the region. And not just people saying that there are good things; they are actually happening. And the conversations between teachers and the understanding about pedagogy has changed.
>
> *(Flo, Numeracy Coach, Tropical City School)*

This recognition of NAPLAN results, including positive expressions of professional practice arising in response to the test, reflects the 'publicness' of the accountability agenda associated with NAPLAN, and of the ability to demand an account of such practices (Bovens et al., 2014). It also reflects how educators were interpreting these data, and seeking to derive educational benefit from the data, rather than simply being dominated by performative logics.

That the emphasis on NAPLAN was a significant factor governing teachers' practices in Queensland, and particularly in the more northern regions of the state where results were lowest, was also reflected in the way the head of curriculum at this school referred to how the focus on explicit teaching (see previous chapter for further details) was a direct result of a push for a broader improvement agenda in the region as a whole, particularly on the part of the Assistant Regional Director (ARD),[6] and in relation to NAPLAN. This entailed collecting data every five weeks as part of a push to ultimately show improved outcomes:

> So, from a regional perspective – it's all based on our NAPLAN results; so, our NAPLAN results as a region are not good. So, the region has gone on its own – what they call 'improvement agenda' – which is 'explicit teaching'. So, the region has employed a mentor, John Fleming from Victoria who kind of drives that, but is also a big stick for the schools – that's my opinion. So often what he advises our ARDs – the Assistant Regional Directors – to do, such as 5 weekly data tracking, is taken on board by our region. So, they then say to the schools, 'Every 5 weeks, we want to see whatever, or you will collect whatever'. And when they come visit the schools, they will say to us, 'We want you to pull up that data'. So, we have to actually have it there. But some of that data might not necessarily be what is best for us, for the school. So sometimes we're doing this as an accountability thing rather than something that we can actually use to improve student outcomes. And because we're being advised by someone else, sometimes what is asked for, from a curriculum point of view, is actually not always accurate in my opinion.
>
> *(Dympha, Head of Curriculum, Tropical City School)*

This expression of concern about the focus of attention on particular kinds of data reveals how even as more performative accountability logics clearly governed practices in schools, and were explicitly acknowledged as such, there was also evidence of critique of such practices – of collecting data for the sake of accountability, rather than to respond to students' learning needs. Such a response reflects a more agentic stand-point, focused on the need to consider what the tests might indicate in relation to student learning. This more 'authentic' approach constitutes a form of accountability to students' actual learning needs – which should be the central focus of teachers' work – rather than in relation to more performative, broader, state-level concerns which simply and unproblematically construe various forms of data and test results as proxies for student learning. These more authentic accountabilities occurred even under clearly challenging conditions in which more performative accountability logics commanded so much time, attention and authority. Concerns about the nature of the data collected as part of the 5-week data tracking cycles, and accountability for the sake of accountability, reflected how more managerial conceptions of accountability exerted significant influence, and with potentially erosive effects on necessary relationships and responsibilities on the part of educators (Biesta, 2004; 2020). However, educators' interrogation of such practices also reveal how such governance processes were not uncontested and how educators strove to reclaim professional autonomy and responsibility in such circumstances. At least to some extent, there was evidence of more active interrogation of NAPLAN and its effects, even as more performative accountability logics clearly reoriented the nature of educators' work.

The clash between more performative and educationally oriented – authentic – accountabilities was also evident in relation to collecting data on students' reading fluency, particularly the request that teachers collect two sets of data about their students' reading capacities. These data were based on standardized readers designed to ascertain students' fluency and reading comprehension. While teachers had been used to collecting data on the 'level' they perceived their students to have attained during the course of the year, they were not used to having to collect additional level-data to reflect the different capacities of students vis-à-vis their reading comprehension and fluency at multiple points in time:

> From a school point of view, we need what we call 'instructional levels' on the kids so that we can figure out this is where they fall down and these are the strategies we can help them to move on. From the explicit teaching regional point of view, they collect 'easy levels' because when he [ARD] comes, he will pull that data, and want to know where the kids are at … So, in the school, I'm saying, 'We need your "easy" level because that's what the region's going to pull, but we also need your "instructional" level because that's what we're actually going to use to help you be a better reader'. And so the teachers are like 'Why do I need two levels?' So that's where the agendas clash.

> (Dympha, Head of Curriculum, Tropical City School)

The collection of the 'easy levels' seemed to serve as a distraction from the collection of the 'instructional levels', which pushed the students further, and which were recognized as more educationally useful. This situation was further complicated by the way in which the region also set specific 'levels' of attainment that students should reach by the end of each year level, and reinforced that schools needed to be able to justify why students had not attained those levels by the end of each year:

> And then the region says, for those levels, [the region] actually says, 'This is the minimum that your kids should leave Prep with'. And, so, from an advisory point of view, they will say to us as a school, 'Any child who's not going to reach that level has to be basically signed off by you. Otherwise what's your reason for not getting your child to that level if there's not something wrong with them?' It's you as a teacher or you as a school that's not doing the right thing. So, it's kind of that big stick – so we don't actually tell the teachers all that stuff because they would be, 'Ugh!' So, it's a fine line to kind of tread.
>
> *(Dympha, Head of Curriculum, Tropical City School)*

Through the collection and use of data such as the 'easy' reading levels, school systems were able to apply more managerial mechanisms to 'steer from a distance' (Kickert, 1995), even as staff in schools, such as this head of curriculum, sought to facilitate enhanced accountability amongst teachers for their work with students. Furthermore, for this head of curriculum, this sense of agency within constraints, and efforts to seek to interrogate and influence the governing of educational practice was also evident in how she sought to determine how much information to share with teachers to encourage them to fulfil external accountability requirements but without discouraging them. In this sense, she was displaying a sense of authentic accountability to her colleagues, as well as students, as she took seriously how to facilitate their learning, rather than using relatively poor NAPLAN results to simply criticize teachers.

The focus on data for its own sake within more performative logics is also evidence of a form of what Lawn (2013) describes as a 'systemless system', with its reliance on various modalities of data to govern what occurs in schools and regions, rather than more traditional modes of governance, such as those associated with inspectors. NAPLAN served as information which stimulated regional concerns about students' literacy (and numeracy) practices, and encouraged an active focus on collecting various forms of associated data (such as the 'levelled' reading data) for accountability purposes (even as more educative concerns were also, arguably, simultaneously in play amongst senior systemic educators).[7] This had particular effects at the local level, with tensions surrounding the collection of 'easy levels' as a baseline of data for accountability purposes, and 'instructional levels' for educative purposes. That it was felt such information could not be divulged to teachers also reflects the sensitivity surrounding governance practices, and how this head of curriculum sought to ameliorate the very substantial pressure originating from the state for improved results on these standardized measures of student achievement, as she sought to enhance teachers' professional capacities. Again, all of these practices provide evidence of her displaying a form of accountability that was oriented to the learning needs of students as the primary responsibility of schools – a more authentic accountability.

In a central Queensland region that was also construed as underperforming through such a comparative logic, pressure for improved results was also understood as emanating at the regional level. And as in the northern parts of the state, the focus on the data collected at the regional level influenced how those in schools responded:

> From the district office, there's obviously a push there to enhance the data. Obviously, we've got to improve every year, and that's something that's a requirement of education. So, I think that's where the big push has come from, and the way in which we produce the tests and the way in which we monitor the test as well. So obviously that's the big thing that came down from up above.
> *(Toby, Year 7 Teacher, Central Mining School)*

As well as this overt recognition of the need to 'enhance the data', and the 'obviousness' of needing to do so to respond to pressures 'from up above', the focus on the number of students achieving at particular levels also revealed how educators' practices were governed by set targets and markers of achievement. This occurred even as the number of actual students in some schools meant it did not make sense to apply broad targets to individual schools in the region as a whole. This was particularly problematic in smaller rural schools dotted throughout central and western areas in Queensland, where small numbers of students meant that limited conclusions could be drawn from these data from year to year. However, even as it was recognized as problematic to make assumptions and extrapolations from these students about NAPLAN and associated results, principals felt that the Assistant Regional Directors responsible for their schools were resolutely focused on NAPLAN results:

> You might have two kids in Year 5 you're collecting and comparing data on. And that's really not accurate … [However], the ARD will sit there and say, 'Yes, we know you've only got 2 kids'. But they still ask – they still push, 'Hey, your NAPLAN data dropped from last year! What's going on?' Even though they say all the right things, they still ask that question! And you think it's all about data to them. It's all about numbers.
> *(Valmae, Principal, Central Mining School)*

This emphasis on it being 'all about data' and 'all about numbers' for the senior members of the schooling apparatus in Queensland reflects more performative logics *par excellence* at play, and how the roles of these senior educators were constituted in ways that made it difficult for them to respond in any other way (see also Lingard & Sellar, 2013).

However, reflecting the contestation that surrounded such numbers, numbers as expressed through NAPLAN (as well as any other form of numeric calibration of students' learning) were recognized as only going so far in expressing students' understandings, and it was more educative understandings which were most valued, including in relation to students' everyday practices:

> I'm not a fan of it because how can you actually prove what a kid knows through numbers.
>
> *(Peter, Year 5 Teacher, South East Urban School)*

> To NAPLAN – how do you know if a child's had a good day or a bad day? How do you know if they've just multi-guessed everything and done well? I think your day-to-day classroom activities – seeing how little Johnny's going with his grammar and punctuation – to me, is a better way of seeing where the gaps are.
>
> *(Sylvia, Music Teacher, South West Rural School)*

While recognition that 'it's all about data', 'all about numbers', reflects the dominance of more enumerative logics more broadly in education (Hardy, 2015), educators not only sought to appropriate the focus on such numbers for more educative purposes (Hardy, 2014), but also critiqued the inappropriate application of such numbers in relation to students' learning. By doing so, they displayed accountability to their students that was oriented towards the actual purposes of schooling – to provide educational opportunities. Again, such intentionality provided evidence of a more authentic conception of the work of teachers and schools, and the limitations of numbers in their efforts to represent student learning.

Nevertheless, the constitutive nature of these figures meant that numbers, construed as part of a broader apparatus of 'objects [that] must be perceived as indisputable, above the fray' (Desrosières, 1998, p. 1), were also clearly productive in relation to more performative conceptions of schooling, and were used unproblematically in this regard. They came to dominate relations between educators in schools, and system personnel (in this case, the Assistant Regional Director from the local regional office) even as they were recognized by all involved as deeply problematic.

In this context, again, comparison as a technology for accountability as a mode of governance (Nóvoa & Yariv-Mashal, 2003) was also evident in the way the same students at different year levels, and different students at the same year level, were compared. Even as NAPLAN was ostensibly supposed to be used to provide broad aggregate data for more systemic purposes, these data were becoming increasingly fine-grained, down to the individual student-level:

> Sometimes they're comparing from last year's Year 7s to this year's Year 7s, but sometimes they're comparing how the Year 7s went in Grade 5 and how

they go in Grade 7. So, they are looking at the improvement. They also look at the questions and which quiz, they can now find out – the data can tell you what questions they get right and what types of questions they get wrong. So analysing that data so the teachers can try and work with the things that the students don't know or struggle with, and focus on that. Because they can do it for every single question – what answer that students gave ... You can see every single answer for every single student; you would be able to see where it sits ... It is quite specific, yes.

(Monica, Music Teacher, Central Mining School)

That these comparative logics could exert strong effects was also evident in how teachers sometimes construed the data unproblematically, and as evidence of students underperforming, and a valid measure against which to benchmark appropriate levels of achievement for students:

I did look back at their results from Year 5 and when I look back at their results from Year 5, they were similar to the results they were putting out at the start of Year 7. So, I went through and said, 'Right, so what's Year 7 standard? This is where I want them to be; let's see if we can get as many as we can up to that standard.' So that was something that I found out here. So, we've got to get them back up and we tried our best to get them back up there.

(Toby, Year 7 Teacher, Central Mining School)

More performative comparative logics were also evident in relation to the pressure of financial incentives associated with NAPLAN, and concerns about schools' competitive standing on the test. Such concerns were a direct result of various forms of incentives provided by the federal government to the individual states, depending on their NAPLAN performance. Under such circumstances, Lingard and Sellar (2013) argue that NAPLAN results act as a form of 'catalyst' data, serving to encourage a 'reaction' amongst those affected, and also leading to the relative diminution of state power relative to the federal government in the arena of education (even as education is the constitutional responsibility of the states in the Australian federal system). While Lingard and Sellar (2013) refer specifically to state systemic personnel, there is also clear evidence of how 'reactions' have been substantive amongst teachers themselves, in how they have responded to the pressure around NAPLAN, and of how the federal government agenda has had significant influence on their work in state/public schools. For personnel working at the state level, the stimulus for increased focus on NAPLAN results included allocation of funding to the state systems in response to particular NAPLAN results.

While they were not familiar with the specificities of such relations, those in schools were aware that funding was attached in some way to the accountability agenda associated with NAPLAN, and that their work was subsequently deeply implicated in such attention to results for more performative reasons. While

NAPLAN was construed as problematic, the pity of the process was that teachers understood that the test could serve a useful function, if the performative accountability processes that governed it, including through various forms of targets, did not exert so much influence:

> We do feel the pressure, I know, being a NAPLAN grade [this year]. It was kind of nice last year, being in Grade 4 – no NAPLAN! Yeah, because like I said, because of all these money targets and this pressure, and this competitiveness, and the way the results are displayed in that way [on the *MySchool* website], it just – it takes away from the benefits of it, which is really disappointing. Because I think it could be a really positive thing, and I think it's kind of not so great at the moment. Because it's got the competition aspect, the big display of, 'Oh gee, Central Mining School, if you didn't do very good at NAPLAN this year, it doesn't look good on the internet and the school reports!' And also, 'We didn't hit our targets; we had these targets, [and] didn't hit the targets!' All this focus on hitting the targets! You're talking about different kids; they're coming from different backgrounds. It's not going to be exactly the same as last year.
>
> *(Winsome, Year 3 Teacher, Central Mining School)*

This emphasis on achieving particular targets reflects the deeply comparative nature of such data, and how more comparative logics dominated as a mode of governance (Nóvoa & Yariv-Mashal, 2003). There was very much a sense in which accountability was exercised through the forum of NAPLAN, and 'the forum promulgates its judgement to the public at large' (Bovens et al., 2014, p. 7) However, that the test was recognized as having the potential to serve educative purposes reflects alternative logics at play, and a much more authentic conception of accountability of teachers to students' actual learning, and not simply representations of their learning.

This constant comparison created angst amongst these teachers, and a blending of the more performative and educative aspects of the test. This was evident in the way the educative potential of the test was recognized, as teachers sought not to be overwhelmed by the more performative demands of the test:

> So yeah, there's a lot of pressure being in a NAPLAN grade; I know I feel it. I know that other teachers who teach NAPLAN grades also probably feel it. It's past now [for this year], which is good, but at the time, you're like, 'Oh, we've got to make sure these kids keep up; we've got to make sure they know the stuff the other states know; we've got to make sure they know how to colour a bubble;[8] got to make sure they know how to do this; got to make sure they know how to do that.' You do feel that pressure – and you're stressed about that a bit. But it's a pity, because it could be really good.
>
> *(Winsome, Year 3 Teacher, Central Mining School)*

For a colleague with prior experience teaching in New Zealand, the focus on improving standards was not seen as a problem, but it was the public display of test results that was concerning. Specifically, the ability to develop league tables (a proxy feature of the *MySchool* website where NAPLAN results are displayed) was seen as particularly problematic.[9] This was seen as particularly concerning for schools serving more disadvantaged communities. For this teacher, the fear was that New Zealand would also adopt what was seen as the 'Australian approach' of focusing on the public spectacle around NAPLAN:

> You guys went to NAPLAN, and ever since you went to NAPLAN, there's been a huge fear in New Zealand that New Zealand's going to follow down the same track. They have so far gone as far as setting New Zealand standards which is a minimum – which is a standard expected of a child. Not everyone will reach it and some will pass it, of course. But that is where we are aiming towards, is [improved] standards. I've got no problems with that [focus on improving standards] because that at least tells a parent where the [child should be]. But the whole thing about NAPLAN, tables of league tables and that sort of thing – they just do absolutely nothing. They just make the poor schools feel poorer, and the rich schools feel richer, because the rich ones have the resources – well, especially the community resources. And the poor schools haven't got that, and it just makes it so much harder. Also, it's harder to attract teachers to those particular areas and everything else.
>
> (Michelle, Literacy & Numeracy Support Teacher, Central Mining School)

This focus on making results public also reflects a response to broader concerns about transparency, and about the need to provide some means of subjecting teachers' work to more public scrutiny, where such publics are wide-ranging, and include educators themselves:

> Testing programs, whether at local, national or international scales, are generally justified by claims about the utility of the data that are generated. The promise is made that measuring outcomes will help to improve efficiency and quality (for example system, school, teacher and student performance) and that more and better data will give insights into the often opaque world of the classroom. Regimes of testing aim to open the classroom to external scrutiny, in order to putatively solve the problem of the unaccountable teacher through making them accountable to and for student performance data. These contestable claims resonate, often among the media, bureaucrats, parents, policymakers and politicians, but also among educational professionals themselves .
>
> (Lingard, Thompson & Sellar, 2016, p. 1)

Reflecting such critique amongst professionals themselves, poor performance was construed by another teacher in the northern regions of the state as having to be responded to more robustly than had previously been the case. For this teacher, the reasons provided previously for poorer performance, such as students being one year younger than in other states, were now inadequate:

> I think Education Queensland now are putting a far greater emphasis on NAPLAN than they did before. It was kind of before, 'Oh well, we're a year behind and woe is me'. And now we really need to step up because there aren't too many more excuses we can make.[10]
>
> *(Desleigh, Year 2 Teacher, Tropical City School)*

Again, a more comparative logic was at play, as this teacher reflected on Queensland's relatively poor standing in relation to most other states and territories in Australia, particularly during the inaugural year of NAPLAN in 2008, when students were effectively 6–12 months younger in Queensland than most of the other states.

However, the way in which teachers also critiqued efforts to enhance students' test results for their own sake, and as simply part of a more performative accountability agenda, also reflects a desire to push back against the more reductive effects of the test:

> I think it's a good way to see where they're at in terms of where all the other kids are at in the nation. But Queensland's been so low for so many years, I think that it's why they've brought in the new curriculum – to sort of push those marks up. But in the end – you can analyse it and you can put it on the report card, but I don't know. How, actually doing the test, how much benefit it has? To be honest, to say, 'Oh your child's not as good as someone in South Australia' – I mean, it's not really about that, is it?
>
> *(Edwina, Year 4 Teacher, Central Mining School)*

For this teacher, the focus on the relative improvement between the states on aggregate national test scores, or a student's individual response in relation to other students in different parts of the country, was not construed as nearly as important as the learning which these students experienced and in which they were actually engaged. Even as these national standardized testing practices exerted so much influence on teachers' work and learning, more test-centric logics were contested by teachers as they sought to consider what such scores might mean for teaching their students, and vis-à-vis their students' learning. Such responses reflect concern for students' actual learning – a more authentic sense of responsibility and accountability to students and the primary, educative purposes of schooling. That the work of educating children was 'not really about that' reflects how, through more active interrogation of testing practices, more educative logics simultaneously exerted influence, even as more test-centric accountability logics governed so many aspects of the field of schooling practices in Queensland.

Targeting and testing specific students

The way in which teachers focused so much attention on specific students at particular times of the year also reflects how accountability pressures associated with
increased test results also governed teachers' practices. The timetable of the learning
support teacher in a school in a western district in the south-east corner of
Queensland reflected how time was allocated to particular year levels according to
when NAPLAN was held (in May). This work involved focusing explicitly on
NAPLAN related test activities, and genres that were to be covered in the test
(most obviously, persuasive and narrative writing), for those grades in which students were examined (Years 3, 5 and 7), in the months prior to the test:

> Yes, [NAPLAN] is [an important focus area]. So, throughout the year,
> I change, because the school's so big that I can't give help to all grades at once.
> So up until May, I take Years 3, 5, 7; sometimes I have a support person to
> help me. We take teaching groups from those year levels, and then we try to
> work on NAPLAN-type things. Like reading strategies, comprehension, trying
> to teach language conventions, sometimes its numeracy also. And the writing;
> we're writing persuasive tasks. Just practising the structure of the persuasive
> format.
>
> *(Bonnie, Learning Support Teacher, South West Urban School)*

This process of targeting specific students at particular times also occurred at a more
micro level, and included giving attention to those students who 'we can make a
difference to' in specific year groups:

> I take groups of children from classrooms, and that can be for enrichment, or
> it can be the children who are lagging behind. It could be the bottom
> children – often it is the second bottom, or the children that we can make a
> difference to. So, we heavily focus on children in Years 1 to 2 and try to get
> their reading ahead when they're young, so that they can access the
> curriculum.
>
> *(Bonnie, Learning Support Teacher, South West Urban School)*

This reference to those students who were 'the second bottom or the children that
we can make a difference to' referred to those students who were performing
below passing benchmarks for the regular curriculum, and who, with additional
assistance, could achieve passing grades. Such 'bubble children' (Booher-Jennings,
2005) tended to receive more attention than some other children, and were construed as more likely to contribute to enhanced outcomes on various forms of
school-based and national standardized testing.

Such responses also reflect a sense of acquiescence to more performative
demands to enhance results for particular cohorts and to do so as quickly as possible, and regardless of how this might be achieved. Teachers could be construed as

primarily passive subjects who were governed by broader processes that determined what they actually did:

> Imperative disciplinary policies like those involved in the standards agenda (that is the drive to continually raise the level of student performance in tests and examinations) produce a primarily passive policy subject, a 'technical professional' whose practice is heavily determined by the requirements of performance and delivery.
>
> *(Ball, Maguire, Braun & Hoskins, 2011, p. 612)*

However, the way teachers responded seemed to reflect both more performative as well as more educative logics at play. This was evident in the focus on targeting specific students at another suburban school in south-east Queensland, who were identified as being 'in the middle' of the NAPLAN cohort. These students were described as 'overlooked' more broadly:

> We've always catered for the kids down in special needs areas or learning support. And they do a good job with that. But I guess, particularly when we started to see results with our NAPLAN that we said, 'Okay, well let's try and get those middle kids up' – and that's one of the ideas behind the drafting process with our English; it's really helped with those [middle students].
>
> *(Simon, Year 7 Teacher, Southern School)*

Such a response indicates the intersection between more performative account-ability logics, and more educative logics. In a context in which teachers were encouraged to increase the proportion of students in the upper two bands of NAPLAN, as part of a broader systemic accountability agenda that sought to ensure improved Queensland's outcomes on NAPLAN, such responses can be seen as evidence of more performative accountabilities. The emphasis on specific students represents a form of 'triage' on the part of educators, as they sought to enhance outcomes for targeted group of students, particularly those construed as 'suitable cases for treatment' (Gillborn & Youdell, 2000, p. 133). It is this suitability for treatment that advantages some students over others, with potentially significant and material repercussions for students so treated (and for those given less atten-tion). However, it could be argued that such a response is also reflective of more educative logics, and a concern for the needs of students 'in the middle' who may not have received as much attention, relative to more struggling and higher achieving students. In this sense, it could be argued these teachers exhibited a form of accountability that was more genuine in relation to the needs of students who may have been receiving less attention, relative to others. However, such an argument is dependent upon accepting NAPLAN as having at least some educa-tional value in the first place.

At a school in the northern regions of Queensland, this focus on NAPLAN influenced the nature of the curriculum experienced by students in more overt ways. That the test governed schooling practices was evident in how those students who had performed poorly on previous NAPLAN or trial tests were allocated additional literacy and numeracy classes in Year 7, as part of an 'Academic Success Program'. This was instead of LOTE (Languages Other than English) classes:

> The kids who passed the NAPLAN benchmarks all go to LOTE; the ones who didn't pass it work with the classroom teachers twice a week for 45 minutes each session.
>
> *(Sadie, Year 7 Teacher, Tropical City School)*

This intensity of intervention was construed as a normalized part of practice in the school. Indeed, the Academic Success Program was considered a valuable vehicle for promoting increased opportunities for students to focus on improving their literacy and numeracy capacities. As part of this work, students were focused on intensively by a small number of adults. These students were tested on an ongoing basis in an effort to ensure they were achieving minimum literacy and numeracy benchmarks:

> Now the Academic Success Program – essentially what we do is we take the bottom cohort of kids, from Prep to Year 3 ... and what they do is they get an extra hour of explicit instruction 4 days a week, which equates to 40 hours a term, which equates to 80 hours a semester which equates to 160 hours [per year] ... And so we use a cohort teacher, we use a learning support teacher and we put two highly trained teacher aides with them. So, we've got four adults working with a group of 25–30 kids. And again, it's more explicit instruction but it's in that small group focus, where we can drill down. And the kids are continually tested. If they've proven that they've caught up, or they have the basic facts, they then migrate out of the system. But they have to do it for a couple of sessions in a row.
>
> *(Cameron, Principal, Tropical City School)*

Under these circumstances, there was a sense in which students were constantly tested to determine whether they should continue to receive intensive, ongoing interventions:

WILMA: And they're constantly tested.
IAN: Okay. Okay to see if there's movement?
WILMA: Yeah. *(Wilma, Year 5 Teacher, Tropical City School)*

This intensification of focus clearly reflects more performative accountabilities, as a particular strategy oriented towards enhancing NAPLAN results. However, concerns about the literacy and numeracy practices of students, and the focused push to try to redress embedded shortcomings amongst students in these areas could also be construed as evidence of more authentic accountabilities, involving teachers/

principal being accountable to students for providing them with additional opportunities to enhance their literacy and numeracy capabilities, at least as evident in shortcomings revealed through NAPLAN. Of course, the complicating and problematic factor in this instance is that students were missing out on other subject areas as part of this intensive focus. Literacy and numeracy seemed to dominate over other learning areas or aspects of schooling.

At a whole-school level, strategizing in relation to specific groups of students also constituted a key part of staff meetings, which could be devoted to analysing NAPLAN data, and ascertaining how to target students in specific bands to address shortcomings identified in school data:

> Sometimes most of the staff meeting – a lot of the time actually, yeah ... they [teachers and school administrators] talk about NAPLAN and bands ... Well they look at the data that the students have, what the students have achieved in previous years and how they're achieving now. And there's lots of coloured boxes about. You've got the red box, which is the students who are below the band that's expected. And then you've got the yellow box which is where they should be. And the green if they're above.
>
> *(Monica, Music Teacher, Central Mining School)*

In the southern regions of the state, the comments from the principal of a large suburban, middle-class school revealed there was a focus on a targeted group of 'middle' performing students, and that part of the 'school improvement agenda' was explicitly oriented to improving the proportion of students in the upper two bands of NAPLAN results. The elaborated way in which improvements on just a few students' results were explicitly explained as advantageously influencing the data reveals the influence of a more performative focus on standardized data:

> We've had two programs going this year, one for Grade 3s and one for Grade 4s on those 'belly kids'.[11] Part of the school improvement agenda is moving students up to the top two bands. So, the target is those children who have got the potential but who are underachieving. And the teachers know who they are. And just if we can engage those students, they can get up to be 'Bs' and 'As'. And that would directly affect all areas of our data. We would, if we just got – if you just think about three or four children in the whole of Grade 3 moving up one or two levels, [that] would completely skew our data to be amazing. Because we have really good children – a fairly significant middle, and a tail which is not significant. It's not like the rest of Queensland, or a lot of Queensland; we have a very big middle. And some children in that middle are under-achieving.
>
> *(Rita, Principal, Southern School)*

The explicit focus on seeking to 'affect all areas of our data' reveals the influence of more performative accountabilities, even as these were not the only accountabilities at play, with the principal clearly concerned about a potentially broad swathe of children under-achieving in her school. Nevertheless, such foci reflect how principals' practices can be influenced by testing regimes, and how attention to such tests can distort teachers and principals' behaviours (Stobart, 2008). That a focus on strategies of targeting particular students 'would directly affect all areas of our data' reveals the data-centric pressure on principals in a context in which earlier results had been used so punishingly to criticize teachers and principals in schools in Queensland.

However, even as these processes of targeting specific students were a common practice in schools, teachers also resisted those more performative practices that construed designated students as worthy of more attention than others. For teachers in another school setting in northern Queensland where the streaming and targeting of students was a dominant logic, some teachers expressed concerns about how this focused attention on specific students could reduce the amount of time available to meet with other students to assist them with their learning:

> They're – they're taking a lot of my time in the classroom, I would say. I'm finding it hard to have one-on-one conferencing with other students.
>
> *(Dorothy, Year 4 Teacher, Northern Coast School)*

This emphasis on particular students was not a diminution of the need to be more responsive to those students who were failing to meet adequate targets for their year level, but giving more attention to some students than others was a cause of angst as teachers simultaneously strove to address the needs of all students:

> Sometimes I'm not sure how many students I should be targeting ... And I don't want anyone to be left behind. So, that's obviously a concern ... It's like I see the value in having 'target' students, but really I want them, as any teacher does, all to be improving.
>
> *(Corinna, Prep Teacher, Northern Coast School)*

Teachers also worried that some students did not always respond positively to the increased attention upon their performance, but instead found the increased pressure to improve to be debilitating:

> I do find some of them, because you work with them so much ... they have got the pressure put on them. And because they are those struggling ones, they can't deal with that – they sort of, in a way, just give up ... Because we've got the pressure to get them up, so they've got the pressure of trying to do what we want ... they struggle still.
>
> *(Faith, Year 4 Teacher, Northern Coast School)*

In these ways, teachers exhibited accountability to all of their students, as they sought to provide the best possible opportunities for learning for their students, in context. Even as teachers' practices were clearly governed by systemic parameters and targets, theirs was also a practice forged through a sense of accountability to the genuine learning needs of all students in their care, and not just systemic account-abilities (Lingard, Martino, Rezai-Rashti & Sellar, 2016). While specific targets governed their practices, teachers also sought to move beyond these systemic pre-rogatives, displaying a more 'authentic' stance in relation to the purported aims of schooling to provide an educative experience for all students. And this was difficult work:

> I like to target all of my students ... I have to keep that balance and I don't want them missing out. And that's where it would be really sad to have, 'Okay I've got my "Ds" to "Cs" but you know what? I didn't get any "Bs" to "As"!' Or, 'My "As" dropped to "Bs" because I didn't give them what they needed'. And that's the spinning plate. Which plate did I drop? And it sma-shed. And that's the nature of our job. It's just so complex.
>
> *(Felicia, Prep Teacher, Northern Coast School)*

For a colleague, there was a similar sense in which she sought to be responsive to all of her students' needs:

> I'm definitely running more than one [target group] ... I don't know if it's supposed to be like that, but that's how it seems to be for me ... I like to target *all* of my students!
>
> *(Jess, Prep Teacher, Northern Coast School)*

Consequently, in the context of teachers' practices being governed by pressure to target specific students, and a focus on enhancing students' results in NAPLAN, there was also concern for the educative functions of NAPLAN, and for all stu-dents' learning, not simply those identified within the remit of NAPLAN as requiring additional attention. At least in part, such responses reflect a more active interrogation of the more performative aspects of such testing, and evidence of a more genuine, authentic form of accountability oriented towards providing for the needs of all students.

NAPLAN as a whole-school responsibility

The normalization around NAPLAN was also apparent in relation to how teachers working with students in the year levels before NAPLAN argued there needed to be greater engagement with teachers teaching NAPLAN in the year level prior to the NAPLAN years. This engagement was seen as vital to inform teachers to better prepare students for NAPLAN:

> I'd like to see a lot more work with the Grade 3 teachers on what they're finding. This is my second year back in Grade 2; I haven't had Grade 2 for a

few years. [I'd like to see] a little bit more on what we should be targeting so that we can ensure that they arrive into Grade 3 with a set of skills that Grade 3 teachers know they will need. Because unless we've had Grade 3, we don't necessarily know what's in NAPLAN to try and know what's important to push or to reteach to ensure that they've got that before they go on ... Because the Grade 3 teachers really only have them for 6 to 7 weeks or something and then they're 'NAPLANing!' So, realistically what they come out with on NAPLAN is a lot to do with what the Year 2 teachers have done with them.

(Desleigh, Year 2 Teacher, Tropical City School)

Concerns about not knowing what students needed to experience prior to Year 3, in preparation for NAPLAN, and the belief teachers needed to be more familiar with what students needed to know for NAPLAN, reveal how strongly standardized testing governed teachers' practices. Even as they themselves were not compelled to engage in particular practices in preparation for NAPLAN, teachers in the years before NAPLAN took it as necessary to be more aware of the nature of the NAPLAN test, and that this would be useful to better prepare students for NAPLAN. The reference to students 'NAPLANing' also reveals how the test and lead-up to the test had taken on something of a life of their own, including the dominance of preparation practices in relation to standardized testing (Nichols & Berliner, 2007; Stobart, 2008; Hursh, 2008), and NAPLAN in particular (Polesel, Rice & Dulfer, 2014). Such responses also intimated how so much of the school year leading up to the test was actually taken up in preparation for the test. This focus on practice occurring in the year before was construed as important, given teachers only had students for a little over a term (approximately 10 weeks) in the year in which they sat NAPLAN:

Yes, yes, very much so, and I think that's what the Year 7 teachers were saying, you know, we only have them for a term, or the [Year] 5s – well we weren't talking to the 5s but they're the same. We have them for a year. They have them for a term. So, really, who – you know, and really you're looking more at the year before. ... I think that's really been [recognized] this year.

(Geraldine, Year 6 Teacher, South West Urban School)

The governance of schooling practices through NAPLAN testing was also evident in the focus on strategic attention to reading groups in the early years in some schools, in preparation for the Year 3 test. Part of this push involved ensuring homogeneity of experience across year levels in the lead-up to the test:

We look over the results – and the results of the NAPLAN test is probably a reason why there's been such a focus on the reading groups in the lower end of the school. Like I said, you know, we've always done reading groups but they wanted ... I'm guessing that they wanted to make it more of a systematic and streamlined process where everybody was doing the same from Prep to Grade 2, leading into Grade 3 for NAPLAN.

(Suzie, Year 1 Teacher, Southern School)

Standardized testing seemed to encourage a form of systematic practices in school sites, oriented towards the test itself. Whether such practices contributed to forms of 'constrained professionalism', in which more centralized curriculum and instructional strategies were advocated (Wills & Sandholtz, 2009), was not immediately apparent in this specific instance, but the focus on homogenizing processes more broadly does suggest the propensity towards such practices. And as indicated in the previous chapters, more standardized approaches to both curriculum and teaching were certainly in evidence.

In one school in central Queensland, attention to NAPLAN meant ensuring students were familiar with the test from Year 1, and ensuring all students engaged in activities similar to what they would experience on the test:

It's a big focus though, I know that … We even talk about it in Grade 1 to our kids. … Because it's just a big focus for the school to achieve well. They have, leading up to NAPLAN, they have meetings with the 3, 5, 7s … But even with the Grade 1s; some of our spelling activities are 'find the missing word', or 'find the word that's spelt wrong', like in NAPLAN tests. Things like that.

(Matilda, Year 1 Teacher, Central Mining School)

For this teacher, the focus on NAPLAN was pervasive. As in other schooling settings in Queensland (Comber, 2011; Comber 2012; Polesel et al., 2014), rather than the broader curriculum, at times, there was a sense in which teachers were teaching to NAPLAN, and this was occurring across the whole school. Furthermore, this was encouraged systemically by the strong focus on particular genres in the regular curriculum/C2C, which was seen as dominated by text-types to be addressed in NAPLAN:

And I think there's also teaching the NAPLAN rather than teaching to the curriculum. I think everything goes out the window. And it's interesting, the fact they've – the genre at the moment is persuasive text. So, there's persuasive test in Preps' C2C, Grade 1, Grade 2 and Grade 3, giving children the foundation that they need to go into that. But there's not that [attention] on every other [genre]; you know what I mean? So, there is a real – [focus on particular genres]. What happens when they change genres?

(Violet, Year 1 Teacher, Central Mining School)

For a colleague in the school with a Year 4/5 composite class, the influence of the test across the school as a whole was evident in her decision to allow her Year 4 students to sit the test at the same time as her Year 5 students: 'I get my 4s to do it

as well' (Daphne, Year 4–5 Teacher, Central Mining School). The focus on persuasive texts across year levels – a dominant genre in writing tasks at the time of the
interview,[12] also reflects the systemic pressure in and on the state education
authority to ensure enhanced student outcomes on NAPLAN, and potential narrowing of the curriculum more broadly as a result (Klenowski & Carter, 2016;
Polesel et al., 2014).

This pressure on teachers in Years 2, 4 and 6, as well as Years 3, 5 and 7 was
also evident in a school in south-east Queensland. At this school, pressure on
teachers in the lead-in years was interpreted as not only a product of the relatively short time frame to prepare the students for the test in the year in which
they would sit the test, but also the result of pressure to try to secure funding
associated with enhanced outcomes on NAPLAN. Various forms of 'National
Partnership' funding, involving contributions of federal government funding to
the states, including to enhance schooling outcomes in more disadvantaged
communities, were felt at the level of the individual schools, not just systemically
(cf. Lingard & Sellar, 2013). This was seen as significant in a school serving a
struggling community in the more disadvantaged western regions of the south-
east Queensland conurbation:

> The National Partnerships meant such a huge, huge difference to the school.
> So, it's all about money. And it's all about getting the results to justify certain
> things. And I think that's a tremendous amount of pressure – not on the
> [Year] 3, 5 and 7 teachers, but on the 2, 4 and 6 teachers. Because I've taught
> Year 3 and – you've only got a short period of time; you can't teach the test;
> you can't do all the things that they say. So, there's a lot of pressure on the
> Year 2, 4 and 6 teachers to get the children NAPLAN-ready.
>
> *(Rachel, Year 1 Teacher, South West Urban School)*

In the effort to get students 'NAPLAN-ready', even at Prep, literacy and numeracy
practices had been rearticulated in relation to NAPLAN, and not just at this school:

> Yes, it's been pushed that from Prep, they're starting to learn about literacy
> and numeracy and that's the building blocks for NAPLAN. So, we're all in it
> together – preparing students for the NAPLAN test.
>
> *(Roberta, Year 2 Teacher, Central Mining School)*

Indeed, NAPLAN was construed as everyone's responsibility across school sites,
not simply teachers teaching in Years 3, 5 and 7. NAPLAN results were also
recognized by teachers as a reflection upon their teaching practice as well on their
school as a whole:

> I think some people feel like it's only the responsibility of the NAPLAN year
> levels, like the 3, 5 and 7, but it starts way before that. Like it's everybody's
> responsibility to get the kids up to scratch. And I think it's just, yeah, a

school-wide thing that you want to do well, I guess. Because it reflects on a school, and reflects on our capabilities as well as teachers.

(Stella, Year 1 Teacher, South West Urban School)

Such responses reflect the increasing datafication of primary and early years education (Bradbury & Roberts-Holmes, 2018), and the pressure upon teachers to ensure that results are perceived as adequate, given the publicness of the whole process (with results published online via the *MySchool* website). In this sense, the accountability agenda seemed oriented towards complying with performative demands for enhanced outcomes, rather than focusing strongly on accountability of teachers to one another's learning, and to their students' learning needs. A more performative accountability agenda, and financial benefit to the school for improved NAPLAN results, contributed to NAPLAN being construed as everyone's responsibility across the school, and the whole curriculum being influenced by the nature of the test.

This sense of cross-school and shared responsibility was also evident in relation to staff meetings in many schools, which served as vehicles to inform all teachers about NAPLAN results:

We don't do NAPLAN in Year 4 but there's still − often in staff meetings, we'll be looking at NAPLAN data and looking at particular concepts that kids have not got. And working out why is that, and where we can cover those concepts and help kids do better with that in the future.

(Noella, Year 4 Teacher, Southern School)

However, and reflecting the complexity that attends more performative practices, even as such insights reveal performative logics at play, the desire to address 'particular concepts that kids have not got' and 'help kids do better … in the future' may also be interpreted as reflective of more authentic accountabilities on the part of teachers to students' learning, as they sought to address those areas of need as indicated by NAPLAN. Even as the test could be deployed for more restrictive and reductive performance-oriented purposes, it had the potential to provide at least some insights into areas in which students struggled, and to be used for more formative assessment purposes.

Preparing and practising for the test

That NAPLAN governed teachers' practices was perhaps most clearly evident in explicit preparation practices associated with the test. As in other school settings in Australia (Polesel et al., 2014; Comber, 2012), these preparation practices occurred at a variety of levels, including preparing students to sit the test in current NAPLAN years, as well as preparing students to sit the test in the year immediately prior to the test. The use of assessment as a tool for governing schooling practices was evident in how teachers engaged with practice tests, to ensure students were prepared for NAPLAN. However, at the same time as providing clear evidence of more performative logics at play, this test preparation could also be construed as beneficial at times, particularly in relation to developing students' capacities in specific areas of the broader curriculum with which students seemed to struggle:

> With the practice test I might go, 'Oh dear, no one really knows about this type of punctuation'. Or, 'I've taught symmetry and a whole bunch of them got the symmetry question wrong'. I might have to go back and reteach that and everything like that.
>
> *(Wilma, Year 5 Teacher, Tropical City School)*

Test preparation was also construed as necessary to ensure students could prove what they actually knew, and were not confused by how the questions were presented, and the test executed:

> I guess as a teacher that's been doing it for a few years, I see the benefit in, I guess, test preparation, because I think there's a disconnection between what students know and how the test is actually conducted. I think it is beneficial for the students to have as much test practice that connects their knowledge to the type of questions.
>
> *(Daphne, Year 4–5 Teacher, Central Mining School)*

That there was a whole apparatus of techniques at play to address concerns about being adequately prepared for the test was evident in the way in which students sat pre-tests (old NAPLAN papers) to ascertain where there might be gaps in their understanding in the upcoming tests. These were also employed to inform other educational experiences, such as the make-up of reading groups, or to make decisions about particular curriculum areas in which students may be struggling:

> We do a pre-test and we try and work out where students could benefit from some help [and] what they seem to be doing fine with. [It] also helps with reading groups and things like that. So streamlining them in other ways, and really what we need to work on. So, it might be a concept in maths – the majority are having trouble with angles.
>
> *(Daphne, Year 4–5 Teacher, Central Mining School)*

Practice tests were an inherent part of a culture of ensuring improved achievement on NAPLAN, even as teachers expressed varied perspectives about the nature and influence of NAPLAN. This focus on test preparation is not surprising, given the Queensland government's take-up of the recommendations of the 'Masters' report (Masters, 2009) undertaken into why Queensland students did so poorly relative to students in other states (particularly the larger, leading states of New South Wales and Victoria). This report recommended that Queensland students needed increased exposure to test preparation activities to make them more familiar with the test. Reflecting how the push towards a standardized accountability agenda could exert influence, there was an acceptance of an array of already established practices associated with the test, and ensuring that students performed as well as they could on the test, even as it was simultaneously downplayed:

> I can honestly say there was no push from up above to say, 'You must do NAPLAN' – like there was no single push but just the inherent push of the idea around NAPLAN and what happens with NAPLAN data. So, it was understood that we had to implement testing, pre-testing – everything like that. Obviously, the principal has told us we had to do pre-tests and every-thing like that, but that was just – you do what you believe you have to do to achieve – the best results ... I have a NAPLAN guide book that I have there. There's a couple of pre-tests and obviously on the NAPLAN website there is a number of activities that you can use to prepare your students there. So that was things that we did with the cohort to get them up.
>
> *(Toby, Year 7 Teacher, Central Mining School)*

> So, when we do – we do that at the beginning of the year, as well, so that with NAPLAN, looking at where their weaker area is, it tends to – we might do external language lessons or extra maths – not so much extra but instead of doing your warm-up for C2C, as they ask you to, you do it in the areas where the kids are lacking for NAPLAN. So, it gives them a push along; so, hope-fully your NAPLAN results will improve, so you look like you're doing a good job.
>
> *(Krystal, Year 7 Teacher, South West Urban School)*

This focus on 'look[ing] like you're doing a good job' exemplifies how more performative logics exert influence, and how testing dominated teachers' practices in school settings in Australia (Comber 2011; 2012; Thompson & Harbaugh, 2013), even as teachers simultaneously sought to downplay the effects of NAPLAN. The taken-for-granted way in which NAPLAN had become a part of the tapestry of schooling – part of the 'inherent push of the idea around NAPLAN' also reveals a social imaginary (Taylor, 2004) increasingly influenced by standar-dized testing.

In a school serving a predominantly Indigenous community in north-western Queensland, these preparation practices exerted strong influence on teachers' practices, including those of more specialist teachers. This included a focus on test-literacy strategies, particularly for lower performing students:

> Last year I was specifically put on the class to help the teacher with NAPLAN support. So, I was specifically taking groups out, working with mainly numeracy; we have done some literacy as well around the persuasive writing task. Having said that, though, this year I'm working with the English teacher.

She does [Year] 7, 8, 9 English and I take a rotation, so we do a lot of rotations in the class, especially in high school. It seems to work because there's so much content to cover. So, I was responsible for the comprehension for Year 7 and 8, so we would actually have examples of NAPLAN-style comprehension tasks. So, reading through them, [we would teach] just the explicit strategies of how to attack a reading task – how to answer comprehension questions; what they're looking for; how they're trying to trick you – that sort of thing. Just those explicit strategies on how to actually complete the task, with a few of the lower students.

(Kimberly, Support Teacher – Literacy and Numeracy, North West Rural School)

In addition, one visiting literacy coach was allocated to specific year levels in the lead-up to NAPLAN testing in this school:

Yeah, she's [visiting literacy coach] in [regional city in north-western Queensland] and I actually knew her very randomly. My mother works at a school in Brisbane [capital of Queensland] and she had taught at the same school as my Mum, so it was kind of like there was a little bit of a link there that I had kind of knew about her. And then, amazingly, last year, she was given to the NAPLAN classes during the first two terms. And then for Term 3 and Term 4, she was given to the QCAT[13] classes and because I had a Grade 6 class, she'd come up every three weeks and see me.

(Felicity, Year 7–8 Teacher, North West Rural School)

In a school in central Queensland, the focus on NAPLAN preparation was even more evident, and particularly palpable in year levels directly affected by the test. The focus on keeping teachers accountable through NAPLAN results was explicitly rendered as responsible for encouraging drilling of students, and reducing the amount of time allocated to more substantive teaching practice:

My last class was in Grade 3 – so I saw the stress the teacher was under to get those results up. So always drilling the students … It takes away quality teaching time; it's more teacher accountability with the NAPLAN results. So, it's not only the students or the school but it's also the teacher [who is affected].

(Violet, Year 1 Teacher, Central Mining School)

This preparation for the test, similarly reflected in other research revealing the narrowing effects of NAPLAN on curriculum and teaching (e.g. Comber 2011; 2012; Thompson & Harbaugh, 2013), was potentially limiting for the teaching that could occur, and influenced the school as a whole, as well as individual teachers and students. Such responses intimate more 'constrained professionalism' on the part of teachers (Wills & Sandholtz, 2009), and reflect how testing had a particularly significant effect on teaching practice.

In some school sites, test preparation included more perfunctory tasks as part of this process, such as ensuring students knew how to shade in 'bubbles' for multiple-choice questions to ensure the computers used could accurately read students' responses:

> I even just helped out with filling out the form, this is how you do it, this is how you correctly shade in a bubble. Because it sounds easy, but it's not always done.
>
> *(Kimberly, Support Teacher – Literacy and Numeracy, North West Rural School)*

> Yeah, just so the kids know how to actually fill in the test. Because our kids, I guess, are still getting used to being formally tested so much. Just for them to know how to answer the questions correctly.
>
> *(Wilma, Year 5 Teacher, Tropical City School)*

There was a sense in which schools were becoming increasingly aware of test preparation strategies and deploying these strategies as part of their ongoing practice. However, this was also increasingly challenging, as other schools employed similar strategies:

> Yes, it's a response to always trying to improve the results. Trying to improve our results compared to 'like-schools'. Trying to improve our results nationally, because it's hard. We did improve but it's hard to keep on improving. And the other schools – some of the other schools are sort of employing all the strategies now. So, we were doing really well compared to all schools, but now we're similar to 'like' schools.
>
> *(Bonnie, Learning Support Teacher, South West Urban School)*

Such a response reflects how the test data served as a catalyst for strategic responses, not only at the system level (Lingard & Sellar, 2013), but also the school level. The way teachers engaged with the test in different parts of Queensland also reflects that even as there was attention to how the test was used to identify areas in which students required further attention and assistance, this always seemed to be within the parameters of the test itself; this is the essence of the quandary of quantification – possibilities within limitations – that attends such testing regimes more broadly (Hardy, 2019). This strategizing included teachers sitting the test themselves to better prepare them to teach it to their students:

> We got together as a grade, or year, and then we … looked at each other's [students' results] and what could have happened and what could be done to improve them for the following year … Some teachers were talking about a whole staff activity, having to look at examples of NAPLAN and the tests …

Sort of doing the tests themselves as teachers, just to get a sense about what's expected. And I think that's a good idea.

(Adrienne, Year 5 Teacher, Southern School)

However, and reflecting the more educative potential of the tests, teachers also recognized the limitations of test-centric practices, and also used the test results to help identify areas in their teaching that needed additional attention. This included the need to focus increased attention on how students sought to justify their responses, such as problem solving in mathematics, and other 'common areas' of difficulty, which needed increased attention:

I think there's good things and bad things about it. I know when I had my Grade 5s, we did NAPLAN practice tests to see how they would cope with the questions, the format of the questions and the type of questions. A lot of the things that came out from that was the justify and the reasoning and stuff. Also, the multi-step problem solving in maths – they were low in that. And so, what we did was we – we put that data into a spreadsheet and then we looked at the questions that most of the class got wrong, and what types of questions they were. And then we targeted that in our maths teaching.

(Josephine, Year 6 Teacher, Central Mining School)

When we get the results back there might be one or two. For example, last year we had to look at – we looked at what the test was; we looked at the data; and then we had to do the test ourselves, just to see where those mistakes are. So that we could then determine what were the common errors, and what were the common areas that needed to be focused on.

(Suzie, Year 1 Teacher, Southern School)

For another teacher in the north-western area of the state, the test results were part of a broader tapestry of data, including standardized reading-level data, that helped inform teachers' teaching, and that sought to challenge teachers about the nature of what they believed their students were capable of achieving:

I don't think at all that your teaching is driven for the test; I think it actually encourages you to challenge the teaching of what you're doing or the level of teaching that you're striving for your kids. You're not dumbing down stuff, and I think this is where the government has gone too. Like, with your Prep [students], the reading is incredible; you talk about children being sponges – we've got kids saying words in Prep and Year 1s who are reading up past the level 10^{14} which is impressive! So, it shows that the children do have what it takes.

(Polly, Year 3 Teacher, Western City School)

Similarly, for a teacher on the other side of the state, while her school was very 'data driven', and there was a sense that there was a focus on 'that number', there also appeared to be an over-riding concern about whether students were actually learning:

> In my reading group, I sat them down and I said to the kids – because you don't want to hide things from them as well – I tell them what levels they were on after my data collection last week. And we talked about what levels that I've got them down to achieve next term, and if they think they can get there, and how we're going to get to that level. And they're only Preppies, but you can still talk to them about that sort of stuff. And yeah, so data, yeah, we're very data driven. Even though, at the end of the day, you're not going to get all kids to that number, we know that we want to get kids succeeding; that's our main goal. Is every child succeeding? Is every child moving? And if they're not moving, what are we doing to help them? What aren't we doing to help them move? So, it's a tough job.
>
> *(Trixie, Prep Teacher, Northern Mountains School)*

In this way, even as teachers were simultaneously influenced by NAPLAN, and the collection of other forms of numeric data for more performative purposes – a logic of enumeration (Hardy, 2015) – teachers exhibited a sense of accountability for more educative purposes to their students in the way they sought to address those areas in which students performed most poorly, or how the test results, and associated data, could serve as a vehicle for ensuring maintenance of high standards. A more genuine, 'authentic' approach to the use and analysis of test data, and associated data, was simultaneously evident.

However, even as NAPLAN and associated data had the potential to influence student and teacher learning for enhanced understanding of particular concepts, and insights into the diversity of student learning, this was also seen as contributing towards preparation for the subsequent NAPLAN test for these students. This was evident in how one principal described how teachers engaged with data at his school:

> We haven't used it [NAPLAN and associated data] very effectively this year so far because we haven't had a literacy coach. But we will next term. However, we use that, I guess, to inform the teachers' planning and to, I guess, try and give the teachers an understanding about the diverse needs of their students. So that's mainly the NAPLAN stuff and in preparation for the following NAPLAN.
>
> *(Rainer, Principal, North West Rural School)*

At the same time, and reflecting how test preparation activities could also be resisted for their own sake, such practices were criticized by some teachers, who recognized them as a resource-intensive undertaking that could take time away from more substantive educational practices. However, again, such interrogation occurred alongside practices of 'preparing [students] properly' in schools to perform as best they could on NAPLAN, including ensuring additional aides were available in NAPLAN years to increase the amount of time available for more intensive engagement with students:

> I can remember when they first talked about NAPLAN, it was 'We will not teach to the test' Huh![15] ... Even this year we're starting – in Year 4, in fourth term, we're starting to bring in persuasive text! Because we know that persuasive text is what they're going to cover next time around ... This year, they went for narrative writing and swapped it to persuasive text. And last year we had a lot of money and that was put into getting people ready to do that ... Aide time. Because to be able to prepare them properly, you really need to have a smaller ratio of adult to child. To have a whole teacher with a whole class at different range of levels, just won't get it through.
>
> *(Enid, Year 2 Teacher, South East Urban School)*

Such responses reflect more active processes of the datafication of primary and early years education, and efforts to ensure enhanced outcomes on all forms of data more broadly (Bradbury and Roberts-Holmes, 2018). In some schools, this deployment of intensive resourcing as part of the strategizing surrounding NAPLAN involved the provision of significant additional personnel (usually teacher aides) in the lead-up to the test, and created some dissonance when these personnel were reallocated to other duties at the conclusion of the test:

> If you'd have asked me that last year [influence of NAPLAN], I would have said, 'Yes a heck of a lot' because they really pushed it. This year it tended to break down a little – a lot of work [support] given to us by the teacher aides and the literacy coach for those first six months. Once NAPLAN finished, I lost everybody, and I'll have one teacher aide, say throughout the whole of the week! Whereas beforehand, I'd have one nearly every day. So, it's sort of inundated, and then that was it! Because the QCATs then came in and they [teacher aides] moved to the QCATs and worked with the other classes ... So that's a hard shock to sort of relate and work around, when you knew you had three groups and you had a person in this group, a person in that group, and yourself. To go back to yourself, with two groups who had to work by themselves [was difficult].
>
> *(Andrew, Year 7 Teacher, South East Urban School)*

While concerns about losing teacher aides and the literacy coach could be construed as reflective of more authentic concerns about providing more intensive time with individual groups of students, the way in which such concerns were construed in relation to NAPLAN also reveals how more performative logics simultaneously governed teachers' practices. As in other settings, even as more educational prerogatives guided teachers' engagement with students, more performative practices associated with NAPLAN loomed large (Comber 2011; 2012).

The governing of teachers' practices was also evident in the way in which teachers were involved in marker training for NAPLAN as another strategy to enhance students' results:

> There was a bit of a push … teaching that genre and how to write that. And then we were trained by a NAPLAN marker on how to mark it. So I've got that knowledge now − that if I was in a NAPLAN class, at least I would know what a NAPLAN marker is looking for. Whereas if you're going in blind, you don't have − this is just writing. And so, then I was able to give really good feedback to my children and their parents.
>
> *(Rona, Full-time Relief Teacher, Central Mining School).*

That this teacher believed NAPLAN marking was a valuable practice reveals how pervasive the focus on testing had become, and how it was construed as a normalized part of teachers' practices in schools − particularly those with the lowest results. It was seen as providing valuable feedback to both students and parents about the test.

However, this focus on preparing for NAPLAN was also interrogated more proactively by teachers in the way they construed it as problematic, and as not providing an accurate reflection of students' actual capacities. Reflecting earlier emphases on test-preparation practices (Masters, 2009), more superficial test preparation practices were also criticized as not contributing to substantive student learning:

> I'm sort of of the mind that NAPLAN shows kids how to colour in a bubble! So I don't use a lot of that personally; that's just me. I know that there was a boy who has done exceptionally well in previous years because he can shade in a bubble! He is severely intellectually impaired and has some of the best NAPLAN data; so that's what NAPLAN teaches me! It's a colouring-in competition! There is some value to it, I guess, in the writing section, but in regards to the [multiple choice] comprehending section, I see no value at all because it doesn't accurately give a representation of any kids, I don't think.
>
> *(Felicity, Year 7−8 Teacher, North West Rural School)*

> It's really hard to gather children's trust in one term and say, 'Here! do this bloody test!' Because it's all the focus on, 'Yeah you can do it! Keep going! Have another go!' All that talk of just moving them on. I mean I'm not a big fan of NAPLAN. A perfect example − a child I had last year. She was illiterate; couldn't read a level 1[16] text. She completed the NAPLAN test with the reading book on the floor − didn't even open it. And got a 4 [on a 10 point scale]! Because the skills we taught her was to colour in buttons!
>
> *(Lindsay, Numeracy Coach, Head of Curriculum, South West Urban School)*

Consequently, even as there was such a strong focus on NAPLAN, the extent to which the test generated sound data, reflective of students' actual learning, was contested. Teachers' interrogations of their students' responses to the test indicated how their work was governed – a form of metagovernance (Rhodes, 2012) – by NAPLAN, but they also sought to promote more educational emphases and foci in the way they construed the test as inaccurate, particularly in relation to those students who struggled the most. Such a more critical response reflects a concern about the authenticity of the test vis-à-vis students' actual learnings, and a sense of enhanced accountability for more substantive, 'authentic' purposes.

Teaching to the test

At times, the governance of schooling practices through standardized testing was even more overtly evident in specific pressures on teachers to engage in practices of teaching directly to NAPLAN. When prompted about whether much time was spent preparing for NAPLAN at a rural school in the central regions of the state, the head of curriculum was explicit that teachers taught to the test, and this was achieved through the new curriculum, C2C, via a focus on maths and English:

> Yes, all Term 1, Year 3, 5, 7 teachers teach to the test …Yes NAPLAN, we teach to the test – so Term 1 basically used to be [teaching to the test]. Now, this year, because it's C2C, they've had to follow C2C, but with a big NAPLAN push for maths and English.
>
> *(Beatrice, Head of Curriculum/Librarian, Central Mining School)*

However, teachers also expressed a more nuanced understanding of this work, even as the focus on standardized testing clearly exerted considerable influence on schools. Teachers critiqued and queried – interrogated – the extent to which NAPLAN was an accurate representation of students' understanding, even as they also identified questions in which students didn't do well and sought to try to enhance students' understandings on the basis of their responses to those questions:

> We do a lot of analysis of NAPLAN. Do I think it's useful for me in the classroom; sometimes, sometimes not. I think that I don't know whether NAPLAN's a really accurate representation of what the kids know and what they don't know. But I think that we look at them to see where our kids are at, at the beginning of the year, and set targets for them, so we can try and extend them and expand them. We look at what questions, as a cohort they got wrong, so that we look at what they're lacking. If there's any in maths; if there's any particular area; if there's any particular area in language – maybe grammar, punctuation, spelling; in reading, what types of reading questions they're getting wrong, which is normally inferential.
>
> *(Krystal, Year 7 Teacher, South West Urban School)*

The focus on inferential reading skills highlighted by this teacher was a common theme across the school sites, and NAPLAN was construed as a useful vehicle for identifying that such skills were lacking amongst students, and that this was an area for further attention and development on the part of teachers:

> Our kids really – they decode really well; and they can find the facts, important facts. But they don't really understand the effect of text or, like as in the mood, and what type of – what the writer is feeling – or the messages. They actually, if you ask them what the message of the text will be, so the inference, they'll tell you what the storyline is. 'But that's the story? That's what's written down in the words, but why did she write the story?' Or, 'Why did he write the story? What was the message behind it?' And they struggle with that. But that's because they don't fully understand the words that they're reading. And NAPLAN gives you that totally – I mean that's one thing that stands out in the NAPLAN.
>
> *(Krystal, Year 7 Teacher, South West Urban School)*

While such elaborations on students' difficulties in light of NAPLAN results reflect how teachers' practices were clearly governed by such testing processes, such responses also reveal how local practices of engagement with data on the part of teachers can occur, and help frame organizational understandings of practice (Little, 2012). Such responses reflect a sense of accountability of teachers to their students in relation to the educative aims of schooling – more 'authentic' accountabilities.

The governance of educators' practices was also evident in the sense in which considerable time was spent on NAPLAN, with much focus on not only specific domains where students struggled, but representations of student learning in the form of various kinds of data, graphs and charts:

> NAPLAN is quite focussed on that sort of language features and I think we definitely touch on that quite a bit … But I think that we do spend a lot of staff meetings … focussed on data and analysing data and making more data … Yes we've got lots of charts and graphs … [showing] how we're performing this year and last year and where we want to go [with] goals and things.
>
> *(Bonnie, Learning Support Teacher, South West Urban School)*

This focus on 'lots of charts and graphs' also reveals how educators' practices were dominated by constructions of teachers' work as a datafied policy space, how students themselves were reconstituted as data, and of how education can be governed through data, thereby shifting the focus from more traditional, external forms of regulation of educational practices to more self-regulatory processes (Ozga, 2009). Whilst giving the appearance of more devolved responsibility, such datafication processes enable increasingly centralized steering of educational processes (cf. Lawn, 2013).

This focus on data was the case across school sites, including in a more suburban middle-class school setting where there appeared, ostensibly, to be less concern/

focus on NAPLAN. However, even in this setting, teachers taught students to engage strategically with the test, determining from the outset how students would need to respond to questions:

> We're driven by the data, and that our goal is to get these kids to strive for higher results, and what we're going to do to help that. We had one big meeting, and we sat down and we went through previous NAPLAN tests. And worked out what the challenges for the kids would be – actually even opening the test and splitting up questions. And [identifying] what they would need to know to complete each answer.
>
> *(Eugenie, Year 1 Teacher, Southern School)*

Even as teachers railed against doing so, they agreed they taught to the test in some fashion. That the test governed teachers' practices was evident in how teachers were anxious about what was in the test, and sought to provide students with as many opportunities as possible to engage with material likely to be in the test, even as this was difficult:

> Yeah, I don't know; you learn not to stress out about it. It is hard because you definitely do teach to the test, unfortunately. But at the same time, I sometimes think that with NAPLAN, because it's such a curve ball – you never know what you're going to get – so, you do teach broadly; it's very broad. But at the same time, you miss bits and you think, 'Oh, I wish I had more time to go back and get their heads around that'. But we're trying to push through and just cover everything that could be on the test, so that they don't stress out and go, 'Oh my God!' And, yeah, you've got to teach them how to sit a test, especially at this age because it's their first one.
>
> *(Prunella, Year 3 Teacher, Central Mining School)*

Such responses reflect how practices of teaching to the test have come to characterize NAPLAN, particularly in lower-socio-economic schools (Comber 2012; Polesel et al., 2014). Interestingly, while this school was located in a relatively wealthy mining region, the comparatively low levels of cultural capital (Bourdieu, 1990) vis-à-vis testing practices and processes meant that concerns about students' test results were a dominant logic in this school context, and governed how teachers made sense of their students' practices.

In a more homogenously middle-class environment in the heavily urbanised south-east corner of the state, there was a sense in which teachers did not feel they were teaching to the test, and that such practices were detrimental to students' learning:

> No not this year, not this year; it's definitely not a teach-to-the-test school. There was no pressure put on us as teachers for that purpose. We were just

told to go ahead with the C2C and work our way through that, which was nice really. Because you don't want to be teaching to the test. The kids aren't really learning that way.

(Barry, Year 7 Teacher, Southern School)

Well we use the NAPLAN data, and that's to kind of inform our teaching in a way, like where the gaps have been in maths, reading and grammar ... what we are doing well, and what we need to work on, and what the students need ... No, not at all; it's [not seen as a concern] – yeah it's just you know, I think [principal] says it's a one-off test, and we shouldn't be teaching to a test. And we don't, which is good.

(Sophie, Year 3 Teacher, Southern School)

In this sense, these teachers' experiences seemed to differ from those in other contexts (and some of their colleagues in this school). While some teachers experienced significant pressure, and notions of 'being burnt at the high stakes' of standardized assessment (Kohn, 2000, p. 315), this was a varied experience for teachers, and reflected multiple factors, including the local contingencies of the circumstances in which they worked.

Interestingly, even as it was not construed as influencing teaching practice as much as other sites, NAPLAN data were still employed to inform teaching practices in this school. In comparing her previous school in suburban Brisbane, another teacher described NAPLAN as part of a broad raft of data that were a priority at this school:

They are actually way more data driven than – well, not driven, but their data trail is very clearly defined here. Yeah, that's good; it's well organized ... I just think it's a priority for them and it's easy for people to pick up where the students are at. And their portfolios are really comprehensive. In terms of – you're teaching James; you pick it [portfolio] up; you have a look; everything in his history is in there; it's easy to see. Of course, with the Oneschool[17] now, we've got all that in the system too that you've got access to. So, it's definitely got better as we've travelled along.

(Eveline, Year 1 Teacher, Southern School).

This focus on data more broadly also reveals how data serve as a significant means of governing schooling – particularly numeric renderings of data, with their capacity to construct particular statistical insights about social practices (Desrosières, 1998; Hacking, 1990; Rose, 1999).

However, teachers also sought to not simply teach to the test, but to use the test to inform their teaching practice. This also related to long-term planning by teachers. NAPLAN was seen as a useful vehicle to inform teachers' teaching of these students in subsequent years.

I mean they do collect, I mean it's a transition year so definitely, all your NAPLAN data. And we did have to look at that. As a Year 4 teacher, you certainly look at the Year 3 NAPLAN data. And look at how it can inform your teaching with those particular children.

(Hilda, Year 4 Teacher, Southern School)

Efforts to utilize data beyond simply teaching to the test were evident in how teachers drew on NAPLAN results from previous years to inform teaching practices in subsequent years:

We sort of look at the NAPLAN results from previous years from Year 5s. We have a look, in our team meetings and staff meetings, we have a look at that NAPLAN data to see what questions, perhaps, these kids need more help on. They're doing poorly on this part or they're doing really well in this part of it. So, we use those NAPLAN results to help with our teaching and delivery.

(Paige, Year 6 Teacher, Southern School)

This focus on 'us[ing] those NAPLAN results to help with our teaching and delivery' gesture towards the educative potential and uses of the test, even as more performative logics and foci were ever-present. While more performative accountabilities were clearly in evidence, more learning-oriented, authentic accountabilities of teachers to their students' learning were simultaneously apparent.

Also, while there was a very strong focus on data in general, there was also critique about the extent to which the collection of data was productive in relation to the learning needs of students. For example, while principals' work has been significantly reconstituted by NAPLAN as a form of standardized testing (Comber & Cormack, 2012), collection of data for its own sake in one school by the previous principal was critiqued, and the extent to which such data were construed as beneficial in terms of student learning was considered a moot point:

The previous principal was very data driven – very, very data driven. I've found over here [Queensland][18] it is very data driven. They collect and collect and collect and collect. And a lot of ... there seems to be assessment and figures and facts – and obviously evidence. And that's fine. Collecting evidence is good and fine. [But] I know that a lot of the staff are quite concerned over the fact that they seem to be collecting data and evidence all the time for no good reason. He[19] certainly did have good reason! Perhaps some of it was for himself and not necessarily feedback to the teachers all the time. But to collect data – it's for a purpose. It's to inform your future teaching. What am I going to do with the test? What happens when Johnny's got the score of whatever? What am I now going to do? He's got this question, this question and this question wrong, so I need to focus on those things. This tells me something. It's not just, 'Here's a piece of data. And I'm putting it into the computer and putting it into the place I'm supposed to be.' It's actually for a reason.

And I don't think the teachers understood that. So, they're getting around to understanding why we want to collect bits and pieces. And it's to help them to help the children in the end.

(*Bianca, Literacy Coach/Learning Support, Central Mining School*)

This emphasis on collecting data for educational/learning purposes reflects a much more 'authentic' sense of self – of generating and collecting data not for its own sake but to enhance teaching practices – for educative purposes. While datafication processes have increasingly characterized primary and early years education (Bradbury & Roberts-Holmes, 2018), and may hollow out associated schooling practices (Mehta, 2013), this literacy coach's interrogation of the nature and value of data collection processes reveals a much more nuanced and educationally oriented conception of schooling. She, like teachers who expressed concern about teaching to the test at other schools, exhibited a more educative focus – more authentic accountability – to the learning needs of her students. This was not straight-forward work, as she sought to work with teachers to strengthen a more educative disposition as an alternative to that instituted through more performative accountabilities.

Conclusion: Challenging performative assessment accountabilities

This chapter reveals that alongside the challenges of performativity, and accountability for the sake of accountability in relation to the use of tests and test scores, teachers can act as agents of transformation, and draw on developed senses of professional judgement to do so. Even as the data reveal clear evidence of the substantive, and often problematic effects of more standardized approaches to assessing students' practice, there was also evidence of alternative practices of assessment beyond more external policy and political concerns and measures. Such alternative practices reflect the nature and influence of more learning-centred applications and understandings, oriented to students' growth and development. This focus on student learning, and how to enhance such learning, rather than test results and scores, reflects a more 'authentic' sense of purpose in relation to schooling. Those instances in which school administrators and teachers promulgated more educative purposes reflect more educative logics, and a sense of more authentic accountabilities of educators to their students.

More deliberative, educationally oriented responses resonate with advocacy for various forms of 'intelligent accountability' (Crooks, 2003). For O'Neill (2002), such intelligent accountability practices are construed in terms of: trust amongst the primary participants in education (teachers, students, parents, school leaders); a strong sense of professional responsibility for the work in which they are engaged; sustained engagement with educational challenges to help instantiate substantive, long-term reform; a focus on multiple forms of evidence, rather than single indicators or particular groupings of indicators (often associated with literacy, numeracy and perhaps science) that do not reflect the broader range of actual educational outcomes; active participation in all aspects of the assessment process to ensure the provision of substantive, meaningful feedback; and close scrutiny of the outcome of the accountability processes to cultivate enhanced engagement amongst participants. Such an approach requires an 'intelligent' approach to accountability that necessarily recognizes the limitations of more standardized measures of student attainment, particularly those associated with standardized tests, and often characterized by numbers generated through such tests. While such numbers have the potential to be useful when used in conjunction with context-relevant understandings of students' learning, heavy reliance upon standardized ways of accounting for educational outcomes cannot support relevant insights into the nature of the actual education processes to which they purportedly pertain:

> Numbers are useful when we have a unit of account: we can count pupils, and we can count the money in school budgets. Many things that are important for education cannot be counted, or added, or ranked because there is no genuine unit of account.
>
> *(O'Neill, 2013, p. 14)*

Such measures are particularly problematic when they are reduced to a single set of figures, such as NAPLAN results, and when used to encourage various kinds of perverse incentives, as evident in some of the performative practices described in this chapter. This included allocating undue attention to particular students deemed most likely to improve schools' overall tests scores, or teaching directly to the test. In contrast, more authentic approaches to accountability entail recognizing the importance of professional judgement in context, and that purportedly more 'objective' measures of attainment are unable to capture the nature of actual educational practice. More authentic approaches were clearly evident in the way in which teachers expressed concern about the nature and effects of performative assessment practices in Queensland. The expression of such concerns – interrogation of more performative practices – reveals a respect for the substantive, daily work of curriculum development, teaching and assessment in context. Such an approach advocates transparency in ways that are internally coherent to the educational enterprise itself, and not in abstracted ways that bear little resemblance to the educational function of schooling.

Notes

1 The subtitle to Desrosières' volume *The politics of large numbers* (Harvard University Press).
2 By late 2018, a decade after the inaugural test was introduced in 2008, Queensland had been recognized as one of the 'most improved' states in its performance on NAPLAN, with improvements in 16 out of 20 test areas over that period.
3 'Like schools' comprise 60 designated schools deemed to have a similar demographic profile in relation to 'socio-educational advantage', an index incorporating such factors as parents' occupation, parents' education, geographical location and proportion of

Indigenous students. The *MySchool* website on which NAPLAN results were displayed included schools' overall results (in comparison with the national average), as well as their relative results (in comparison with these 'similar' or 'like' schools).

4 Expressed with sarcasm and some exasperation.

5 A reference to red wine in a 'bottle shop' – a colloquial term for a liquor dispensary in the Australian context.

6 In the Queensland context, the Director of each of the seven educational regions is responsible for schooling and vocational education, and is assisted by several Assistant Regional Directors (ARDs) who are each responsible for specific schools in that region.

7 Further empirical research at a regional and whole-system level is necessary to better substantiate this claim.

8 A reference to test preparation practices to ensure students filled out multiple choice questions properly.

9 Even though the *MySchool* website does not provide schools listed in league tables, such tables can be manually crafted from the data displayed on the site.

10 In 2008, all students sitting NAPLAN in Queensland were approximately 12 months younger than students at the same year level in other states. An additional year (Prep) was introduced in 2007, and became mandatory in 2017. The requirement that students in Year One be at least six months older than previously, in conjunction with the introduction of Prep, effectively increased the age of primary school students by approximately 12 months, in line with other Australian states.

11 At this school, students performing in the mid-range of NAPLAN results were referred to as 'belly students' – students in 'the middle' of the NAPLAN distribution.

12 The NAPLAN writing task oscillated between persuasive texts, and narrative texts. In the year of this particular interview, persuasive text types were a dominant genre in the test.

13 QCAT – Queensland Comparable Assessment Tasks. QCATs were annual, standards-based assessment tasks in English, maths and science, undertaken in Years 4, 6 and 9, and designed to ensure comparability in relation to standards across the state. They were also used to enable moderation of teacher assessment across the state.

14 A reference to the 'PM Benchmark' reading series; at the time of the data collection, Prep students were approximately 5 years of age, and a level 9 was seen as approximating a reading age between 5 and 6 years.

15 Expressed in an exasperated, disbelieving tone.

16 A Level 1 text, as part of the benchmarked reading series from Level 0 (Prep) to Level 30 (Year 6) used as a standardized measure of students' fluency and comprehension, reflected a very low level of reading fluency and comprehension, relative to this student's age.

17 OneSchool, a data management system supported by Education Queensland, was designed to act as a centralized data repository for all aspects of students' schooling, including attendance, behaviour, ongoing academic performance and exiting credentials. NAPLAN data were also uploaded to this portal.

18 This teacher had moved relatively recently from a mining community in Western Australia to the mining community in Queensland which this school served.

19 This comment reflected the previous principal's concerns about relatively low results in the school, particularly as indicated by NAPLAN. The subsequent reference to 'collecting it for himself' could also relate to pressure to collect data in the school because of pressure to do so from the Assistant Regional Director. (This was a common claim made by principals, as indicated elsewhere in this volume.)

References

Anagnostopoulos, D., Rutledge, S., & Jacobsen, R. (2013). Introduction: Mapping the information infrastructure of accountability. In D. Anagnostopoulos, S. Rutledge & R.

Jacobsen,(Eds), *The infrastructure of accountability: Data use and the transformation of American education*. Cambridge, MA: Harvard Education Press.

Andrews, P.*et al.* (2014). OECD and PISA tests are damaging education worldwide – academics, *The Guardian*, 6 May. Downloaded 25 June 2016 from: http://www.theguardian.com/education/2014/may/06/oecd-pisa-tests-damaging-education-adademics

Ball, S. (2013). *Foucault, power and education*. London: Routledge.

Ball, S., Maguire, M., Braun, A., & Hoskins, K. (2011) Policy subjects and policy actors in schools: Some necessary but insufficient analyses. *Discourse: Studies in the Cultural Politics of Education*, 32(4), 611–624.

Beck, U. (1992). *Risk society: Towards a new modernity*. London: Sage.

Bernstein, B. (1971) On the classification and framing of educational knowledge. In M.F.D. Young (Ed.), *Knowledge and control: New directions for the sociology of education* (pp. 47–69). London: Collier-Macmillan.

Biesta, G. (2004). Education, accountability and the ethical demand: Can the democratic potential of accountability be regained? *Educational Theory*, 54(3), 233–250.

Biesta, G. (2020). *Educational research: An unorthodox introduction*. London: Bloomsbury.

Booher-Jennings, J. (2005). Below the bubble: 'Educational triage' and the Texas accountability system. *American Educational Research Journal*, 42(2), 231–268.

Bourdieu, P. (1990). *In other words: Essays towards a reflexive sociology*. Stanford, CA: Stanford University Press.

Bovens, M., Goodin, R., & Schillemans, T. (2014). *The Oxford handbook of public accountability*. Oxford: Oxford University Press.

Bradbury, A., & Roberts-Holmes, G. (2018). *The datafication of primary and early years education: Playing with numbers*. London: Routledge.

Care, E., & Beswick, B. (2016). Comparison and countries. In D. Wyse, L. Hayward & J. Pandya (Eds), *The Sage handbook of curriculum, pedagogy and assessment* (pp. 928–945). Los Angeles, CA: Sage.

Comber, B. (2011). Changing literacies, changing populations, changing places – English teachers' work in an age of rampant standardisation. *English Teaching: Practice & Technique*, 10(4), 5–22.

Comber, B. (2012). Mandated literacy assessment and the reorganisation of teachers' work: Federal policy, local effects. *Critical Studies in Education*, 53(2), 119–136.

Comber, B., & Cormack, P. (2012). Education policy mediation: Principals' work with mandated literacy assessment. *English in Australia*, 46(2), 77–86.

Crooks, T. (2003). *Some criteria for intelligent accountability applied to accountability in New Zealand*. Paper presented at the annual conference of the American Educational Research Association, Chicago, Illinois,22 April. Downloaded 20 June 2016 from: http://www.fairtest.org/some-criteria-intelligent-accountability-applied-a.

Cukier, K., & Mayer-Schönberger, V. (2013). *Big data: A revolution that will transform how we live, work and think*. London: John Murray.

Desrosières, A. (1998). *The politics of large numbers: A history of statistical reasoning*. Cambridge, MA: Harvard.

Foucault, M. (2007). *Security, territory, population: Lectures at the Collége de France*. Basingstoke: Palgrave Macmillan.

Gardner, J., & Galanouli, D. (2016). Teachers' perceptions of assessment. In D. Wyse, L. Hayward & J. Pandya (Eds), *The Sage handbook of curriculum, pedagogy and assessment* (pp. 710–724). Los Angeles, CA: Sage.

Gillborn, D., & Youdell, D. (2000). *Rationing education: Policy, practice, reform and equity*. Buckingham: Open University Press.

Hacking, I. (1982). Biopower and the avalanche of printed numbers. *Humanities in Society*, 5, 279–295.

Hacking, I. (1986). Making up people. In T. Heller *et al*. (Eds), *Reconstructing individualism* (pp. 222–236). Stanford: Stanford University Press.

Hacking, I. (1990). *The taming of chance*. Cambridge: Cambridge University Press.

Hardy, I. (2014). A logic of appropriation: Enacting national testing in Australia. *Journal of Education Policy*, 29(1), 1–18.

Hardy, I. (2015). A logic of enumeration: The nature and effects of national literacy and numeracy testing in Australia. *Journal of Education Policy*, 30(3), 335–362.

Hardy, I. (2019). The quandary of quantification: Data, numbers and teachers' learning. *Journal of Education Policy*. doi:10.1080/02680939.2019.1672211

Henig, J. (2012). The politics of data use. *Teachers College Record*, 114(11), 1–32.

Holloway, J. (2019). Teacher evaluation as an onto-epistemic framework. *British Journal of Sociology of Education*, 40(2), 174–189.

Hursh, D. (2008). *High stakes testing and the decline of teaching and learning: The real crisis in education*. Lanham, MD: Rowman & Littlefield.

Hursh, D. (2016). *The end of public schools: The corporate reform agenda to privatize education*. New York: Routledge.

Kemmis, S., Wilkinson, J., Edwards-Groves, C., Hardy, I., Grootenboer, P., and Bristol, L. (2014). *Changing practices, changing education*. Singapore: Springer.

Kickert, W. (1995). Steering at a distance: A new paradigm of public governance in Dutch higher education. *Governance: An International Journal of Policy and Administration*, 8(1), 135–157.

Klenowski, V., & Carter, M. (2016) Curriculum reform in testing and accountability contexts. In D. Wyse, L. Hayward & J. Pandya (Eds), *The Sage handbook of curriculum, pedagogy and assessment* (pp. 790–804). Los Angeles, CA: Sage.

Kohn, A. (2000). Burnt at the high stakes. *Journal of Teacher Education*, 51(4), 315–327.

Lawn, M. (2013). A systemless system: Designing the disarticulation of English state education. *European Educational Research Journal*, 12(2), 231–241.

Lingard, B., Creagh, S., & Vass, G. (2012). Education policy as numbers: Data categories and two Australian cases of misrecognition. *Journal of Education Policy*, 27(3), 315–333.

Lingard, B., Martino, W., Rezai-Rashti, G., & Sellar, S. (2016) *Globalizing educational accountabilities*. New York: Routledge.

Lingard, B., & Sellar, S. (2013). 'Catalyst data': Perverse systemic effects of audit and accountability in Australian schooling. *Journal of Education Policy*, 28(5), 634–656.

Lingard, B., Thompson, G., & Sellar, S. (2016). National testing from an Australian perspective. In B. Lingard, G. Thompson & S. Sellar (Eds), *National testing in schools: An Australian assessment* (pp. 1–17). London: Routledge.

Little, J.W. (2012). Understanding data use practice among teachers: The contribution of micro-process studies. *American Journal of Education*, 118, 143–166.

Masters, G. (2009). *The shared challenge: Improving literacy, numeracy and science learning in Queensland primary schools*. Melbourne: ACER.

Mehta, J. (2013). The penetration of technocratic logic into the educational field: Rationalizing schooling from the progressives to the present. *Teachers College Record*, 115(5), 1–36.

Nichols, S., & Berliner, D. (2007). *Collateral damage: How high-stakes testing corrupts America's schools*. Cambridge, MA: Harvard Education Books.

Nóvoa, A., & Yariv-Mashal, T. (2003). Comparative research in education: A mode of governance or a historical journey? *Comparative Education*, 39(4), 423–438.

O'Neill, O. (2002). *A question of trust: The BBC Reith Lectures, 2002*. Cambridge: Cambridge University Press.

O'Neill, O. (2013). Intelligent accountability in education. *Oxford Review of Education*, 39, 4–16.

Ozga, J. (2009). Governing education through data in England: From regulation to self-evaluation. *Journal of Education Policy*, 24(2), 149–162.

Ozga, J., Segerholm, C., & Simola, H. (2011). The governance turn. In J. Ozga, P. Dahler-Larsen, C. Segerholm & H. Simola, *Fabricating quality in education* (pp. 85–95). London: Routledge.

Pederson, P. (2007). What is measured is treasured: The impact of the No Child Left Behind Act on non-assessed subjects. *The Clearing House: A Journal of Educational Strategies, Issues and Ideas*, 80, 287–291.

Polesel, J., Rice, S., & Dulfer, N. (2014). The impact of high-stakes testing on curriculum and pedagogy: A teacher perspective from Australia. *Journal of Education Policy*, 29(5), 640–657.

Rhodes, R. (2012). Waves of governance. In D. Levi-Faur (Ed.), *The Oxford handbook of governance* (pp. 33–44). Oxford: Oxford University Press.

Rizvi, F., & Lingard, B. (2010). *Globalizing education policy*. London: Routledge.

Rose, N. (1999). *Powers of freedom: Reframing political thought*. Cambridge: Cambridge University Press.

Schatzki, T. (2002). *The site of the social: A philosophical account of the constitution of social life and change*. University Park, PA: The Pennsylvania State University Press.

Schleicher, A. (2016). International assessments of student learning outcomes. In D. Wyse, L. Hayward & J. Pandya (Eds), *The Sage handbook of curriculum, pedagogy and assessment* (pp. 913–927). Los Angeles, CA: Sage.

Slavin, R. E. (2008). Perspectives on evidence-based research in education: What works? Issues in synthesizing educational program evaluations. *Educational Researcher*, 37(1), 5–14.

Smith, K. (2016). Assessment for learning: A pedagogical tool. In D. Wyse, L. Hayward & J. Pandya (Eds), *The Sage handbook of curriculum, pedagogy and assessment* (pp. 740–755). Los Angeles, CA: Sage.

Stobart, G. (2008). *Testing times: The uses and abuses of assessment*. Abingdon: Routledge.

Takekawa, S. (2016). Effects of globalised assessment on local curricula: What Japanese teachers face and how they challenge it. In D. Wyse, L. Hayward & J. Pandya (Eds), *The Sage handbook of curriculum, pedagogy and assessment* (pp. 946–965). Los Angeles, CA: Sage.

Taylor, C. (2004). *Modern social imaginaries*. Durham: Duke University Press.

Venugopal, R. (2015). Neoliberalism as concept, *Economy and Society*, 44(2), 165–187.

Thompson, G., & Harbaugh, A. (2013). A preliminary analysis of teacher perceptions of the effects of NAPLAN on pedagogy and curriculum. *Australian Educational Researcher*, 40(3), 299–314.

Verger, A., Parcerisa, L. & Fontdevila, C. (2019) The growth and spread of large-scale assessments and test-based accountabilities: A political sociology of global education reforms, *Educational Review*, 71(1), 5–30.

von der Embse, N., Pendergast, L, Segool, N., Saeki, E., & Ryan, S. (2016). The influence of test-based accountability policies on school climate and teacher stress across four states. *Teaching and Teacher Education*, 59, 492–502.

Wills, J., & Sandholtz, J. (2009). Constrained professionalism: Dilemmas of teaching in the face of test-based accountability. *Teachers College Record*, 111(4), 1065–1114.

Wiseman, A. (2010). The uses of evidence for educational policymaking: Global contexts and international trends. In A. Luke, J. Green & G. Kelly (Eds), *What counts as evidence and equity? Review of research in education*, vol. 34 (pp. 1–24). New York, NY: AREA, Sage.

7

BEYOND STANDARDIZATION OF EDUCATIONAL PROVISION

The case for authentic accountabilities

Introduction

Throughout this book, I have argued that schooling has been governed by practices and processes of accountability that have led to considerable standardization of educational provision – in curriculum, teaching and assessment. However, and at the same time, I have also revealed how those engaged in educational provision in schools have endeavoured to exert influence in ways that challenge the more reductive effects of educational standardization, and attendant performative practices. Processes of educational accountability have been particularly significant within these governance processes, and have sought to reconstitute what it is to educate under current conditions. Foucauldian inspired conceptions of governance, alongside Bourdieuian inspired notions of contestation, have proved fruitful for better understanding schooling practices under current policy conditions. Rhodes' (2012) concept of interpretive governance has been generative for analysing and further developing understandings of educational practices more broadly.

At the same time as providing an account of why and how more performative accountability logics have exerted significant influence on schooling practices, and how those affected have sought to make sense of – interpret – these accountability processes, this volume has built on notions of interpretive governance to make the argument for what is described as 'interrogative governance' as a form of more agentic 'interpretation' on the part of those most influenced by these accountability practices. Such a standpoint is an indicator of the way in which more performative practices 'interrogate' the actions of teachers and other school administrators, but, perhaps more significantly in terms of educators' agency, how these school-based personnel 'interrogate' such logics themselves.

This chapter provides a summative account of the nature of interrogative governance for curriculum reform, in relation to the standardization of teaching, and vis-à-vis testing practices and processes. It concludes with a call for more 'authentic accountabilities' as a mechanism to foster greater attention to the more genuinely educational work of teachers – work designed to help bring about a more sustainable world for all (Kemmis et al, 2014) – involving more active interrogation of educators' practices and active interrogation on the part of educators. This is in clear contrast with the more performative accountabilities that have characterized so much of schooling practices to date. In its entirety, the chapter provides an overview of the need for further inquiry into the nature of such interrogative practices, the more authentic accountabilities that can arise through such practices, and how these might serve as principled alternatives to more performative accountabilities.

Interrogative governance for curriculum reform

The research reported here reveals that what was significant about teachers' responses to curricula standardization was not only that teachers were governed by these practices, or that they were critical and resisted such practices, but the robust way in which they engaged with and interpreted these practices. While teachers were clearly governed by broader pressures to engage with the C2C, the way in which they actively sought to make sense of the C2C – to not just interpret but actively 'interrogate' it on its own terms, and in relation to more educative logics – was striking. While the sheer volume of documentation meant they struggled to engage with the C2C, and to identify the intent of the units, and there was a sense in which they were sometimes striving to 'cover everything' (particularly in the early stages of its roll-out), they also sought to interrogate these circumstances such that they became much more active participants in the reconceptualization of this work. Teachers wanted to respond back to the producers of the C2C, and to have their say about how the curriculum should be organized. There was also a sense in which teachers were not happy about how quickly the curriculum was enacted, and the relative lack of opportunity to revisit work undertaken earlier in a unit, or earlier units, with detrimental effects for those students who struggled the most. The regularity of assessment – every five weeks – was construed as burdensome, and challenged as such. Teachers were also concerned about the largely academic focus, with a subsequent reduction in concerns about the development of the whole child.

The conception of engaged professionalism on the part of these teachers was palpable, and they were not prepared to simply comply with the curriculum as it stood but instead sought to refashion it to enhance student learning. At the same time, they also interpreted the curriculum as valuable and valid in parts, and potentially useful for students who were transient, and for whom stability in schooling provision could not be taken for granted. There was a sense in which the curriculum had the potential to provide forms of powerful knowledge (Young, 2008) to students, and helped to provide justification for why particular approaches to language, for example, were taught in schools, even as some approaches were simultaneously construed as restrictive. Such a curriculum could also promote culturally relevant pedagogies, even as its enactment was often restrictive of such pedagogies.

Furthermore, even as teachers interrogated testing practices in relation to curriculum reform, and were highly critical of the nature of the NAPLAN assessment practices undertaken in lieu of a richer, more comprehensive curriculum, they also felt 'interrogated' by the pressure to ensure compliance with the C2C. They too were asked to account for their teaching practices and subsequent results, and this was challenging. Even as they questioned the standardization practices that characterized their schools, they too were questioned in relation to these practices. Processes of interrogation appeared to operate in a two-way process – both from teachers towards standardization processes and from such processes to teachers.

This sense of being interrogated reflects the pervasive effects of more performative pressures, even as these were resisted. Such performative pressures contributed to practices such as streaming of teaching in relation to the C2C, which were justified in part to manage workloads; as a result, more exclusionary practices (Slee, 2011) were indeed part and parcel of curricula standardization, and often construed unproblematically. However, some teachers expressed concern about streaming practices for the potentially limiting effects such practices had for those students who struggled the most, and for whom access to examples and instances of more substantive learning were limited. The expression of these hesitations reflect more substantive concerns about the learning needs of all students, regardless of their circumstances, and reflect a more encompassing, holistic – 'authentic' – expression of concern for students' learning. However, such stances also struggled to gain traction under conditions in which streaming practices were sometimes justified on the grounds of enabling students to better access the curriculum. Teachers also seemed overwhelmed at times with the sheer volume of the new curriculum and how to ensure coverage. Testing appeared to have reductive effects, with some classes seen as conforming to more test-centric practices, even as these were purportedly resisted.

Consequently, teachers were governed by the curriculum, at the same time they simultaneously not just interpreted it, but actively re-interpreted it – indeed, interrogated the curriculum; this occurred in light of what they perceived as the palpable and very real limitations but also possibilities of the curriculum. What was evident was not only a form of interpretive governance, but, arguably, interrogative governance, whereby teachers actively scrutinized and critiqued the more reductive effects of standardized governing practices, even as such practices also clearly exerted influence, and led to more reductive and exclusionary practices. Such effects had significant impacts on the work and learning of teachers and students – both productive and problematic.

In this way, more interrogative governance processes reflect not just the contestation that characterizes curriculum standardization processes more broadly, but gestures towards the intensity of the effects of standardization, and the intensity of the push-back on the part of educators against the more reductive effects of such standardization processes.

Interrogative governance and teaching practice

Similarly, in relation to teaching, the focus on explicit teaching led to teachers interrogating the value and validity of particular approaches to teaching, even as teachers' practices were also interrogated in response to concerns about poor teaching practice and performance across the state as a whole. In relation to the latter, explicit teaching practices were construed as part of the solution to the 'problem' (Bacchi, 2009) of underperformance amongst students, which was interpreted as attributable to problematic pedagogies on the part of teachers.

Amongst some teachers, such interrogation was interpreted as beneficial, including for fostering higher expectations amongst younger/Prep students who may have previously been construed as not able to cope with more robust curricula and teaching practices. The focus on explicit teaching seemed to accord more with teachers of younger students, even as advocacy for explicit teaching was far from unanimous. That some teachers found the focus on explicit teaching productive of the need for higher standards for students was a beneficial outcome of such a focus, and evidence of genuine concern for the learning of students and how to enhance such learning. A more 'authentic' disposition seemed to be at play, beyond the performative.

At the same time, the insights of teachers engaging in standardized teaching practices, including various explicit teaching approaches, clearly reflected the overt governance of teachers' work and learning. When focused on ensuring teachers were engaging in particular kinds of predetermined, and sometimes heavily scripted practices, there was clear evidence of how teachers' work was being interrogated through broader governance processes that construed teachers' work and learning as problematic, and as requiring urgent and ongoing intervention. The way in which observations of explicit teaching approaches transpired reveals the potentially reductive effects of standardized approaches to teaching and learning, and the limited and limiting way in which teachers and students engaged with such practices.

However, when undertaken as more 'micro-teaching' opportunities, focusing on particular aspects of teachers' delivery, such as introducing new material to students, such explicit teaching approaches could also be appropriated for more educative purposes on the part of educators, and used to interrogate more performative practices; in part, a logic of appropriation of more performative practices for more educative purposes was evident (cf. Hardy, 2014). Close scrutiny of teachers' practices could be helpful for refining teachers' techniques and skills. The way in which more senior members of staff, particularly some of the principals, sought to manage this process (such as not providing too much information amongst members of the school leadership team to avoid cultivating fear amongst the staff more broadly) also reveals how accountability logics were being constantly interrogated along the way, even as they simultaneously exerted influence.

The ways in which teachers sought to appropriate the potentially reductive approaches to observations of explicit teaching for more learning-oriented purposes were also evident in teachers' openness to scrutiny, and desire to use the process to elicit feedback to enhance their practice. While such preparedness to engage with the observations could be construed as evidence of acquiescence to broader governance processes of standardization, such engagement also indicates, arguably, a desire to appropriate performative requirements for potentially more educative purposes.

More overt criticism of explicit teaching, and particularly the reductive effects of observations, and concerns about having to organize lessons to satisfy observation schedules of members of the administration teams of respective schools also reveal teachers' more active and interrogative governance of such practices. Advocacy for analyses of teaching practice through 'watching others work' also represent potential alternatives to more reductive accountability-oriented logics influencing teachers' practices. In one way, such approaches could be construed as vehicles for 'softening up' teachers to processes of observation more broadly – for further interrogation for performative purposes. However, the multiple ways in which such observations were engaged by teachers, and the variety of practices associated with these observations, reflect advocacy for alternative practices, and a form of interrogation of the governing practices of teachers that were much broader in scope and potentially more productive.

Consequently, there were multiple levels of 'interrogation' occurring in relation to the standardization processes associated with explicit teaching, and teaching more broadly. Such interrogation was evident in the way these standardized approaches were construed as pushing teachers' practices in restricted and restrictive ways. However, processes of interrogation were also evident in the way these standardized practices served as a vehicle to stimulate critique of teachers' sometimes problematic practices – such as perhaps not having sufficiently high standards for all students, including younger (e.g. Prep) students. At the same time, a sense of authenticity on the part of teachers was evident in relation to governance processes in the way teachers interrogated and problematized those practices of standardization which they construed as limited and limiting, as inhibiting the sorts of more substantive practices they sought to foster amongst their students, and of simply getting in the way of good teaching.

Interrogative governance and testing

Processes of interrogative governance were clearly in evidence in relation to assessment practices in Queensland. That teachers and administrators in schools in Queensland were under much pressure to improve on their original 2008 NAPLAN results reveals how standardized testing practices had become a significant tool for governing teachers' and school-based administrators' work. Explicit targets of 3% improvement year-on-year in the poorest performing regions throughout the state meant that testing practices became significant foci of attention, even as they were downplayed in many school settings. Constant references to having to respond to 'a sea of red' or 'we're all red' acted as forms of shorthand that characterized discourses surrounding the governing of assessment practices throughout the state, and poor educational practices more broadly. Processes of constant comparison as spectacle (Nóvoa & Yariv-Mashal, 2003) – between schools, between regions, between earlier and later results, and between year levels, to name but a few permutations – ensured ongoing surveillance of educators' practices and a propensity to downplay any other forms of success beyond improvements in the numbers associated with standardized tests and testing.

Focusing on particular students to enhance results also reflects problematic effects of broader accountability logics and processes of governance. Teachers' practices were heavily oriented towards responding to enhancing results of particular groups of students – especially those not achieving minimum national benchmarks. There was also considerable focus on students in the 'upper two bands of NAPLAN' – and such students in these categories were frequently referred to in this way. The discourses that attended such descriptions reinforce how a logic of enumeration (Hardy, 2015) – in this case, the number of students achieving particular benchmarks – dominated over student learning per se. The focus on targeting those students whose results could be most readily manipulated, and a systemic push to focus on such students, also reflects how more inclusive logics were challenged by more performative logics, and how practices of educational triage (Booher-Jennings, 2005) were clearly in operation.

Practices of preparing and practising for the test also provided clear evidence of how testing was governed by more standardized logics of accountability. These were no more obvious than in relation to explicit practices of teaching to the test. Even as teachers recognized the problems of doing so, and endeavoured not to, they also succumbed to these pressures on multiple occasions. Sometimes this teaching to the test was explicit, and a dominant practice, even as it was resisted.

However, interrogative governance was also evident in how teachers and educators in schools interrogated the focus on NAPLAN, and openly critiqued and criticized the more reductive effects of the test on teaching practice, and the organization of schooling more broadly. That more performative accountability logics were explicitly recognized as such, and as influencing the nature of more substantive educational practices, reflects how such logics could be contested, even as they exerted significant and ongoing influence. Teachers critiqued whole-school foci of testing for its own sake, including the way staff meetings were dominated by NAPLAN-related activities. They also criticized the focus on funding associated with results, and how this diminished the educational potential of the tests. Reflecting broader media discourses focusing on distrust, choice and performance (Mockler, 2013), concerns about undue emphasis on performance and performative concerns more broadly were also recognized as detracting from the educative potential of the test, and distracting from actual evidence of students' learning. Also, efforts to utilize the test data to inform teachers' practices vis-à-vis student learning reflect a more nuanced approach to NAPLAN, and attempts on the part of teachers to utilize the data for more educative purposes. While there sometimes appeared to be an acquiescence in relation to targeting particular students to enable enhanced outcomes, 'to make the data look good', there was also unease amongst teachers about the relative neglect of some students over others, and disquiet about how processes of governance associated with NAPLAN had reconstituted teachers' work in sometimes dramatic ways. A sense of accountability to all students, not just those targeted for additional attention, pervaded the work of many of these educators. Teachers' hesitations about teaching to the test, and their efforts to utilize the test data for more educative purposes – to inform their teaching in particular domains that appeared to require additional attention – also reflect how they interrogated the data even as they were interrogated by it. Even as this process was fraught, they sought to appropriate the focus on more performative practice for more educative purposes.

Beyond standardized schooling practices: The case for 'authentic accountabilities'

These processes of interrogation reveal how educators are simultaneously constituted by, even as they challenge, broader processes of accountability. These accountability logics were clearly problematic at times, even as they had the potential to be used for more productive (read educative) purposes. The more agentic, educative forms of interrogation presented in this volume reveal that teachers and educators do wish to provide substantive opportunities for their students. Consequently, what is required are various forms of 'intelligent accountability' (O'Neill, 2013) that actually have the potential to foster more substantive learning on the part of both students and teachers. Rather than focusing on 'second order' expressions of performance, as do various performance-oriented accountability systems, it is necessary to focus more strongly and substantively on 'first order' actions and activities of teachers and educators working in schools to enhance students' learning. Such activities need to attract much more substantive attention than the second order parameters and influences that currently exert influence. Such approaches foreground the need to build professional responsibility and trust amongst educators, and to avoid emphasis on external measures of performance, such as in relation to imposed curricula, scripted teaching, and external and standardized tests.

However, accessing such forms of 'first order' accountabilities requires a level of trust in teachers that is premised on a belief in their capacity and desire to effect more substantive change. Such forms of accountability, that draw on teachers' own knowledges, concerns, insights, perspectives, and hesitancies – their active interrogation of practice – constitute a more 'authentic' form of accountability than other forms that are removed from their work. More authentic forms of accountability can be informed by data presented through more standardized criteria, including in relation to particular curriculum, teaching and testing practices.

However, they are not simply limited to such foci, but instead seek to foreground the capacities and needs of all students, in context, drawing on evidence of their current capabilities to inform decision-making about future approaches and foci. The broader social and academic learning capacities of students are foregrounded in such an approach, and serve as a necessary vehicle to develop students' capacities as contributing members of their communities, now and into the future.

Such 'authentic accountabilities' also focus attention on the conditions for teaching and learning that inform teachers' practices. As with more 'rich account-abilities' (Lingard, Martino, Rezai-Rashti & Sellar, 2016), such approaches consider the broader social and systemic supports that are essential for enabling teachers to work effectively with their students, and without which the work and learning of teachers and students would be unable to proceed in schooling settings. This also resonates with forms of 'resource accountability' that constitutes part of Darling-Hammond, Wilhoit and Pittenger's (2014) notion of 'genuine accountability'. For Darling-Hammond et al. (2014), there is a need to cultivate a) meaningful learning on the part of students (including various 'soft skills' of problem formulation, interpretation and communication) which engages with multiple measures of attainment; b) resource accountability, which focuses attention on ensuring ade-quate resource provision at a system level to enable such meaningful learning; and c) professional capacity and accountability, which emphasizes the cultivation of professional judgement amongst individual educators and supports for doing so at school and system levels. The second and third of these foci, focusing on resources and the cultivation of professional capacity, like Lingard et al.'s (2016) notion of 'rich accountabilities', draw heavily on ensuring the broader conditions are con-ducive to the cultivation of meaningful learning on the part of educators and students.

However, more 'authentic accountabilities' not only acknowledge and recognize the importance of these broader conditions for cultivating substantive educational practice, but they also include attention to the nature of these conditions as they pertain to the key tasks of curriculum development, teaching practice and assess-ment processes as they unfold in schooling settings, including in relation to tea-chers' daily practices. This work of curriculum development, teaching and assessing constitute the core work of teachers and schools, and seeking to ensure that this work is maximized through ongoing scrutiny – interrogation – should be the focus of individual educators, schools and schooling systems. This entails collecting and collating different forms of evidence of the nature and effects of specific curricula, teaching approaches and assessment practices, and interrogating these in relation to the extent to which they genuinely seek to maximize the learning needs of all students, in context. Such an approach foregrounds how it is actual instances of student learning that transpire in response to these curricula, teaching and assess-ment practices that are most crucial, rather than the numeric or alphabetic indica-tors that can only ever serve as proxy measures of learning. Consequently, the focus of attention should be a rich array of practices that conform to what MacIntyre (2007) refers to as various 'standards of excellence' within the tradition of a practice – in this case, education. These are 'standards of excellence which are appropriate to, and partially definitive of, that form of activity [education], with the result that human powers to achieve excellence, and human conceptions of the ends and goods involved are systematically extended' (MacIntyre, 2007, p. 186). Importantly, these efforts at always 'extending' human conceptions of ends and goods in relation to education demand a schooling tradition which is not static, but one that is always subject to scrutiny and inquiry for how to enhance the learning experiences of all students (Carr, 1987); again, ongoing and constant scrutiny – interrogation – of practice is the key to enhanced governance of educational practices. The focus of attention on a rich array of student learning practices, rather than on the representations of such learning, are likely to provide more substantive evidence of the extent to which teachers, schools and systems have been successful in promoting the learning of the students in their care.

Drawing on and beyond the research presented in this book, such authentic accountabilities also entail the interrogation of more performative logics that characterize so much of schooling practice. It is the capacity of educators to resist more performative logics that characterizes them as engaging in genuinely 'authentic' work for their students. More 'authentic' accountabilities are simultaneously focused on cultivating conditions to foster more educative practices, and attention to multiple accounts of students' work and learning as evidence of growth and development, and to help identify those domains and fields requiring further attention and development.

Advocacy for such accountabilities entails a complex awareness of the influence and effects of more performative approaches, and the broader neoliberal logics that foster such approaches, and how these might be resisted. More authentic accountabilities are framed by understandings that broader global processes that seek to foster more neoliberal logics are not simply automatic or inevitable, but are the result of ongoing practices and processes by those involved (Peck, 2010). Such ongoing practices and processes, in all their seeming triviality, are instances of what Ball (2012) describes as 'attention to the mundane', and it is through analyses of such micro-processes, *in situ,* that it becomes possible to see how more neoliberal logics that inform more performative accountability processes are always actively constructed:

> Attention to the mundane also serves to highlight neoliberalism as a process, not something that is realised as a set of grand strategies and ruptural changes but rather made up of numerous moves, incremental reforms, displacements and re-inscriptions, complicated and stuttering trajectories of small changes and tactics which work together on systems, organizations and individuals – to make these isomorphic. They are made into enterprises. These ensembles of changes work together to produce new practices, subjectivities and opportunities. This constitutes a process of attrition which gradually renders the social into the commodity form and amenable to profit. Neoliberalism is also polymorphic and evolving, it morphs and adapts, taking on local characteristics from the geographies of existing political economic circumstances and institutional frameworks

where variability, internal constitution, societal influences and individual agency all play a role in (re)producing, circulating, and facilitating its advance. It can 'materialise' differently in mutated and hybrid forms.

(Ball, 2012, p. 30)

Several lessons can be learned from recognition of the way in which more neo-liberal logics exert influence. Just as more neoliberal practices are 1) made up of numerous moves; 2) characterized by complicated and uncertain trajectories that influence individuals, organizations and systems; 3) polymorphic and ever changing and adapting; 4) able to learn from local characteristics associated with existing political and economic circumstances and institutional frameworks; and 5) expres-sed in various mutations and hybrid forms, so too are more authentic account-abilities, foci and approaches. Such accountabilities, with their focus on varied accounts and evidence of student learning from multiple sources: 1) require time to develop and can be generated through several sequences of events/moves; 2) are similarly uncertain and complicated and not always clear in their organization and intent; 3) are ever changing and adapting to their circumstances; 4) are similarly attuned to and influenced by local features and foci associated with existing policies and economic circumstances and institutional frameworks; and 5) exist in multi-faceted and hybridized forms that may not necessarily be easily recognized at first glance. Just as 'the neoliberal ascendency was never a sure thing' (Peck 2010, p. 4), and its rise was never inevitable, so too is advocacy for and the development of authentic accountabilities an ongoing process of continual development. In the same way that more neoliberal logics that inform standardized, performative approaches to accountability 'w[ere] not guided by some secret formula or deter-minant blueprint' (p. 4), but instead reflect a 'zigzagging course [that] was impro-vised, and more often than not enabled by crisis' (Peck, 2010, p. 4), more authentic accountabilities are the result of ongoing and hard work to bring them into being. This should give hope to those who may despair about the possibility to 'do differently' in relation to more authentic curriculum, teaching and assess-ment practices under current conditions.

Such authenticity also resonates with an 'ethics of accountability' focused on deliberate and contemplative choice-making about how best to proceed. As Aris-totle (1976) argued in his *Ethics*:

no process is set going by mere thought – only by purposive and practical thought, for it is this that also originates productive thought. Everyone who makes anything makes it for some purpose, and the product is not an end in itself but only a relative or particular end. But an action is an end in itself, because good action is an end, and the object of appetition.

(pp. 205–206)

Such ethically oriented action is important, because governing entails a variety of actions and activities on the part of individuals and groups in society to influence social practices. Governing is not simply the product of some 'external' being or force exerting influence, but a product of the actions and activities of those involved. As Kooiman (2003) argues:

> Governing *can be considered as the totality of interactions, in which public as well as private actors participate, aimed at solving societal problems or creating societal opportunities; attending to the institutions as contexts for these governing interactions; and establishing a normative foundation for all those activities.*
>
> *(p. 4; emphasis original)*

Such an approach reinstates the agentic within conceptions of practice, and seeks to provide hope for the more challenging circumstances that attend broader processes of standardization that govern performative processes of accountability. Hursh (2016) argues, with some justification, that the broader conditions in which educators undertake their work have become more challenging because of the nature and influence of broader global processes. Such processes have had disempowering effects on those, such as teachers and educators in schools, who operate at more localized levels, without necessarily the resources or connections to those making these decisions:

> Where education policy is made has shifted up the geopolitical scale from the local and state to the federal, national, and international (corporations, foundations, and nongovernmental organizations), disempowering those who lack the financial and political clout to affect policy decisions at the upper levels.
>
> *(Hursh, 2016, p. 7)*

However, and while the governance of educational accountabilities has indeed been influenced by the more performative logics that characterize neoliberal instantiations of standardization in schooling settings, and been influenced by more economistic decision-makers far removed from schools and classrooms, alternative, more authentic accountabilities can be and are supported by educators working in local situations and settings; this is apparent in the way educators advocate for the substantive learning needs of their students. This includes endeavouring to be the best possible educators they can for their students, and working collectively to challenge those more dominant, external logics and influences that mitigate against such work. More neoliberal instantiations of schooling practice cannot simply be taken for granted, and do not simply arise 'automatically', but instead transpire through the active and ongoing processes and steps taken by those involved in their ascendency. In the same way, and through practices and processes of more interrogative governance, more authentic accountabilities can and need to be similarly actively pursued, even as this is challenging and sometimes thankless work.

Limitations

It is recognized that the final manuscript of any work is always a compromise in relation to the research process that informed that work. As Ball, Maguire and Braun (2012) acknowledge, '[t]here is much more to the research process than ever goes onto the pages of articles and books' (p. 17). This is certainly the case here. The research informing the final text is part of a broader, ongoing program of work focused on the politics of policy development and enactment in schooling (and other educational) settings in different national contexts. While the Australian/Queensland data that comprise this research are certainly generative for understanding how more performative accountability logics play out in relation to policy development and enactment in other settings where such logics have become dominant in recent times, they can best be understood as a stimulus for the empirical work that needs to be undertaken in these contexts to know how such logics have actually played out. While the research resonates strongly with much of the cognate literature in relation to accountability in schooling practice under current conditions in other (often Anglo-) sub-national and national contexts, schooling practices are always necessarily deeply situated in context. Indeed, the work, learning and perspectives of those presented in this volume are themselves only a partial account of such practices. I hope I have rendered the experience of the educators described here as 'authentically' as possible, but I am also deeply aware that any account of their work, such as presented in this volume, can only ever capture but a portion of the actual work and learning of educators *in situ*. These insights always necessarily have to be interpreted, and reinterpreted – indeed interrogated – in light of the specific circumstances at play in these and other contexts. They cannot simply be 'read' across national and sub-national borders without deep consideration of the particular social, political and economic circumstances at play therein.

Authentic accountabilities, trust and ways forward

While this volume is a critique of performative policy, curriculum, teaching and testing practices that characterize so much of schooling, it also seeks to advance a normative agenda around more authentic accountabilities, and the interrogative logics on the part of teachers that will help to facilitate such accountabilities. At the heart of issues of accountability is what O'Neill (2002) referred to in her 2002 Reith Lectures as 'A question of trust'. A key part of the malaise in which educators find themselves pertains to issues of trust. More authentic accountabilities, with their focus on teachers as active participants in deliberating about and developing context-specific, multifaceted accounts of their students' capacities, will hopefully serve to provide better accounts of and for the work of teachers, and serve to cultivate more robust conceptions of trust in the profession more broadly.

The preface to O'Neill's (2002) summary of her lectures begins with both a concern and a hope about the current state of trust. O'Neill (2002) questions the extent to which we believe in trust, while at the same time arguing that trust continues to be placed in others. Importantly, in making her inquiry into the extent to which 'we have stopped trusting', she makes an explicit connection between issues of trust, and efforts to 'manage' activities through various forms of control and audit:

> Is it true that we have stopped trusting? Has untrustworthy action made trust too risky? Is trust obsolete? In giving the Reith Lectures in the spring of 2002, I began with these questions. It quickly became clear that the evidence that we face a 'crisis of trust' is very mixed. We often express suspicion, yet we constantly place trust in others. Our attitudes and our action diverge. Should we put our money where our mouths are, and give up on trust? Or would giving up on trust just be a matter of placing more trust in abstract systems of control and audit?
>
> *(p. vii)*

It is this possibility of placing more 'trust' in processes of 'control and audit' that has helped stimulate the development to the ideas presented in this volume. Indeed, O'Neill (2002) explicitly asks the question 'Can a revolution in accountability remedy our "crisis of trust"' (p. 4)?

In a sense, what is required is a paradigm shift from dominant approaches to performative educational accountabilities to a much more context-relevant, and context-productive conception of practice – more authentic accountabilities. This does entail something of a 'scientific revolution' (Kuhn, 2012). Such extraordinary ruptures come about when established means of inquiry are found to be wanting – 'when, that is, the profession can no longer evade anomalies that subvert the existing tradition of scientific practice' (Kuhn, 2012, p. 6). Such responses are 'the tradition-shattering complements to the tradition-bound activity of normal science' (p. 6). In a sense, the 'normal science' that surrounds the accounting of teacher and schooling practice is infused with a lack of trust in educators in schools as willing and able to effect substantive and necessary change to foster enhanced student learning. The end result is undue confidence in standardized approaches to curriculum, teaching and assessment as vehicles to ensure 'quality' provision of education. And as has been documented here, through both relevant literature and reflection on detailed accounts of actual practice, such confidence in technicist approaches has been found wanting. Where more performative accountability logics have dominated over educators' practices, instead of excellence and integrity in relation to the educative functions that should characterize schooling, we can identify incoherence and lack of engagement. However, where more performative accountability logics have been actively challenged/interrogated for their negative effects on student and teacher learning, and where educators seek to foster more productive, robust approaches to learning, we see evidence of coherence, engagement and much more substantial learning. In other words, educators can indeed be trusted to seek to strive for improved educational practice for their students, and this is evident in the ways they interrogate and critique problematic practices. Even as teachers and administrators in schools are governed by more standardized accountability logics, they also simultaneously resist such logics. It is through such productive analysis and critique, together with the energy and enthusiasm attending educators' efforts to address students' learning needs in context, that the seeds of and for more authentic accountabilities are and can be sown for the advancement of all.

References

Aristotle (1976). *The ethics of Aristotle: The Nicomachean ethics* (Trans J.A.K. Thomson). Harmondsworth: Penguin.

Bacchi, C. (2009). *Analysing policy: What's the problem represented to be?* Frenchs Forest: Pearson Education.

Ball, S. (2012). *Global Education Inc.: New policy networks and the neoliberal imaginary.* Abingdon: Routledge.

Ball, S., Maguire, M., & Braun, A. (2012). *How schools do policy: Policy enactments in secondary schools.* London: Routledge.

Booher-Jennings, J. (2005). Below the bubble: Educational triage and the Texas accountability system. *American Educational Research Journal, 42*(2), 231–268.

Carr, W. (1987). What is an educational practice? *Journal of Philosophy of Education, 21*(2), 163–175.

Darling-Hammond, L., Wilhoit, G., & Pittenger, L. (2014). *Accountability for college and career readiness: Developing a new paradigm.* Stanford, CA: Stanford Centre for Opportunity Policy in Education.

Hardy, I. (2014). A logic of appropriation: Enacting national testing in Australia. *Journal of Education Policy, 29*(1), 1–18.

Hardy, I. (2015). A logic of enumeration: The nature and effects of national literacy and numeracy testing in Australia. *Journal of Education Policy, 30*(3), 335–362.

Hursh, D. (2016). *The end of public schools: The corporate reform agenda to privatize education.* New York: Routledge.

Kemmis, S., Wilkinson, J., Edwards-Groves, C., Hardy, I., Grootenboer, P., & Bristol, L. (2014). *Changing practices, changing education.* Singapore: Springer.

Kooiman, J. (2003). *Governing as governance.* London: Sage.

Kuhn, T. (2012). *The structure of scientific revolutions.* Fourth edition (50th anniversary edition). Chicago, IL: The University of Chicago Press.

Lingard, B., Martino, W., Rezai-Rashti, G., & Sellar, S. (2016). *Globalising educational accountabilities.* New York: Routledge.

MacIntyre, A. (2007). *After virtue: A study in moral theory.* Third edition. Notre Dame, Indiana: University of Notre Dame.

Mockler, N. (2013). Reporting the 'education revolution': MySchool.edu.au in the print media. *Discourse: Studies in the Cultural Politics of Education, 34*(1), 1–16.

Nóvoa, A., & Yariv-Mashal, T. (2003). Comparative research in education: A mode of governance or a historical journey? *Comparative Education, 39*(4), 423–438.

O'Neill, O. (2002). *A question of trust: The BBC Reith Lectures, 2002.* Cambridge: Cambridge University Press.

O'Neill, O. (2013). Intelligent accountability in education. *Oxford Review of Education, 39*, 4–16.

Peck, J. (2010). *Constructions of neoliberal reason*. Oxford: Oxford University Press.

Rhodes, R. (2012). Waves of governance. In D. Levi-Faur (Ed.), *The Oxford handbook of governance* (pp. 33–44). Oxford: Oxford University Press.

Slee, R. (2011). *The irregular school: Exclusion, schooling and inclusive education*. London: Routledge.

Young, M. (2008). *Bringing knowledge back in: From social constructivism to social realism in the sociology of education*. London: Routledge.

INDEX

Printed in the United States
By Bookmasters